ARCHITECTS OF OUR FORTUNES

Architects of Our Fortunes

The Journal of

ELIZA A. W. OTIS

1860–1863

with Letters and Civil War Journal of

HARRISON GRAY OTIS

Edited and with an introduction by Ann Gorman Condon

HUNTINGTON LIBRARY   SAN MARINO, CALIFORNIA

Printed in the United States of America

Published by the Huntington Library Press
1151 Oxford Road, San Marino, California 91108
www.huntington.org/HLPress/HEHPubs.html

Library of Congress Cataloging-in-Publication Data

Otis, Eliza A., 1833–1904.
Architects of our fortunes: the journal of Eliza A. W. Otis,
1860–1863 with letters and Civil War journal of Harrison Gray Otis /
[edited by Ann Gorman Condon].
p. cm.
Includes bibliographical references.
ISBN 0-87328-181-0 (alk. paper)
1. Otis, Eliza A., 1833–1904—Diaries. 2. Otis, Harrison Gray, 1837–1917—Correspondence. 3. Otis, Harrison Gray, 1837–1917—Diaries. 4. United States—History—Civil War, 1861–1865—Personal narratives. 5. Louisville (Ky.)—History—Civil War, 1861–1865—Personal narratives. 6. Military spouses—Kentucky—Louisville—Diaries. 7. Soldiers—United States—Correspondence. 8. Soldiers—United States—Diaries. I. Condon, Ann Gorman, 1936– II. Otis, Harrison Gray, 1837–1917. III. Title.
E601 .087 2000
973.7′81—dc21 00-035048

FRONTISPIECE

Eliza Otis in 1856 (top).
Harrison Gray Otis at age sixteen (bottom).
Pencil sketches by Jane Purcell.

For Gwen and Guil and our families

Yet I don't believe that we need be creatures of circumstances, but rather the creators *of them, and thus the architects of our own fortunes.*

ELIZA ANN OTIS, January 6, 1860

ACKNOWLEDGMENTS

I owe much to the staff and readers at the Huntington Library in San Marino, California, for encouraging this project. Martin Ridge and Robert Ritchie took an early interest in these documents, and William Deverell provided invaluable information on the historical context of the Otis generation. A three-month fellowship permitted me to work in the library's rich collection. Craig St. Clair, the archivist at the History Center of the *Los Angeles Times* in 1993, was exceptionally generous in sharing his knowledge of the Otises' California years. Mike Lange, communications director at the *Times*, helped find Otis family photos for the project, as did Dan Lewis of the Huntington's manuscript staff. Darl Stephenson, a military historian working on the Scout operations in West Virginia during the Civil War, gave me much insight into the treacherous fighting conditions in that state.

Several institutions in the Midwest opened their archives and their photography collections to me: the Filson Society in Louisville; the Marietta Historical Society in Ohio; the Ohio Library/Archives in Columbus; the Cincinnati Historical Society; and the West Virginia Archives in Charleston. The courtesy and strong interest shown by staff members at these institutions made my field trips unusually rewarding. My colleagues at the University of New Brunswick patiently listened to two versions of my introduction. Gwendolyn Garland Babcock and David McPherron Leaf made the manuscripts published here available to me and the Huntington Library. As always, my husband, Thomas J. Condon, cast his discerning eye over the manuscript and made many helpful suggestions. I hope all who contributed will find pleasure in the final result.

A.G.C. *Saint John, New Brunswick, Canada, 2000*

CONTENTS

ILLUSTRATIONS

INTRODUCTION

The Civil War papers of Eliza Ann and Harrison Gray Otis consist of three sets of documents written during the American Civil War. The largest text is Eliza's journal, which runs sporadically from January 1860 to September 1863. Harrison's contribution includes four letters written to Eliza in 1859 soon after they were married and an action-packed diary recording his Civil War experiences in 1862 and 1863. Eliza's journal is written in the highly legible, curvilinear script favored by American schools of that era. Harrison's letters also conform to the conventions of the day, but his wartime diary is a barely legible, often slanted scrawl, suggesting he was using his knee or perhaps the bare ground as support.

Contained within these texts are two personal stories. The first concerns the poet Eliza Ann Wetherby Otis, who was twenty-six years old when she began the journal. Born and educated in New England but living then in Louisville, Kentucky, Eliza was a new bride. Although deeply in love and eager to display her talents as a wife, she was confined to the limited environment of a boardinghouse while her husband sought work and then, in the summer of 1861, joined the Union army. The second story is that of the soldier-husband Harrison Gray Otis. A printer's apprentice before the war, Otis was a native of Marietta, Ohio, the last born into a family of sixteen children. During the Civil War, Otis compiled an outstanding record of courage under fire and rose from the rank of private in 1861 to major by 1865. A few letters written during the first year of his marriage plus Eliza's accounts of their time together indicate that Harrison Otis was a devoted husband and an unusually zealous supporter of the effort to preserve the American Union and defeat what they both regarded as Southern treason.[1]

Over time the idealism of these two young people was severely tested by the multiple pressures on their lives, especially the anxiety of prolonged separation from each other, the sudden death of their first child, and repeated encounters with the grisly reality of the Civil War. By the time the journal ends, both Eliza and Harrison have become much tougher personalities: more realistic in their personal goals, more rigid in their moral standards, more fatalistic about life and death, and more devoted, if possible, to their sense of America's national mission.

These texts provide an intimate glimpse into the personal responses of two ordinary, middle-class, white Americans to a period of national crisis. They take on added importance, however, because these are the only known private documents describing the ideological perspective of what became one of America's great publishing families. The twenty years following the Civil War were times of earnest but discouraging struggle. Business failure, frequent changes of residence, and poor health plagued the Otises. Then, in the early 1880s, Harrison and Eliza made one more move and took one last desperate gamble: they bought a quarter share in the newly founded *Los Angeles Daily Times*. Four years later, in 1886, they scraped together enough capital to become sole owners and publishers of the newspaper, rechristening it the *Los Angeles Times*. From that moment forward, the pace of their success matched the

1. For fine, pre–Civil War descriptions of the cities mentioned in these texts, see John A. Jakle, *Image of the Ohio Valley: A Historical Geography of Travel* (New York: Oxford University Press, 1977).

exponential growth in population and wealth of Southern California itself. By the time of their deaths, Harrison and Eliza owned the largest newspaper in the nation in terms of size and in the number of lines devoted to advertising.[2] They were hailed by some and feared by others as the prophets, the rhetorical architects, of California's political and cultural future.[3]

While the Otises' public views are documented extensively and readily available, their Civil War documents remain the only substantial source of information on the personal life of this remarkable husband-and-wife team. This introduction explores the documents' major themes and identifies the characteristics of these two young people as they began their life together amidst the turmoil of a society at war. All of the texts are presented verbatim, as they were originally written by Harrison and Eliza, complete with occasional misspellings and nineteenth-century punctuation.

Eliza Ann Wetherby Otis was born in Keene, New Hampshire, in 1833, the daughter of Charles T. Wetherby (1807–67) and Nancy Hyde Wetherby (1809–49). Her father was a not-very-successful woolen manufacturer and part-time Congregational minister.[4] In the journal, Eliza described her childhood as supremely happy, even though she had to endure the death

2. Susan Henry, "'Journalistic Comrade': Eliza Otis and the Beginnings of a Newspaper Dynasty" (*Los Angeles Times* Archives, 1986), 11.

3. No noteworthy biography of either Harrison or Eliza Otis has yet been published. The article by Susan Henry cited above is the best overview of Eliza Otis's career. For Harrison, by far the best study is Richard Connolly Miller, "Otis and His *Times*: The Career of Harrison Gray Otis of Los Angeles" (Ph.D. diss., University of California, Berkeley, 1961).

4. The declining status of Congregational ministers in the nineteenth century and its effect on woman's culture is traced in Ann Douglas, *The Feminization of American Culture* (New York: Knopf, 1977).

of two young brothers, two sisters, and her own mother before she reached the age of sixteen.[5] No doubt her strong religious faith carried her through these losses and explained her public optimism in the face of adversity, but her journal reveals a preoccupation with death and frequent periods of depression, suggesting that these family losses took a heavy toll. Eliza certainly encountered unpredictable, devastating moments in her adult life as well and felt keenly the impact of these blows, but her belief in the Puritan values of fortitude and faith proved a recurrent source of strength.

Following the death of his wife in 1849, Charles Wetherby married again and decided to move to Ohio to try his fortune in that flourishing state. He settled in Lowell, a small town ten miles north of Marietta, where he served as founding minister of the First Congregational Church and began Wetherby Academy.[6] Eliza was permitted to stay in New England to finish her education at the Castleton Seminary in Vermont, where she won several prizes for poetry, including the distinction of having one poem published in the *New York Tribune*, surely a signal honor for a sixteen-year-old. Once graduated, Eliza rejoined her family in Lowell, and although no records exist, it seems

5. Gwendolyn Garland Babcock, *The Ancestry of Marian Otis Chandler* (San Marino, California: privately printed, 1991), 17–22, 35, 37.

6. Wetherby was so esteemed by his congregation that, after his retirement, the church formally requested his return to the pulpit. See Minutes of the Consociation of the Congregational Church, 1858 (Marietta County Historical Society). See also Martin R. Andrews, ed. and comp., *History of Marietta and Washington County, Ohio, and Representative Citizens*, vol. 1 (Chicago: Biographical Publishing Company, 1902), 380. There is no public record of Wetherby Academy, although Harrison Otis cites it in his "Milestones: Marking Some High Spots in the Pathway of a Strenuous Life" (Otis-Chandler Family Papers, *Los Angeles Times* Archives, 1913), 5.

likely that she helped her father with the teaching duties at the Academy. There she met Harrison Gray Otis, an aspiring printer, who returned to school to augment the very thin instruction he had received as a youth. After completing his five-month course, Harrison (also known as Harry) went to Columbus, Ohio, to take a job there and enroll in additional courses. In 1859, three years after their first meeting, Harrison returned to Lowell to marry Eliza. She was twenty-six and he was twenty-two. They began married life, as Harry later recorded, "without money and without scrip, and with no surplus raiment to speak of. But we were happy and hopeful on 8 dollars a week."[7]

While it is risky to project opinions backwards in time, we do know that marriage, and especially finding the right partner, was a preoccupation in mid-nineteenth-century America.[8] Thus we can at least speculate that the union of the cultivated Miss Wetherby with a man three and one-half years her junior, of no obvious promise, would have created quite a stir in the small town of Lowell. One can almost hear the sniffing behind the handkerchiefs of the local gossips. Yet Eliza's journal makes clear that she found many admirable qualities in this rough-hewn young man. His devotion to her, which can be seen in his letters and diary, surely appealed to her romantic disposition. And Eliza's own desire to live a meaningful life complemented

7. Harrison Gray Otis, "Milestones," 6.

8. For contemporary courtship patterns, see Karen Lystra, *Searching the Heart: Women, Men, and Romantic Love in Nineteenth-Century America* (New York: Oxford University Press, 1989), especially 157–91. Also informative is Carl Degler, *At Odds: Women and the Family in America from the Revolution to the Present* (Oxford: Oxford University Press, 1980), 18–25.

Harry's intense ambition and willingness to work hard. Above all, Eliza and Harry shared a deep moral fervor, a religious devotion to God, America, and the abolition of slavery.

Who was he, this Harry? And how did he acquire such characteristics? Harry was born in 1837 in Marietta, Ohio, the sixteenth child of Stephen Otis and the eighth child of Stephen's second wife, Sarah Dyar Otis.[9] Stephen's roots were in Vermont, and he was distantly related to Senator Harrison Gray Otis of Massachusetts and to James Otis, the fiery tribune of the American Revolution. Like so many New Englanders, the Otises resettled in Ohio after the American Revolution. Harrison Otis grew up on his father's farm and attended the log-cabin school for three months each winter and the Methodist Church every Sunday. He overcame the dullness of farm life by reading voraciously the epic stories of the old frontier and by helping his father in the antislavery movement. Stephen Otis was a bold abolitionist, a Liberty Party man, whose house became a station on the Underground Railroad. The excitement of this "Great Cause" posed real dangers for the Otises because many people around Marietta were proslavery. For Harrison, the Underground Railroad provided an unusual intensity and sense of purpose to one so young.[10]

When he was fourteen, Harrison began the long apprenticeship to become a printer. He worked in many shops in Ohio and

9. Miller, "Otis and His *Times*," 5–10; Babcock, *Ancestry of Marian Otis Chandler*, 11–12.

10. The most recent work on the Liberty Party is Vernon L. Volpe, *Forlorn Hope of Freedom: The Liberty Party in the Old Northwest, 1838–1948* (Kent, Ohio: Kent State University, 1990). The origins of both the Liberty Party and the Republican Party are traced in Eric Foner, *Free Soil, Free Labor, Free Men: The Ideology of the Republican Party before the Civil War* (New York: Oxford University Press, 1970).

Illinois and in the process joined the Republican Party. It was during this period that he enrolled for five months in the Wetherby Academy, where he met and later married Eliza Wetherby. For a brief while after their marriage, Eliza continued to live at home while Harry scouted job possibilities in Cincinnati, only to report ironically that "I don't find a demand for more than a million printers in Cincinnati."[11] Rather than sit around Cincinnati, Harry proposed to Eliza that they should go to Louisville, live in a boardinghouse, and try their luck in Kentucky's major metropolis. It was from this site that Eliza began her journal on January 1, 1860.

Confined to a boardinghouse room, with her husband away working long days, and all her meals and household needs met by the staff, the young poetess was bored, and so she took up writing a journal to pass the time. She jokes at one point that it will give her something to read in her old age; it is clear that publishing the journal never entered Eliza's mind.[12] As a result it has an intimacy and spontaneity that are both credible and winning. The manuscript has occasional crossed-out words, spelling corrections, and phrases added in a different ink, suggesting that Eliza set her thoughts down directly on the page, without making previous drafts or notes.

The journal, written over a three-year period, reflects Eliza's maturation in response to the pressure of events. In the beginning she was an idealistic, effusive young woman, enthralled by the new doctrines of transcendentalism spreading through America. The concept of self-reliance, that one *can* and indeed *must* be the architect of one's own fortune, had great appeal

11. HGO letter, October 17, 1859.
12. EAO journal, January 31, 1860.

for her. She also embraced the heightened importance the transcendentalists assigned to nature, "the embodied thought of God." Love of nature would characterize Eliza's writing throughout her life, and many pages of the journal are filled with descriptions of the natural scenery and her own investment of spiritual meaning in mountains, treetops, clouds, and the starry night. She believed equally in the importance of intuition and the creative imagination. Finally her journal reflects Eliza's deep religious faith and her fervent wish to do something useful with her life, to live nobly, and especially to express her love of life artistically, in poetry or painting.[13]

At the same time, Eliza was a committed Christian. She and Harry attended the Unitarian Church two or three times a week, and she often summarized the sermon in her journal. She believed in the Christian God, the divinity of Christ, and the promise of an afterlife as well as the constant presence in the world of human depravity and sin. Eliza stated these beliefs matter-of-factly and with total confidence, as if she had learned them as a child. The final element in her spiritual world was a conviction that religious truth can be found in all faiths. She visited Catholic, Jewish, and African-American places of worship in a sincere attempt to discover their insights into spiritual matters. In fact, Eliza was quite progressive in her openness to alternative belief systems, although she does not seem aware she is crossing theological borders.

She spent much of her time touring Louisville with women

13. There is no evidence that Eliza ever read Ralph Waldo Emerson or the other transcendentalist pioneers. It may be that she received these beliefs second-hand, most likely through her father. For a concise summary of these doctrines, see Paul F. Boller Jr., *American Transcendentalism, 1830–1860: An Intellectual Inquiry* (New York: G. P. Putnam's Sons, 1974).

lodgers from the boardinghouse. As they made their rounds, Eliza made an effort to practice the virtues of "tolerance" and "compassion" for all beings, all beliefs. She also looked into the faces of strangers she met along the way—a mad woman, a beggar, black children, even a portrait of Napoleon and Josephine—and tried to discern from their expressions the moral lessons of their lives. Her description of a madwoman is a fine example of her powers of observation and empathy:

> I was in at Mrs. Churchill's today, and there came a poor, miserable feeble old beggar woman, who held out her shrivelled hands, and in a faint voice uttered the one word "*money.*" In her eye was a wild vacant stare, that showed at once that reason was dethroned and the poor mind was a wreck, tossed on the dark, terrible, muddy waters of idiocy. Her face was full of deep furrows, in every one of which was written a long story of care, and want, and misery, and perhaps of crime. Life is a terrible thing when it comes to this, when its bright morning ends in such a long blank night. But perhaps the poor spirit looks out from what seems to us its mental muck into the clear light and sunshine of God's love.[14]

Real change in Eliza's life came not from overt efforts at self-improvement but as the result of three crises. The first was the death of her baby boy. Born after Harrison had joined the army, baby Harry quickly became the enchanting center of Eliza's life. She, Harrison, and the baby were able to spend Christmas 1861 together, but by then the infant had developed a "pneuma,"[15] which grew worse until he died on February 17, 1862, a mere ten months old. With her husband away at war,

14. EAO journal, February 8, 1860.

15. A vague term apparently indicating difficulty in breathing, possibly the beginning of pneumonia.

Eliza had to face the shock alone, and she was utterly devastated. No other event in her journal imparts the sense of loss bordering on despair that gripped Eliza in the days that followed. Although she tried valiantly to reassure herself that the baby was happy in heaven and that she was selfish in wanting to cling to him, such exhortations provided little relief. She even took the unprecedented step of tearing a page out of her journal, apparently not wanting to remember the thoughts it contained, and two years later, in marking the anniversary of the baby's death, she noted how very ill she was after the funeral.[16]

Although most young mothers would be devastated by such a loss, Eliza's feelings were surely intensified by the record of death within her own family. In the decade before her marriage, she had lost five members of her immediate family, including her mother and her beloved sister Mary. In the journal Eliza frequently reminisces about these loved ones and even conducts imaginary conversations with them. Yet she clearly felt a moral obligation to be cheerful—the phrase "I live in the sunshine" runs like a leitmotif through the text. The sad fact is that Eliza was often obsessed with death and subject to "gloomy" feelings. Funerals particularly upset her, especially those for the very young.[17]

Her anxiety about death is the proper perspective for understanding Eliza's second crisis, the Civil War itself. At the conscious level, Eliza was intensely patriotic. The war in her view was a battle to end slavery: "a conflict between the mighty host of evil and the opposing battalions of Freedom and right."[18] She was proud of Harry's heroism and willing to accept the

16. EAO journal, March 28, 1863.
17. EAO journal, March 26 and 27, 1860.
18. EAO journal, March 19, 1860.

loneliness this meant for her. Over time, however, as newspaper reports of casualties came in and the wounded appeared in the streets in increasing numbers, the horror of war impinged more deeply upon Eliza's imagination. One anecdote that she recorded in her journal shows how chilling these reports could be:

> In one place, near South Mountain, I think, they said it was, sixty dead bodies were thrown into a deep old well—that was their only sepulcher—they were those of the rebel soldiers, and were placed by our men who were three days burying the dead, and time and various duties gave them no opportunities to afford the fallen foe a better mausoleum. General Burnside offered a dollar to every citizen who would bury a dead body, but few were willing after this great harvest of death was over.[19]

A few months after baby Harry's death, in the spring of 1862, Eliza took the unusual step of writing letters to Harry's comrades. Although they are perfectly proper in tone, they express a sort of frenzied cheerfulness. She assured the men that "every true American woman" cherished their sacrifice and prayed earnestly for their deliverance. She even rebuked one soldier for living in "Doubting Castle" because he is skeptical of the support on the home front, and she closed this letter with a glowing description of life after the war when the soldiers and their wives would live close to one another, in "pleasant Houses," and continue the rich friendships forged on the battlefront.[20]

These buoyant letters are perplexing. Why so cheerful? So determinedly optimistic? Certainly the year 1862 was not a

19. EAO journal, June 19 [1862]. For details on the treatment of dead bodies during the war, see Gary Laderman, *The Sacred Remains: American Attitudes Toward Death, 1799–1883* (New Haven: Yale University Press, 1996).

20. EAO journal, July 1, 1862.

cheering one for the Union army. The motive behind this unusual correspondence finally surfaces in a letter to Frank Fornshell,[21] a comrade of Harry. After several paragraphs of pleasantries, Eliza raises the delicate question of Harry's fate:

> You see Mr. Otis often, don't you? I am glad that he has so good a friend as you with him. And wont you let me ask a favor of you, just such an one as I would ask of a dear brother? I am *sure* you will. I know as well as any one all the dangers of the battle-field, and all that may possibly happen to my Husband, and you'll let me ask you, Frank, to care for him, if he should be wounded, and to send me word; and if he should fall in the strife you would take him up *tenderly*, wouldn't you and send all that death would leave to earth, home to me? Promise me *this*, and I will *bless* you always.[22]

With wonderful sensitivity, Eliza finally articulates her fear of Harry's peril. All military wives live with this fear, but the death of baby Harry increased Eliza's anxiety. In describing for the soldiers their happy life after the war, she was clearly consoling herself as much as them. It seems significant that, in this period of desperation, she turns to Harry's comrades for comfort rather than her own family.

Indeed the third crisis mentioned obliquely in the journal is an undefined family crisis, a scandal involving Eliza that, according to Harry, threatened to "ruin her pure name." Harry dismissed the charges contemptuously: "Her unwaver-

21. Frank Fornshell, Twelfth Regiment, Ohio Volunteers, appointed sergeant in 1863, was wounded at the Battle of South Mountain and reduced in rank at his own request. See J. B. Foraker, Henry Axline, and J. S. Robinson, comps., *Official Roster of the Soldiers of the State of Ohio in the War of Rebellion, 1861–66* (hereafter *Roster*), vol. 2 (Cincinnati, 1886), 368.

22. EAO journal, May 31 [1862].

ing constancy gives the lie to their every calumnious tale." Inevitably, the conscientious Eliza was upset "by the wrongs that others do me" to the extent that Harry urged her not to "go back to Lowell again where everything is so unpleasant."[23]

Unfortunately, the Victorian habit of reticence prevented Harry and Eliza from delineating specific details of Eliza's supposedly "improper" behavior. The likeliest explanation is that the family was censorious of Eliza's traveling alone around the South, an unattended married woman, and alleged, according to Harry, that "she is not true."[24] They may even have pressed her to return home to Lowell for the duration of the war and resume her teaching duties at Wetherby Academy, thus helping out the family enterprise. Whatever the nub of the matter, both Eliza and Harry were outraged, and the effect of the incident was to separate Eliza from her family. She still returned to Lowell when Harry was on duty and stayed with her sister Jenny, but she rarely mentions her family in her journal. Henceforth, Eliza noted with great poignancy, Harry was her "home."[25]

The journal ends with some wonderful moments. Two visits by Eliza to Harry's camp in West Virginia were filled with fun and camaraderie. Eliza's account provides a vivid picture of herself and Harry at play. She decorated their makeshift

23. EAO journal, October 24, 1862, and April 1, 1863; HGO diary, September 15, 1862.

24. Historian Anne C. Rose noted that, while definitely unconventional, many Victorian wives and other kin followed their soldiers in a similar manner. Eliza's situation may have been aggravated by submerged tension with her stepmother, since she is never mentioned in her journal or as a correspondent. See Anne C. Rose, *Victorian America and the Civil War* (New York: Cambridge University Press, 1992), 184–92.

25. EAO journal, June 8, 1863. For Harry's outraged reaction to the slurs on his wife's character, see HGO diary for Monday, September 15, 1862, and Thursday, January 22, 1863.

quarters with illustrations from *Harper's Weekly* and with wildflowers arranged in a jelly jar. She socialized with the company officers and was flattered when they came by one night to serenade her—"one of the pleasantest days of my life." She climbed the local mountains and rode on Harry's back "a la mule" when the heights were too steep. She even engaged in a mild flirtation with the handsome army doctor, a young bachelor, when he extended the wives' stay in camp. These two and a half weeks in camp were special, offering the kind of companionship and fun that appealed so much to Eliza but which she rarely experienced.

In the final section of the journal she recorded a second trip through the Kanawha Valley to visit Harry. It offers some of Eliza's best descriptions of nature as well as some astute comments on West Virginia's "poor whites," whose cabins dotted the road and whose slovenly lifestyles stirred Eliza's moral outrage. The most interesting part of this trip is her conversation with a companion, a young man of sixteen or seventeen named Henry, a native of West Virginia. They speak of many topics, in the midst of which Eliza confesses that, as a child, she was full of hope and yearning, that she studied hard to prepare herself to be "great," but now that she is an adult she finds her hopes unfulfilled and her life incomplete. Eliza closes these reflections by reaffirming that "all life is noble if we choose to make it so," but the entire passage is quite different in tone than her earlier reveries. The romantic impulses and the gloomy moods have been refined over three years into a more tranquil, accepting frame of mind. The desolation of war and the "pitiful little children" are visible everywhere, but Eliza rides on, enjoying the majestic landscape and the knowledge she will soon be with Harry. She bids her young companion good-bye and writes in her journal that "almost everyday has its farewells." There is a new maturity in Eliza's character; henceforth she will probably enjoy life more and be less vulnerable to crisis.

Above all, Eliza's journal is a tribute to her love of language. Perfectly chosen adjectives and rich metaphors point to her craftsmanship as a writer. She was adept at evoking moods from whimsy to grief, and she was masterful in her personifications of nature. She had distinguished herself as a poet in school and would go on to become a much-published professional poet after the Civil War when she and Harry went into the newspaper business.[26] Her language of course was that of Victorian America: dramatic, fanciful, highly moral.[27] Although the journal is prose, it inevitably has many poetic features. A good example is Eliza's description of her place in the cosmos:

> My heart is full of solemn thoughts tonite—big, throbbing with the mystery of life. On the telegraphic system of the universe what words are my actions writing? On the vast picture gallery of immensity what portraits have my life-deeds painted? To what is my influence tending—to the weal or woe of those with whom I am intimately associated?[28]

26. Eliza Ann Otis, *California, "Where Sets the Sun": The Writings of Eliza Ann Otis in Poetry and Prose, 1876–1904*, Harrison Gray Otis, comp. (Los Angeles: Times-Mirror Company, 1905). This is Harry's magnificent, folio-sized compilation of the best of Eliza's public poetry. She wrote for all the newspapers they managed in Marietta, Ohio, Santa Barbara, California, and, of course, Los Angeles.

27. For an illuminating discussion of Victorian women poets, see David S. Reynolds, *Beneath the American Renaissance: The Subversive Imagination in the Age of Emerson and Melville* (Cambridge: Harvard University Press, 1989), 335–67.

28. EAO journal, January 29, 1860.

Although these questions are unusually grave, Eliza could also be dainty and humorous. Her description of the prostitutes in Louisville has a festive tone: "With faces of their own make . . . daubed with rouge and carmine, and the sallow complexion made of almost pearly whiteness by the free use of . . . 'Lilly White.' "[29] And the wind becomes quite sensuous in her account of her mountain quarters: "The wind comes in, in a dancing, saucy way as if it had all the privileges of an old acquaintance."[30]

Other passages that express her longing for departed loved ones or for Harry reveal Eliza's emotional depths. One of the most affecting moments in the journal is the description of a young mulatto girl she saw on a steamboat trip:

> There was a sweet little mulatto girl on board; a bright eyed little darling, with sprightly winning ways, and a charming, dark, little face. I did wish that I could take the poor lamb to my heart and shelter her. I trembled as I thought of her future, belonging as she did to a wronged and outraged race. The soul, bright with its native intelligence, looked out of those dark eyes and you could look down depth on depth and yet not fathom the world of feeling which lay mirrored in them. But, poor little one! The iron hand of tyranny will fetter your spirit! It may flutter and throw itself ever so wildly against its prison bars, but it will be all in vain. Darkness and Ignorance will chain it down and hold it there forever. And yet *not* forever! Thank God, *Death* will set it free.[31]

Eliza's journal is sufficiently long and varied to provide a solid sense of her personality. By contrast, the two sets of documents written by Harrison Otis during the period 1859–63 are

29. EAO journal, March 17, 1860.
30. EAO journal, June 7, 1863.
31. EAO journal, May 6, 1860.

quite short. The first set consists of four letters sent to Eliza in 1859. Although not important in terms of events, these letters do reveal the feelings and anxieties of a young man recently married and now trying to find a job as a printer in Cincinnati, a major commercial center. The letters describe his daily routine, emphasizing his loneliness and his longing to be reunited with Eliza. They are very polite letters, correct in grammar and refined in sentiment, as if written with painstaking care. Early in the first letter Harry resolved "to do a better and braver work for my wife" and added the hope that someday his efforts would "aid ourselves and the world too."[32]

Harry's expressions of love alternated between fervent avowals of his devotion and such delicate teasing as "don't forget that you are married." In one extended metaphor he cheerfully declared his dependency upon Eliza:

> Lizzie it would never do for me to be a missionary, a sailor, or a fisherman, or if I were to turn my attention to any of these occupations you would most certainly have to prepare yourself to be a *voyageur* along with me: I couldn't get on without my wife. If at any future time I should chance to become the recipient of Presidential favors, and be appointed *charge d'affaires* to the Hottentot Country, or to the Unexplored Region where they converse in the unknown tongue, and live on dirt, I guess you would have to bundle up and *charge* with me. I couldn't treat with the dirt eaters without my wife. . . . Who would drive away the weakness and waywardness that come from desolation in the heart? My inner feeling tells me "none but your Bride."[33]

This is a charming passage, full of imagination and affection. It also provides a brief glimpse into Harry's ambitions. How many

32. HGO letter, October 15 [1859].
33. HGO letter, October 17 [1859].

American printers, aged twenty-two, would imagine themselves receiving presidential favors or serving on diplomatic missions? Although Harry was clearly teasing, such grand fancies provide a hint of his aspirations.

This idyllic mood contrasts sharply with the most poignant moment in the letters. Harry was plainly discouraged by his inability to find work. Money was certainly a factor but so was his manhood. Feeling defensive, he asked Eliza not to think that "I am devoid of 'pluck' for I don't believe it is true. I know sometimes I evince something like a timid spirit, but you know it is more the shrinking from certain associations than from a hard task."[34] Harry's dilemma was genuine. He was a poor farmer's son, a churchgoer and teetotaler who abstained as a matter of conscience from the drinking, gambling, and wrestling bouts that many young men used to display their virility.[35] Work is Harry's main source of self-affirmation. It must have been acutely distressing to be without work in the first days of his marriage.

Otherwise Harry's voice is rather quiet in these letters. He sent regards to friends and relatives and gave Eliza detailed instructions for her trip to Louisville. His only rhetorical outbursts occurred when describing his love for her: "Ah, here I am, *Wife of My Heart, My Darling*, with a great, long, sweet, soul-born offspring of your love—your high, heaven-like affection, like even unto that of our Father's angels in the realms

34. HGO letter, October 17 [1859].

35. See Nicole Etcheson, "Manliness and the Political Culture of the Old Northwest, 1790–1860," *Journal of the Early American Republic* 15, no. 1 (1995): 59–77, and E. Anthony Rotundo, *American Manhood: Transformations in Masculinity from the Revolution to the Modern Era* (New York: Basic Books, 1993), 56–74.

above."[36] This is an exceptionally flowery passage, but it is not the only one. At another point he swore ("with my hand on my heart") that only Eliza could give him the strength his life needed.[37]

Harry's romantic effusions echo Eliza's many references to heaven and the power of the soul as well as to the fervent devotion required in a marriage. Yet Harry's writing is much funnier than Eliza's, showing his ability to see the humorous side of events even when in distress. Over time his prose will become more taut and muscular. The first evidence of his developing style is the final text of our series, the Civil War diary, written over a period of seven months in 1862 and 1863.

The diary introduces a new man: confident, resourceful, and aggressive. Before it begins, Harry has risen from the rank of private to first sergeant and has fought in the battles of Scary Creek and Carnifax Ferry in West Virginia. During the course of the diary, Harry will see action at South Mountain, the second Manassas (Bull Run), and Antietam. Thus Harry was by 1862 a seasoned soldier, used to long marches, foraging for food, and meeting the enemy on fields where thousands will die in just one day.

Harry's account is a simple soldier's story. There is no grand talk of strategy or headquarters. Food, sleep, dust, and letters from "Lizzie" preoccupied Harry. He became angry when his comrades got drunk and woke him up or when someone sent back a false alarm of enemy movement, but by and large Harry was remarkably single-minded. For him the Civil War was a great cause: "The Country must be saved. God be with the

36. HGO letter, Saturday [October 22, 1859].
37. HGO letter, October 17 [1859].

nation's defenders," he exclaimed on hearing of the Union victory at Harper's Ferry.[38] Occasionally he took time to notice the beauty of the Maryland countryside or to sneer at the captured North Carolinians who once called the Union soldiers "hirelings."[39] And the sight of the dead and wounded at South Mountain Gap stirred his sympathy: "The fighting was indeed desperate. . . . The ground lay strewn with dead and dying. . . . The sight was awful to look at."[40]

Yet the overall tone of the diary is one of exhilaration. At last Harry had found a cause worth fighting for and an enemy who must be defeated. The challenge to Harry's abilities was total, and he would earn promotion after promotion for his leadership and bravery on the field. The excitement of combat ripples through the diary. At the news of the victory at Harper's Ferry, he reported being "churned up. Ready to fight to the death."[41] He was proud of his regiment and noted that at Bull's Run Bridge the Twelfth "came into Battle in good style. . . . Bullets fly like hail. . . . I fire at flag & then 'get up & dust.'" In the midst of this deadly encounter, Harry drops back to help a wounded comrade. "Rebel Calvary came dashing up, crying '*Halt!*' 'Nary Halt for me—'Light out,' with two guns & a sword."[42]

This vivid account conveys the tension and danger of war from the soldier's perspective. In fact, the only moments of

38. HGO diary, September 4 [1862].

39. HGO diary, September 10 and 15 [1862].

40. HGO diary, September 16, 1862. James M. McPherson presents a fine study of the motivation of both Northern and Confederate soldiers in *For Cause and Comrades: Why Men Fought in the Civil War* (New York: Oxford University Press, 1997).

41. HGO diary, September 4 [1862].

42. HGO diary, August 27 [1862].

tedium occur when Harry is in winter camp, studying for his officer's examination. He would clearly much rather be in the field. Yet he is a good soldier—cautiously aggressive, obedient to orders, constantly checking his food and equipment so that he is ready to go on short notice. Temperamentally he presents a paradox in these texts. With Eliza, Harry is the embodiment of Victorian courtesy and moderation. Yet in war he is ferocity itself. These contrasting traits seem to be grounded in Harry's origins in a pious, evangelical family combined with his experience with the Underground Railroad, an earlier "great cause" that involved constant danger and painstaking caution. Exposure to high risk for the sake of an ideal galvanized Harrison Otis. Later, in his newspaper editorials, he would unleash similar passion as either the strenuous advocate of certain causes or the unrelenting critic of men and measures he opposed.[43]

Since the diary was specifically written for Eliza, Harry probably omitted many of the cruder or more ghastly aspects of war. Yet the diary marks a remarkable step forward in his writing style and his personality. The flowery, sentimental adjectives have simply disappeared. He provides excellent detail, but the prose resembles shorthand or a telegram, using truncated sentences to express the kernel of his experience. Such short, robust messages would form the basis of his editorial style after the war.

Harry wrote to Eliza frequently and waited impatiently for her letters. She was clearly his touchstone, but Harry was now so confident of himself and his marriage that romantic flights of fancy were no longer necessary. The diary ends with an exuber-

43. See Miller, "Otis and His *Times*," 128–328, for numerous examples of Harry's editorial style.

ant declaration of his loyalties: "My birthday! Twenty six years of my life gone! They have not been wholly spent in vain, I hope. I am today a soldier for my Country which is worth living for, and deserves dying for, and I have a glorious wife to Cheer me on to noble deeds. May God preserve her and my Country too, and my poor self."[44]

In addition to their personal information, these three texts provide new and important information about the Otis marriage. Modern scholarship has devoted intense study to the Victorian marriage. "Republican Motherhood," "separate spheres," "the cult of true womanhood," "the female world of love and ritual," and "companionate marriage" are only some of the descriptions applied to nineteenth-century women and men and their most intimate bonds.[45] Inevitably Harry and Eliza fit into some of these categories but not others. Certainly their personal attributes fit the typical Victorian image of the middle class: conspicuous politeness, religious piety, and a romantic ideal of the marriage bond. The texts also suggest that they enjoyed physical and sexual intimacy with each other, although the references are rare and very restrained.[46]

In other ways the Otises deviated from Victorian norms. They did not maintain close kinship ties after their marriage. More-

44. HGO diary, February 10 [1863].

45. A fine review of recent scholarship on nineteenth-century women is provided in Linda Kerber, "Separate Spheres, Female Worlds, Women's Place: The Rhetoric of Women's History," *Journal of American History* 75 (June 1988): 9–39.

46. For example, Harry's letter of October 15, 1859, in which he wrote that he longed to "rest on the same couch" with Eliza and make "her breast my pillow." Eliza refers on several occasions to highly emotional good-bye kisses when she and Harry had to part, but this is the extent of her references to physical contact. See journal entry for June 29, 1863.

over, despite her advanced education and strong moral convictions, Eliza did not become an *active* supporter of the temperance movement, or abolition, or women's suffrage.[47] Nor was Harry, despite his vigor on the field, an overbearing patriarch at home. Quite the opposite. There was within the Otis marriage a bond of mutual support and mutual decision making that left room for real autonomy within the basic commitment.[48] The best example of this interaction occurred in 1863 when Harry told Eliza he was thinking of enlisting in the regular army at the war's end:

> The thought chilled me. I told him I never could consent to it, that I wouldn't feel as if there was any brightness in the future for me if he would do that. That while his country needed him in this great strife for Freedom, and National existence I would not say one word to keep him from the field, but when this war was over, I should feel, that I had some claim upon him, and with him I should want a home.[49]

47. Anne Rose notes that many Civil War wives pursued lives of domesticity after the war in *Victorian America and the Civil War*, 184. Eliza may have been a bit unusual in that she did help Harry manage the various family newspapers and wrote poetry for all of them, but she never showed interest in a public role for herself. She and Harry seemed therefore to have escaped the role conflicts that Lystra found in many Victorian marriages in *Searching the Heart*, 121–56.

48. For an insightful description of this type of American marriage, see Degler, *At Odds*, 17, 26–51.

49. EAO journal, April 4, 1863. Harrison did resign from the Ohio Volunteers in 1865. However, two years later he applied to the Army for a second lieutenant's commission, took the required examination, but failed the section on arithmetic. Harrison begged to be allowed to take the exam again but was refused. Smudges on the exam suggest that Harrison's marks were deliberately lowered. There is no record of Eliza's feelings about Harrison's renewed interest in a military career. It certainly would have changed their lives as well as the history of Southern California. (See Miller, "Otis and His *Times*," 32, and thanks to Darl Stephenson for documents in the National Archives, Washington, D.C.)

Harry bowed to the strength of his wife's feelings on this all-important question of his future career. He returned to civilian life in 1865, and, with the three young daughters who joined their family beginning in 1864, they began the long quest for a successful newspaper.[50]

This quest was made possible by certain personal traits that both Otises had developed. The first, certainly, was mobility. The journal shows Eliza moving from place to place in the upper South, traveling alone on public transportation, and then taking lodgings in a boardinghouse if there were no friends nearby. In the 1830s the French statesman and author Alexis de Tocqueville remarked with astonishment on the practice of respectable American women traveling alone in public, quite safely.[51] It was still a fairly unusual practice in the 1860s, but Eliza took it in stride. Harry was equally mobile, going from place to place to look for jobs; and he was, of course, constantly on the move while in the army. The Otises would uproot their family several times in search of opportunity: to Marietta, Ohio, in 1865; to Washington, D.C., in 1867; to Santa Barbara, California, in 1876, including a two-year stint for Harry on the Seal Islands in Alaska to superintend the seal-fur trade; and finally permanent settlement in Los Angeles in 1882.

This kind of mobility is associated by historians and sociologists with individualism.[52] One must be independent to survive

50. Beulah Lilian was born in 1864, Emma Marian in 1866, and Mabel in 1871. Esther, born in 1875, died in infancy. All three surviving girls worked for the *Los Angeles Times* as young women. See Babcock, *Ancestry of Marian Otis Chandler*, 1–2.

51. Alexis de Tocqueville, *Democracy in America*, vol. 2, J. P. Mayer and Max Lerner, eds. (New York: Harper and Row, 1966), 578.

52. For a powerful critique of individualism by Americans and visiting Europeans in the nineteenth century, see Fred Somkin, *Unquiet Eagle: Memory and*

the constant breaking of ties and the challenge of new surroundings. There is no documentary evidence of the Otises' reaction to this constant moving about. Eliza's early experience of moving as a teenager from New England to Ohio and then to Kentucky after her marriage may have prepared her for later moves. Harry seemed to care little for place; he was intent on owning an influential newspaper and acquiring political power. It would take twenty years to accomplish these goals, but he was a man of fierce determination.

Mobility and individualism coupled with the yearning for a better life are quite common among the pioneering men and women who went west after the Civil War. Most traveled on wagon trains and endured three months or more of hardship to cross the Great Plains. Recently there have been several studies of this pioneer experience and its impact on the families who rode in the wagons. Generally men took the initiative in deciding to go west. Often wives were very reluctant to give up home, kin, and roots. The trip itself was harsh, and women, who were responsible for children, food, and clothing, bore a heavy burden. Their migration was made physically more comfortable when the railroads began to reach points on the Pacific Coast in the 1870s, although the loss of kinship ties and remembered places remained a source of regret. Some of these families realized their dreams and began new, fruitful lives, while others rued the day they had ever crossed the Mississippi.[53]

Desire in the Idea of American Freedom, 1815–60 (Ithaca: Cornell University Press, 1970), chap. 5.

53. For a fine description of life in the pioneer wagons, see John Mack Faragher, *Women and Men on the Overland Trail* (New Haven: Yale University Press, 1979). A more romantic picture is painted in Henry Nash Smith, *Virgin Land: The American West as Symbol and Myth* (Cambridge: Harvard University Press, 1950), 184–8, 250–60.

Harrison and Eliza Otis went west in comparative splendor, taking the railroad to San Francisco and a steamboat to Santa Barbara. Yet there is a remarkable affinity between the Otises and the families that rolled across the continent in wagons or trains. These migrants came overwhelmingly from the Midwest. All had experienced the Civil War in some form. All had cut their ties with the land and people back east. All had summoned within themselves a spirit of self-sufficiency. And all had made opportunity and a new life their primary goals. For Harry and Eliza, this great gamble brought both happiness and success. Eliza wrote hundreds of poems and several travelogues celebrating her love of California's climate and landscape, especially its flowers. Harry's acquisition of a major, expanding newspaper brought him national prominence and immense personal satisfaction.[54]

It is often said that the success of the *Los Angeles Times* was due to the arrival of a second railroad, the Santa Fe, into the city. That was certainly a factor; yet this explanation overlooks the great ideological affinity between the Otis newspaper and the hosts of migrants who flowed into Southern California by rail, wagon, or ship. Both the *Times* and its readers felt the intense patriotism generated by the Civil War. Harry's editorials and Eliza's poetry repeatedly invoked the glorious cause and the gallant heroism. Equally strong in the minds of the Otises and their readers was their belief in the unfolding progress of

54. An excellent account of the new western communities is provided in Richard White, *"It's Your Misfortune and None of My Own": A History of the American West* (Norman: Oklahoma University Press, 1991), including descriptions of women's roles on pages 311–15, 627–31. A different but imaginative account of the origins of Southern California is presented in Kevin Starr, *Inventing the Dream: California through the Progressive Era* (New York: Oxford University Press, 1984), 31–98.

America and its special destiny, guided by the firm standards of Protestant morality. The *Times* became a leader in campaigns for civic improvement, for the encouragement of the arts and cultural institutions, and for the growth of free-enterprise capitalism. Naturally this was not an outlook favored by all. The extraordinary success of the *Times* does suggest, however, that the Otises had an instinctive bond with their readers. This is a story that awaits its historian. One can only observe in conclusion that the sacrifices Eliza and Harry made during the Civil War and the ordeal of their long search for a permanent base were the necessary preconditions for their triumph at the *Times*. Their lives offer a striking example of how ideas moved from east to west in late-nineteenth-century America and how a newspaper's success arose directly from the publishers' sensitivity to the values of their community.

ARCHITECTS OF OUR FORTUNES

SECTION ONE

The Correspondence of Harrison Gray Otis, 1859

Panorama of Cincinnati in the 1850s. (Cincinnati Museum Center)

CINCINNATI, OCTOBER 15 [1859]
SATURDAY EVE.

Dear Lizzie—*Darling Wife!*

I'm lonely without you, my Blessing. It is harder now to be away from you than ever before! All alone away from your woman's heart, the *only home* I have, it's a cheerless task to try to have a happy heart and a smiling face. And there I don't succeed in doing anything worthy for you—that troubles me more. Not that I mean to speak now of anything I've attempted since I reached here at 11 o'clock this morning, but when I'm away out in the world, where we'll both be sometime, there I feel more than ever how much I ought to do, and yet how little I have ever yet done for you. O, I must do a better and braver work for my wife than I have ever done in my life! It makes me almost ashamed to think that I yield to circumstances rather than make them yield to me. The fact is, I wish I didn't do a petty business in the world! If I could only aid ourselves and the world too! Happy thought! But this is not like myself when I've work before me—it's *trifling*. You'll just remember that I've a young wife up among the Muskingum hills, and she's good and true, and it makes my poor heart tremble to leave her. I'll tell you, Lizzie, for you are an old friend, and intimate and

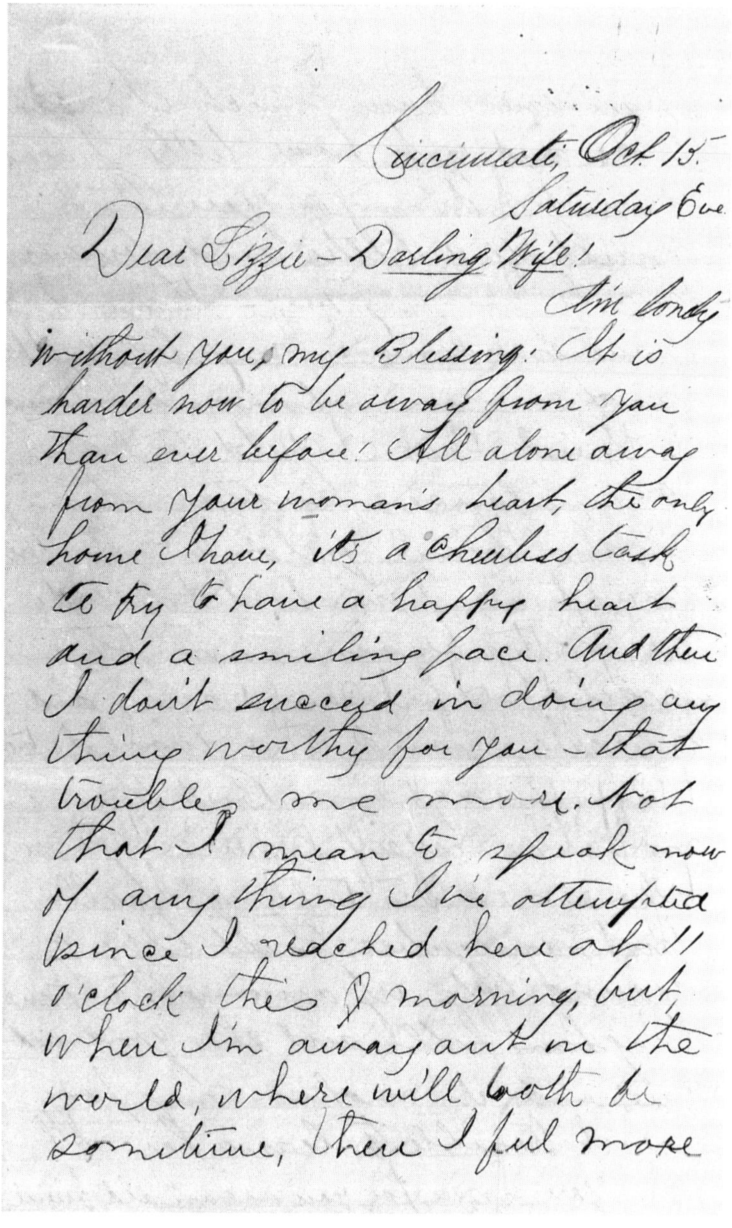
Cincinnati, Oct 15.
Saturday Eve.

Dear Lizzie—Darling Wife!

I'm lonely without you, my Blessing. It is harder now to be away from you than ever before. All alone away from your woman's heart, the only home I have, it's a cheerless task to try to have a happy heart and a smiling face. And then I don't succeed in doing any thing worthy for you—that troubles me more. Not that I mean to speak now of any thing I've attempted since I reached here at 11 o'clock this morning, but, when I'm away out in the world, where will both be sometime, there I feel more

Page from letter showing Harry's script.
(Los Angeles Times History Center)

confidential as ever I had friend, that she didn't like to part with me very well. She put her white arms around my neck and almost refused to let me go—and that dear embrace!—dear but sad!—would I had never again to feel other than the melting clash of her dear arms! Forever may I rest on the same couch with her, and forever be her breast my pillow.

Sunday Morning—I commenced this a little before night yesterday, and expected to finish in time for the mail, but as I did not know just when it left I concluded to wait until this morning before closing. As I was tired, and, what is unusual for me, troubled with a headache, I wrote but little after dark but went out into the air for an hour or two. I am well this morning. I'll go to church this morning, because I think a sermon will afford me food for pleasant and profitable reflection, and if that prove true, it may take the place of misanthropic and unprofitable musings. I'll go to hear Mr. Stores if he preaches today.

I would have dropped you a few lines from some point on the river, but as I had written nothing when we reached Portsmouth (probably the most favorable place for mailing) I thought that my letter would get to you about as soon by waiting to mail it at Cincinnati.

The *Ohio* had a hard time getting over the bars at Blennerhasset and Buffington Islands. The boat passed both places finally by dint of much steaming and "sparring" and the aid of a rope attached to a tree on shore. At Buffington Island we passed nine steamboats all hard aground.

From Parkersburg to Gallipolis we had the company of an attractive young lady. There was a number of ladies aboard, but I speak of this one in particular because she "took my eye"—that is to say, I "made up my mind" about her. She is a "stunning" singer—and didn't she know it? The next time I stop at Gallipolis, "I've got my mind made up" about whom I'm going to see.

Afternoon. What a glad surprise it was, Lizzie Darling, when your letter was handed me this morning at the office! It was my first visit to the Post Office since I reached the city, and need I tell my Wife that it was a joyful one? Heaven bless you, Dearest, for your loving remembrance and your more loving words!

And you too have felt with me how hard it is to be away! You feel it now and will feel it so long as each is not near the heart and the breast of the other. When I say this do I not say what your heart tells you is true? Lizzie, I can now speak for you and you can speak for me in whatever the heart would utter. The language of one is that of the other.

I went after reading your letter to hear Mr. Stores, but heard instead President Smith of College Hill Seminary. (Love, I suppose). He delivered a most masterly and powerful sermon in defense of evangelical truth. He has received a call from the Second Presbyterian Church of this city lately, and an offer of a $25,000 salary,[1] but declines to leave his post in the Theological Seminary.

I was am glad to hear from father and that he reached his destination in safety; and I hope he will get back as well.

I am right glad you feel less of that chilly sensation. I think all you want is a better circulation and a little more *fire*. Don't sit in cold rooms, Lizzie, or you shan't be my music teacher—I'll go to *Gallipolis*. I could have a grand time grinding groans out of a "piano forty" which means, I suppose, forty pianos.

Read "Love" while you are not courting preachers, and don't

1. Probably Harry has added an extra zero inadvertently. A salary of $2,500 would be quite handsome for a minister in the 1850s.

Presbyterian Church in Cincinnati, where Harry heard a powerful evangelical sermon. (Cincinnati Museum Center)

forget that you are married. Is it essential that a pupil should tell his music teacher—she being a young lady, blonde, auburn hair, classic features, blue eyes, pretty form, intellectual—that he is a married gentleman? If you think it is, why all right.

You had a pleasant visit from Dr. Lindner's folk, I venture to say. I am sorry I was not at home. Thank them for the visit on my behalf, and tender my compliments—a poor return by the way.

I hope Dr. Tenney's family did not feel hurt by my sudden vacation of their premises. I was sorry, after enjoying their hospitality, to be compelled to leave so abruptly. Mrs. Tenney is good and kind, and I thank her for her hospitality and friendly interest. If I read her aright, there are few such matrons.

I will mail this now, as I think it may go out early in the morning and you shall hear again soon from Harry.

Jones boards me. I shall not stay long with Jones.

I delivered Charles'[2] letter to Glazier, he being the gentleman with whom Mr. Clark has his office. The latter gentleman was away in the city somewhere.

You will probably get a letter from Churchill[3] soon. Open and read it and then please send it to me with any suggestions you may wish to make. I will write to him again immediately.

Of course I can't tell anything much about business here as yet.

2. Charles T. Wetherby, born in 1804, was Eliza's older brother. A successful businessman in Lowell, Ohio, he with other partners incorporated the Lowell Woolen Factory in 1867 with forty thousand dollars in capital stock and built a woolen mill. See Norris F. Schneider, *History of Lowell and Adams Townships* (Lowell, Ohio, 1940), 12.

3. Elroy Churchill was a printer and owner of the boardinghouse where the Otises stayed in 1860; *Louisville Directory and Business Advertiser, 1859–60.*

Goodbye, and My Darling shall get another letter, imperfect though it be, within a few days from

Harry

Miss E. A. Wetherby Otis

. . . (Good joke, ain't it? I wrote Miss before I thought how you had changed it for me . . . But let it stand.)

CINCINNATI, OCT. 17 [1859]
MONDAY EVE.

Dear, Darling Wife:

My Own Lizzie! How could I live without you? I wish you were with me, God bless you!—then I would have a happier face and a lighter heart—and you, too, wouldn't you, Love? The rain might fall ever so fast and the night glow ever so dark, as they do tonight, but if you were close to my heart, no lonely feeling would be there.

Lizzie, it would never do for me to be a missionary, a sailor, or a fisherman, or if I were to turn my attention to any of those occupations you would most certainly have to prepare yourself to be a *voyageur* along with me: I couldn't get on without my wife. If at any future time I should chance to become the recipient of Presidential favors, and be appointed *charge d'affaires* to the Hottentot Country, or to the Unexplored Region where they converse in the unknown tongue, and live on dirt, I guess you would have to bundle up and *charge* with me: I couldn't treat with dirt eaters without the aid of my wife. Not that I would always need the assistance of a third party so much, but I could not do my work without renewed strength *here* (with my hand on my heart) and who could supply that strength, that vitality, that life-essence but my Lizzie? Who could drive away the weakness and waywardness that come from desolation in the heart? My inner feeling tells me "none but your Bride."

But while I must be away from my young wife, I will try to have the nerve that I believe rightly belongs to me, though I won't warrant the attempt to prove successful always. But there, it won't be long that I'll have to be alone, and that thought does me good.

Did your brother Frank[4] marry any one of your acquaintance? His marriage surprised me too. But I don't know him. I hope he will be happy.

Tell Ellen[5] in your next letter that it isn't half so hard to be away from your parents as it is from your wife, and that I think she don't have a hard time "a bit"—that is, compared with mine.

I don't find a demand for more than a million printers in Cincinnati. The daily newspapers furnish the most employment and the most opportunities for situations; I guess if I don't get something to do at Bradley's book office (who promised to send me a note if there should be any demand for additional compositors in his concern.) I will try to get a little work on one of the morning papers, so as to earn enough to prevent my trip down here from being a losing one. That wouldn't do, you know.—There, a noisy, but clever chap has just come into my room, and I must wind up for tonight—"cos why," he talks much and loud.

4. "Brother Frank" married Eliza's sister Mary Jane (born 1835) in 1855. She died later the same year. Presumably Otis is referring to a second marriage. Babcock, *The Ancestry of Marian Otis Chandler*, 35.

5. Ellen Augusta Wetherby, born in 1842, was one of Eliza's younger sisters.

Tuesday Morning—A happy, healthful "good morning" to you, Lizzie. May these bright sun-risings find you well and strong. I would that your body might always have the healthy warmth of your heart.

I will mail this without increasing its length beyond a single sheet. Short but frequent letters shall be the rule with us when it can't be otherwise.

I would not have you think, My Lizzie, brave good woman that you are, that I am devoid of "pluck" for I don't believe it is true. I know sometimes I evince something like a timid spirit, but you know it is more the shrinking from certain associations than from a hard task.

Your——

Harry

FRIDAY AFTERNOON [1859]

Strange I don't hear again from you, Dearest Lizzie! A waiting heart *will* grow anxious, you know, sometimes, and mine is almost so because *five days* have come and gone without any word from my young wife. Don't smile at me, Lizzie, because I've a long face, which I fancy you may almost see when you read my letters, for it requires *fortitude* to brave all this waiting.

I must mail this in a very short time, so you will excuse a very brief letter this time, won't you, Dear?

I have not yet succeeded in obtaining any business, and have been thinking for a day or two past that it will hardly pay to stay here any time. I have even been on the eve of writing to request

Stephen Otis, father of Harrison Gray Otis.
(Family Collection)

Sarah Dyar Otis, mother of Harrison Gray Otis.
(Family Collection)

you to join me as soon as you could, when we would proceed directly to Louisville, but I will not do that until I hear again from you. Besides, there is some prospect of obtaining work at a book office here in a few days, the *authority* re-assuring me today that he expected every day to need the assistance of a number of compositors. And I want to hear from Churchill, too, for it will be better for us to have him, if possible, ready for our reception when we arrive there, so that it will not become necessary to stop at a hotel. There is not, of course, much to be gained by any extended stay here, inasmuch as I can earn about the same in either city, provided I work; but now that I have spent nearly a week here on expense, (which is slight,) I don't like to leave without earning enough to pay my necessary expenses, and be square, at least, when you join me. But I'm ready to say, *positively*, that it won't be long that I wait here without you, *My Own*. If you please, Lizzie, I would like to have you make yourself ready, so that you may start at any time; and, if the river is not navigable for safe and comfortable boats, you will have to take the cars, won't you? If there is any immediate danger on the Railroad, of course, I would not wish you to come in that way, but I believe it is thought by those who know to be about as safe as any of them. The fact is, there is no choice to speak of now-a-days in the thoroughfares.

I had a letter from Jant yesterday. He preceded it by one addressed to Lowell, which I suppose you have, or else it is on its way to me.

There must have been some delay in the mails, as you did most certainly write to me several days ago, perhaps on Sunday or Monday. The fault is not in *Lizzie*; *She* is always prompt.

But I hope to be greeted by a letter full of your sweet words, conveying sweeter feelings and sentiments—sentiments right from your heart, and feelings, that find their birthplace in your innermost soul—such a letter I hope will reach me tomorrow.

One embrace, Darling and know me as

Your

Harry.

Mrs. E. A. Wetherby Otis
Cincinnati, Oct. 21/'59

SATURDAY MORNING

Ah, here I am, *Wife of My Heart, My Darling*, with a great, long, sweet, soul-born offspring of your love—your high, heaven-like affection, like even unto that of Our Father's angels in the realms above—and with the reading of this tender, sweet reflex of your soul comes the natural and necessary result, a *smiling face*. And haven't I a glad heart? You *know* it, Lizzie! But its gladness won't be complete till you can feel its beating.

But must I pass by without reply all the sweet sayings that swell up from your soul, and only tell you in brief that they are treasured in my heart? Yes, I must do it, for I have three or four letters to write today and then how can my poor pen do the office of the heart's interpreter?

It's true enough that Churchill asks a "great price." We wouldn't get rich very fast with that expense, would we? But I don't see what better course there is to pursue than to accept the offer for the present, and we can make some change in the course of a few weeks if necessary—and it *will* be necessary. We can live in Louisville for less money than that. I expect the best way—and cheapest—will be to rent a cottage in the suburbs where we live just as we please. True, we might have fine times at Mr. Churchill's, but there's that "pesky" expense! We will have a better opportunity to find a suitable location after we live there a short time, and we can make the change at our leisure. Churchill evidently means a furnished room for that price; we can furnish it ourselves. But since you have no further suggestions to make, I will write to him today requesting him to be in readiness for us. And you will please accordingly start as soon as convenient after receiving this. I am sorry I cannot be with you before you reach Cin. but it would cost me eight dollars to go and come, and I trust you will therefore excuse me for not being the attendant of my wife on the proposed trip. I hope father will be able to accompany you. If he can't come all the way, he will be with you certainly as you leave Marietta. I would much prefer the river route, if there was a good stage of water, but I fear that won't be the case. But you can come much quicker by rail, and that would please me much—*very much*, need I say? You will, however, make your own choice and write me when you start, how and what time you will probably reach here. The best time to get here will be in the forenoon as the Louisville mail boats leave at 12 M. I will of course meet you as soon as you touch.

Don't you know you were fully authorized and empowered to open Jant's letter, as well as any others that may fall into your hands! I would rather you would take all such liberties, if such they be.

Ain't Jant a "*trump?*" I like him.

But I will close now and hope to greet you very soon—don't your heart *know* what that greeting will be?

Heaven bless you my best friend, My Love, My Angel-Wife! and God guard you in safety to your husband, your

Harry

Mrs. E. A. Wetherby Otis
Cincinnati, Oct. 22. [1859]

SECTION TWO

The Civil War Journal of Eliza Ann Otis, 1860–1863

Louisville, Kentucky, on the Ohio River. (Filson Society, Louisville, Kentucky)

CHAPTER I

"I Am by Nature Gay, Light-Hearted, Joyous— a Thing of Romance"

SUNDAY, JANUARY 1, 1860.

This first-day of the new year is full of sunshine, although it is cold and frosty. I'd almost think that the climate was New England's own. Did not attend church today, but the evening was so bright Harry and I ventured out. Attended service at a Unitarian Church. Subject of discourse "The Mission of Christ." Received a letter from Sister Ellen tonight. It was welcome indeed, as *all* letters from home are. My heart is light, full of faith and hope.

MONDAY, JANUARY 2. [1860]

Still cold. I haven't ventured out to day. Miss Williams[1] called upon me and I passed the afternoon quietly with her.

1. Williams was apparently a fellow boarder. Most of Eliza's female friends cannot be traced through the *Louisville Directory and Business Advertiser,*

TUESDAY, JANUARY 3. [1860]

The beauty of the afternoon tempted me out of doors. Called upon Mrs. Hull from whom I received a hearty welcome. On my return made Mrs. Smith and Mrs. Mathis a call. Came home with a heart full of gladness. My soul wakes up to a glad paean now and then, and holy thoughts frame themselves into sweet psalms that stir a wondrous melody in the spirit sometimes. I am by nature gay, light-hearted, joyous—a thing of romance indulging in the intoxication of delightful fancies. And my life has been bright—with the exception of here and there a shadow. Childhood was full of pleasant things, of rare delights—of wondrous hopes, and sweet love—And the *Present* is not less fair—To the pictured Past it is a beautiful foreground—

Reflecting all the gleams that glimmer
In the sunlight of the long Ago.
The summer sunlight of the long ago.[2]

WEDNESDAY, JANUARY 4. [1860]

This has been really a happy day to me—such an one as I love to live. It was snowing a little at breakfast time, but soon the clouds gave place to the clear sky and calm sunshine. At ten o'clock set out with Mrs. Smith for our morning's walk. Was gone an hour or so, and came back greatly refreshed. These clear cold days are glorious, life-renewing.

The afternoon found me out again in company with Mrs. Williams and lots of pleasant things we saw. I wrote of them to Ellen

---

1859–60 because no first names are given and the directory only listed property owners.

2. The poet is unknown but quite possibly could have been Eliza herself.

as follows—beautiful pictures—one of a sweet young girl with bright blue eyes, fair hair and cheeks rivalling the roses, with which the head was twined. Then there was another—a charming picture entitled "Sympathy." Two fair girls with faces such as we see only in our dreams, full of thoughts such as the soul *feels* but for which it finds no utterance.

And still another—a representation of Mozart—he with the great soul of song, and about him were gathered lovely women, sitting in an attitude of listening silence, while he sat at the piano, drawing out from it the melody of his great spirit. I almost held my breath as I looked at it, half waiting to catch the sound of the music. But—I heard only the wild rushing of the winter wind as it swept past me touching my cheek with its chilling breath.

Wrote Mrs. Tenney to-day. Speaking of painting I told her that I had a perfect passion, an enthusiastic love for such works of art. That I believed that I had an artist's *soul* without an artist's power to embody on canvass all the wondrous pictures that the mind conceives and paints within its vast picture gallery. I can feel the poetry of these beautiful creations and as I gaze upon them I feel that there's something in my nature that may claim kindred with them. I don't believe that I was made for practical life—it just isn't my element. I wish that I could work out what I dream of

———

I wonder if she wont think me a strange girl, just as others do.

THURSDAY, JANUARY 5. [1860]

The new year continues smiling and bright, and it is warming gradually. Took a short walk this morning, but not feeling well

Opening page of manuscript with Eliza's signature. (Huntington Library)

I did not enjoy it greatly. How intimate the connection between the physical and the mental of our being. How quickly the mind is depressed when the body suffers. Strange union, that of soul and body—matter, perishable and decaying matter, and spirit imperishable, undecaying and invisible spirit. The wide world offers nothing so mysterious as man.

Mr. Minor and Miss Wilhams spent the evening with me. Had a nice time—quite an extensive political canvass. These hori-blous[3] times are a fruitful topic for thought and conversation. The political horizon is dark and clouded, but mayhaps the storm will pass over, with a few fitful gusts, a few lightning flashes, and faint mutterings of thunder. But let every lightning flash, every mutter of the thunder of that political storm and raging be a warning, and an admonition to the lover of his home and country.

FRIDAY, JANUARY 6. [1860]

Every day should be a record of usefulness, and every night should find us higher in our progressive life. But my advance I fear is somewhat snail-like, and not always certain at that. My life, I fear, is one of *thought* more than of action.

But it is earnest, active life that we need. Our *inner* life makes the world no better, be it ever so high and holy, unless we em-body it in deeds.

It's raining tonight, and there's something in the music of the battering drops as they dash against the window panes that's in keeping with the mood I'm in tonight. I seem to feel the rain drop on my *heart* as well as hear it dash upon the roof and yet

3. This seems a deliberate exaggeration of the word "horrible."

I'm hardly sad. There's a feeling though within me as if I was not true to myself—true to my life mission. I yield too much to circumstances, and settle down into an inaction that is not life. Yet I don't believe that we need be creatures of circumstances, but rather the *creators* of them, and thus the architects of our own fortunes.

SATURDAY, JANUARY 7. [1860]

Gloomy and dark today—not one ray of sunshine but warm as a spring day which breathes life into plant and tree.

I've been employed in my room all day. In the morning I worked busily trying to make it look nice and cheerful when Harry should come home. Ah, isn't there pleasure in seeking to make home look bright to a loved one? Pleasant to ask yourself in every little thing you do, will it please *him*, will *he* be gladdened by it? How truthful the saying that life is made up of *little things*. I've felt it to be so many a time. A smile and one endearing word have brought me hours of quiet happiness. Memory has been wondrous busy today. A child again! Shall I weep that it was only in fancy that I was such! No there are no tears in my heart for my vanished childhood, beautiful though it was.

I see my old home where some of life's happiest hours were passed. I can see it as it looked when the soft summer sunlight was stealing through the thick maple boughs, and casting its golden glory on the numberless buds and blossoms that grew in the pleasant nooks about it everywhere. The roses! I can almost breathe in their fragrance hanging as I see them in their modest beauty, some just faintly blushing, others deep red, others dark, almost crimson, rich and velvety. O how beautiful.

I remember as well as though twere yesterday how when a

Charles Thomas Wetherby, Eliza's older brother. (Family Collection)

Front Street, Lowell, Ohio, in the 1890s. Eliza's father moved to Lowell in 1849; Eliza spent much time here with her family in the 1850s and 1860s. It was a small village, about twelve miles from Marietta, the regional center. (Ohio Historical Society)

child I stood at one time in our large south chamber, at the window which opened to the west. It was a summer Sabbath evening and the sun had just gone down, but the west was full of beauty. I scarcely ever witnessed a more gorgeous sunset. It thrilled my very spirit and awoke intense, immortal longing. How my heart yearned to feel itself in sympathy with the God who could in a moment paint the broad sky so gloriously, and my poor little child heart made many a promise to be good and holy, and I think it must have dipped its pencil in the colors of the sky as it drew there its glowing picture of the future. But ah me, where is that child dream of goodness now? how faintly is it realized.

Dear old home! I wish that I could write of all the pleasant things that I've shared with you. You stood on the sunny side of life, didn't you, out of the reach of its shadows? O no, not *quite*, for the shadow of death did fall upon you, and twice we bent over little coffins, and folded little hands to rest on guiltless bosoms. Twice we pushed back the fair hair from the cold brows of our darlings, closed the white lids over the bright eyes, and sorrowing, o *so* sadly followed our little Austin and Baxter[4] to their one grave on the hillside.

Well the tears of sorrow were only a baptism that made you dearer—a consecration that makes you sacred.

How cheerfully Thanksgiving Day always came to us there. A bevy of little smiling faces welcomed its dawning, and the fair, sweet face of our mother seemed to grow more beautiful as she ministered to the happy hearts God had given to her keeping. O

4. Eliza's two brothers, Austin (born 1845) and Baxter (born 1847), both died in 1851. See Babcock, *Marian Otis Chandler*, 35.

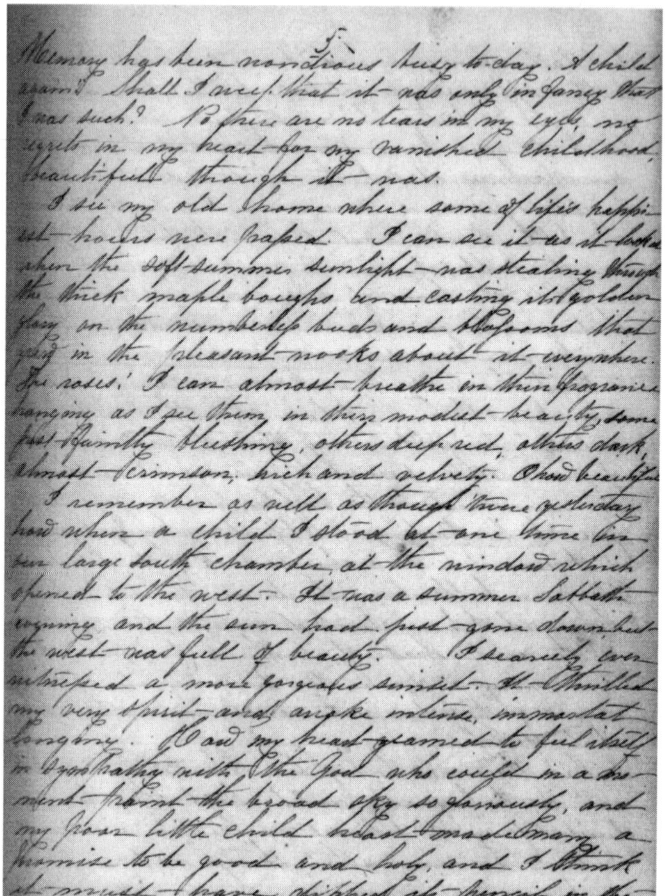

5

Memory has been wondrous busy to-day. A child again! Shall I weep that it was only in fancy that I was such? No there are no tears in my eyes, no regrets in my heart for my vanished childhood, beautiful though it was.

I see my old home where some of life's happiest hours were passed. I can see it as it looked when the soft summer sunlight was stealing through the thick maple boughs and casting its golden glory on the numberless buds and blossoms that grew in the pleasant nooks about it everywhere. The roses! I can almost breathe in their fragrance hanging as I see them in their modest beauty, some just faintly blushing, others deep red, others dark, almost crimson, rich and velvety. Oh how beautiful!

I remember as well as though twere yesterday how when a child I stood at one time in our large south chamber, at the window which opened to the west. It was a summer Sabbath evening and the sun had just gone down but the west was full of beauty. I scarcely ever witnessed a more gorgeous sunset. It thrilled my very spirit and awoke intense, immortal longing. How my heart yearned to feel itself in sympathy with the God who could in a moment paint the broad sky so gorgeously, and my poor little child heart made many a promise to be good and holy, and I think it must have dipped its pencil in the colors of the sky as it drew there its glowing picture of the future. But ah me! where is that child dream of goodness now?—how faintly is it realized.

Dear old home! I wish that I could write of all the pleasant things that I've shared with you. You stood on the sunny side of life, didn't you, out of the reach of its shadows? O no, not quite, for the shadow of death

A page from Eliza's journal dated January 7, 1860. It details one of her many nostalgic recollections of her childhood and old New Hampshire home. (Huntington Library)

life, it was a long Thanksgiving then! I remember the orchard back of the house, with its green hillside; with its one tree into which Mary[5] and I have climbed many a time, and sat in the cool shade of its thick boughs. Ah, how many a dream I've had in its old arms—dreams of the future, with no coloring in them but that of Hope.

Then there was the "high tree—Charlie's"[6] we used to call it; the boys only could climb that for the fruit, so juicy it almost melted in our mouths—but it was sour without, though not unpleasant—

Next his was "Mary's tree" with great red apples, but hard and acid; tempting looking fruit—but what disappointment its taste I thought. Ah, *dear one* how like your life! Bright, beautiful it looked to you then, but as you tasted it you found it not what you hoped for, and willingly you laid it down and went to rest. Next was my tree which stood to the south, bathing all the day long in the sunshine; all the summer time drinking in the soft southern breezes and when autumn came, it was hanging full of golden apples, sweet, tempting, luscious ones, the best by far that the orchard afforded.

Under the shadow of that tree, bright hours have passed and dreams have been dreamed that were only dreams. There is one who I often think of in connection with that spot, a strange, dark being who is ever a mystery to me. His life is lonely, but he himself has made it so. He used to whisper soft words sometimes under the shadow of those old trees I love, and perhaps his heart felt them, but I fear not. But the words were not to me.

5. Mary Jane Wetherby (born 1835), Eliza's sister, married Frank Chopin and died three months later in 1855. Ibid.

6. Charles Wetherby; see Section One, footnote 2, page 8.

I remember the last social gathering we had in our old home.[7] All the beauty, the loveliness, the talent, the genius of the place was there. Wit and song, and merry laughter all charmed us on that bright eve. Our table was spread bounteously, and flowers, and evergreens made our dining hall look like a charmed bower. Sentiments and speeches, grave and gay, enlivened the hour after we had done justice to the good things before us, and after them came our return to the parlors. It was late before our good night song was sung, yet after that there were some who lingered over favored guests. Ah, and you linger yet in my memory, kind friends—linger there yet though we wander far apart, and our lips perhaps have spoken in the long ago in which your tones come back to one through the vanished years, clear, dear days as of old.

I lean my head on my hand, and wish that the world wasn't so full of change. I wish that friends didn't go out from each other so far, and after a few brief, bright hours, and a sad farewell wander on henceforth as strangers.

But such is life. Here am I at the far south, and my home is home no longer. Other feet than those of our home circle wander there. Our Mother is at rest in her last home.[8] Mary, with her loving smile, her gentle words, and her bright, beautiful face, fairer than summer sunshine, is sleeping too with her white hands folded softly and her bosom stiff and cold, and Etta[9]—

7. This was presumably the last before the family moved from New Hampshire to Ohio. See Introduction.

8. Nancy Hyde Wetherby died in 1849. Babcock, *Marian Otis Chandler*, 37.

9. Etta Juliette Wetherby (born 1844), another of Eliza's sisters, died in 1854. Ibid., 35.

her golden curls are under the coffin lid and side by side they sleep, she and our darling brothers.

SUNDAY, JANUARY 8. [1860]

As I sat at my window today watching the passers by, there came a man with a hard, rough looking face, not a bit of beauty in it, that I could see, and the thought arose at once, almost to my lips, "I wonder if there's anybody in the world who loves him?"

And this is the way we are apt to judge of men: regarding only the rough exterior, there are many perhaps whom we scorn, but whom God loves. There are many rough hewn forms, hiding hearts which take in a world. Many who seem wholly lost to goodness, in whose hearts live yet the germs of many virtues.

Went out to church this evening. Listened to an impressive discourse from Rev. Mr. Hoyt.[10] He announced his text in such a low tone of voice I did not understand where it was found. I remember the last clause of it—"Pardon my iniquity for it is great." It sounds to me like one of the prayers of the sweet Psalmist of Israel, and I am sure that it must be David's own. Through the lapse of how many long years have these sacred strains come down to us. From the far-away Past, when Israel was a people, and Jerusalem, the joy of the whole earth do they come breathing a melody that is not of time.

10. Minister of the Unitarian Church on the corner of Fifth and Walnut in downtown Louisville.

First Unitarian Church, Louisville, built in the classic New England design. Harry and Eliza attended frequently. (Filson Society, Louisville, Kentucky)

MONDAY, JANUARY 9. [1860]

The day has been one of balm and sunshine, bright and warm as the spring. I've been out walking twice today. It was too beautiful to stay within doors. I opened my window too to the sunshine this morning, and as I did so a wild, sweet gush of bird music greeted me. 'Twas full of melody.

I have at times today been tortured with a feeling of disquiet, of unrest, of dissatisfaction, not with the world, but with myself. But I quieted it with one thought, one sweet solemn thought which came to me over and over as Discontent whispered that my Life was a useless thing—it was this—if you can make one life happier, bring joy to *one* heart, aid *one* spirit to throw off the snares of temptation and help it in its struggle to be *good*, your life will be worth the living, your work will be *noble*.

And that thought was enough to cheer me, for there is *one* heart that I would joy to make happy, *one* dear, noble, loving friend for whose sake I would strive to attain all that is good, or great, or noble in woman—one whom I would woo to happiness, and win to Heaven.

Darling you little dream how wholly in my soul you live enshrined! "And they shall no more be man, but one flesh." Don't I feel the force, the health, the *beauty* of this! How wholly *his* life is mine: Mine is colored by it; moulded by it; gladdened, beautified, and perfected by it. His love is my air, my light, my sunshine.

TUESDAY, JANUARY 10. [1860]

Took a long walk with Mrs. Mathis and Mrs. Churchill[11] this morning. Enjoyed it much. Saw on Market Street a little "*colored child*," as white and fair as the cherubs of our own households. Ah, sweet bird, to what will not those bright eyes and that fair, dimpled face expose thee! God of Heaven, have pity upon the beautiful of that poor oppressed down-trodden race, and let thine own Arm defend them!

WEDNESDAY, JANUARY 11. [1860]

Not able to go out today, but I'll enjoy myself in my room.

Sad, *sad* tidings came to us today by telegraph. The Pemberton Mills at Lawrence, Massachusetts[12] have fallen, and hundreds are buried beneath their ruins. In how many ways Death comes, and how often suddenly. How many fresh, young hearts he has stilled all at once by this stroke. How many bright eyes closed forever! Sad, fearfully sad.

11. Wife of Elroy Churchill, the printer and owner of the house on Breckinridge Street where Eliza and Harrison Otis boarded.

12. The collapse of the Pemberton Mills in Lawrence, Massachusetts, was the worst national disaster in America up to the year 1860. The columns holding the roof gave way, crashing to the ground and starting a fire. More than a hundred people were killed, mainly Irish immigrants. Their bodies were laid in the city hall, and many Americans came to pay their respects, including Abraham Lincoln, who was campaigning in New England for the presidency. Subsequent investigation showed that the tragedy was caused by the faulty reinforced concrete used in the columns. I thank Ken Skulski of the Immigrant City Archives in Lawrence for this information.

No organization in Congress yet. The friends of Sherman[13] show the *true metal* in their firm adhesion to him and to their principles.

THURSDAY, JANUARY 12. [1860]

How quickly the days glide into weeks into months. They'll all be gone to us soon, and we, ah where shall we be then? I've not been out today. It looks somewhat wintry out of doors, although it's not cold. There was a slight fall of snow last night, and the ground is white this morning. Harry attended a lecture this evening, given by the Rev. Mr. Robinson of this city. Subject—"Union of Church and State."

The speaker seemed to think that the law early prevalent in New England, obliging each citizen of the State to contribute towards the support of the church led to the founding of so many different denominations, because each, if compelled to sustain a share in the support of any Christian body would of course prefer to contribute to one which embodied the nearest his peculiar views and tenets. Perhaps the speaker's views in this subject may be correct, but it seems to me that these differences of opinion would arise under any circumstances, for each one of the human race occupies his own individual standpoint, and therefore the many different views we have of truth.

No organization as yet of the House. The members are still wrangling, fighting their daily "war of words," and retiring each day apparently just as far from conquest as ever.

13. Congressman John Sherman of Ohio, whose fight for the speakership of the House revealed how deeply divided the proslavery and antislavery forces had

FRIDAY, JANUARY 13. [1860]

It's storming tonight, and the sweeping, sobbing blast affects me mournfully. Harry come home for I feel lonely, but your presence will dispel this gloom.

Not any intelligence of importance from our Nation's Capitol. The remarks of Mr. Bingham[14] in the house, in reference to Helper's Book,[15] were manly and just. I'll quote a few lines: The resolution in reference to this book (Helper's) denounces all the beautiful words of that distinguished Gov. of Virginia, McDowell[16] viz: "You make the yoke of your slave to labor like an ox; you may compel him to live to work, and work to live, and yet the idea that he was created free will abide with him because he has the right to the hope of immortality." The resolution denounces the living sentiment of Jefferson copied from his notes on Virginia, viz: "I tremble for my country when I reflect that God is just and has no attribute to take sides against the struggle of slaves for their rights and liberty."[17] The denunciation in the resolution is a denunciation of the words of the Continen-

---

become. Like Harrison Otis, Sherman was a Republican by 1860. See James M. McPherson, *Battle Cry of Freedom: The Civil War Era* (New York: Oxford University Press, 1988), 200–201.

14. John Armor Bingham, a forceful speaker, was a member of the House of Representatives from 1854 to 1873. *Dictionary of American Biography*, s.v.

15. Hinton Rowan Helper, a white Southerner, wrote a vitriolic book, *Impending Crisis of the South* (1857), that condemned slavery and enraged the South.

16. Governor James McDowell (died 1858) was noted for his efforts to avert a civil war. *Dictionary of American Biography*, s.v.

17. Thomas Jefferson, *Notes on the State of Virginia* [1781], Query 18, William Peden, ed. (Chapel Hill: University of North Carolina Press, 1955).

tal Congress when about entering on the seven years' war[18] wherein it was said in the articles of Association by the members thereof that they "Held every man, or community of men as enemies of American Liberty who were not opposed to the traffic in slaves."[19]

SATURDAY, JANUARY 14. [1860]

Been at home all day. Wrote Mrs. Newman and Cousin Eliza this evening. To Mrs. Newman I wrote—

You remember how in the solemn twilight, while the holy stars were stealing out and looking down some with trembling eyes upon us, we with hands clasped, and voices which were not quite firm said "good-bye," and with a shadow on my heart, as on the world, I left you. You know that I've seen sorrow since then. I've bent over Mary's coffin, and looked my last look of her bright, sweet face and I turned away from her grave feeling that the bright hopes of which I had whispered to you were mockery—that life was desolation, and what could I have to do with joy? But after awhile Hope came back to my heart, and joy nestled there again.—

The fire is burning brightly in our little parlor stove, sending

18. This refers to the American Revolution.

19. Eliza seems to be referring to the Articles of Confederation (1777), yet there is nothing in that document about slavery; see Samuel Eliot Morison, *Sources and Documents Illustrating the American Revolution, 1764–1788, and the Formation of the Federal Constitution* (New York: Oxford University Press, 1965). Indeed the Founding Fathers deliberately avoided the slave issue for fear it would divide their ranks. The moral rhetoric of the sentence quoted by Eliza seems to date from the Abolitionist period.

out gleams of pleasant light, and *roaring* a song that lilts of comfort and warmth. I'm sitting over the tops of the trees that have sprung up with their thick leaved boughs on the warm carpet that covers the floor. The "Lunar Lamp"[20] casts its clear, bright light upon my paper. My neat table is full of books, only a little corner excepted on which I'm writing, and on the mantel are pictures of loved faces, faces that have blessed me many a time with their smiles and affectionate glances.

My wax flowers that I have learned to make are in their place in one corner, and a look at them would almost make you think that summer had come with its roses, and blushing pinks; its climbing woodbines and morning glories, so like life and the blossoms.

My large arm chair is waiting before the fire for *my husband* and let me whisper the truth to you ever so softly the room will look doubly pleasant to me, when he shall take his seat there, and I can sit down beside him.

To Cousin Eliza I wrote. *Later to Mrs. Newton.*[21] I visit you often in a quiet invisible way; sit down with you in the parlor and at the table, let you laugh at me just as much as you please, or talk quietly as we used to sometimes. Eddie,[22] I remember my good bye to him; He didn't like to let me go and we sat sometime by the wayside so sad that the leaves over our heads almost sobbed with us as the wind swept through them.

20. This crescent-shaped lamp imitative of the moon was the latest thing in Louisville, according to an advertisement in the *Louisville Weekly Courier*: "Cheapest, best, and most brilliant artificial light in the world. Better than oil, cheaper than candles." January 7, 1860, 3.

21. Rebecca Newton and her husband, Dave, ran a boardinghouse in Charleston, West Virginia, where Eliza stayed. It is possible that they were both from Lowell, Ohio, originally.

22. A son of the Newtons.

SUNDAY, JANUARY 15. [1860]

I do not feel rightly when I do not attend church, yet I've not been out today. It has been lovely overhead, with the sunny skies, but mud and water underneath. The evening has passed delightfully in pleasant chat. Harry and I passed it alone in our room. We talked of olden days; of our first meeting, and our hearts grown warmer in the sunlight of these memories.

"Ten o'clock?" I exclaimed, as the bell rang for that hour—"O no it cannot be more than eight"—said Harry. And surely the hours had passed so charmingly it did not seem that it could be later. But time had cheated us and ten o'clock had come.

MONDAY, JANUARY 16. [1860]

I'll give my journal but a few words tonight. My thoughts have been busy with the Past today, and its shadow of death, and I have therefore been sad.

Our grief for the dead is indeed a sorrow from which we refuse to be divorced. Ah, who would forget the silent sleepers whom in life we loved so well? Not I!

My love is stronger than death. It is a part of my life, and in memory and affection the dead are with me still.

TUESDAY, JANUARY 17. [1860]

I could not resist the allurements of the morning, so bright and clear was it—so nine o'clock found Mrs. Smith and myself tripping about here and there drinking in enjoyment as we would water when athirst.

A short walk took us to Main Street, and before leaving it we visited two picture galleries, where were some fine specimens of the limner's art.

One sweet, lovely face of the Grecian cult of beauty attracted my attention. It was pensive in expression, the large dark eyes in which you could look down depth on depth and yet not fathom the soul which lay mirrored in them, were downcast and shadowed not less with thought than with the long thick lashes which shaded them.

"Too bad, Mrs. Smith, isn't it," said I ["]that we can't see as much beauty in the *real* world, as in the ideal?"

There was another picture, which as I looked upon it my thoughts went backward through the ages—backward to time's childhood, when the world was fresh and young, and the echo of Creation's birthsong had scarce died out among the stars.

It was entitled "The First Birth." Out under the blue, bending heavens; out in the glory of the golden sunset lying, the green flower decked earth for her couch, and the breast of that dear, *dear* loved one who had sinned with and for her as her pillow, was our Mother Eve. All the *mother* was in the glance of those eyes, as they were lifted so languidly to the little one in its father's arms. There he sits holding it up before her, and the sweet face is full of love and tenderness, not for the baby *only*, but for him too whose strong heart was throbbing like her own, thrilling with new joy, the sweetest they had known since they had been shut out from Eden.

The divorce of Napoleon and Josephine was finely executed. It brought the painful scene vividly before me. On the table lay the document which signed would be fatal to her happiness. Hortense, the faithful Hortense is standing by the table, and close by her side, her head laying upon her shoulder as if to hide her uncontrollable anguish, stands the agitated Empress.

The crown upon her fair brow, and her robes of royalty seem like mockery in the presence of her grief.

Gloomy, sad and stern in his chair of state sits the Emperor. His dark eye is fixed upon Josephine; there is tenderness in it, yet firm determination. Ambition conquers love. Not even the memory of all her devotion, of her undying love for him can move his iron will. There he sits, and she must go out from his presence, his wife no longer.

There was another, "The Mother's Dream," which was beautifully delineated. The young mother sat by the bedside of her little one. His eyes were closed, and the sweet, cherub face rested softly on the pillow, and the fair curls lay softly beside it, lending a charm to its innocent beauty.

The Mother had fallen asleep in her chair, and above her were spread the wings of the angel watchers. There was a smile on her face, for she *felt* their presence, and she felt that she was not alone in her care for her darling.

Ah, such dreams are not all dreams. Invisible ones *are* about us, and angelic eyes look down like stars in the clear night time, and keep watch over our slumbers.

WEDNESDAY, JANUARY 18. [1860]

I'm a sort of good-for-nothing piece of humanity. I wonder how Harry ever happened to pick me up for a "helpmeet." I'm a *helpeat* and that's all, and not a bit the heavier is his purse for my sharing it with him. I write letters and wash stockings and pocket handkerchiefs, and eat breakfast, dinner and supper, and walk out once a day, and this is about the sum total of my exertions both physical and mental.

Ain't I a glorious demonstration of the truthfulness of the quoted saying of Longfellow's—"Life is real, life is earnest."[23] Would anybody doubt it after a glance even at my life?

Noticed yesterday the announcement of the death of Lord Macaulay, the great English historian.[24] How soon he has followed our noble Washington Irving.[25] Ah, Death doesn't spare the great, does it, any more than the humble? And the world hardly pauses as they go.

THURSDAY, JANUARY 19. [1860]

Received a call from Mrs. Dr. Benson[26] this afternoon. She is a very pleasant, accomplished lady, and I like her much. Mrs. Smith spent the afternoon with me. Passed the time in conversing of home friends, and telling of our young, joyous days at home, *childhood's home*.

FRIDAY, JANUARY 20. [1860]

Such a bright, beautiful, balmy day as this has been seldom comes to the world at this season. It's warm and sunny as a May smile, and as full of sunshine.

23. Henry Wadsworth Longfellow, *A Psalm of Life* (1839).

24. Thomas Babington Macaulay, the prolific Whig historian, was widely read and esteemed in the United States as well as in England. Among his numerous works, the most famous and enduring is the *History of England*, 6 vols. (London, 1848–60).

25. Much-loved American novelist, essayist, and historian. "The Legend of Sleepy Hollow" and "Rip Van Winkle" are his most popular tales, published in *The Sketch Book* (1819–20).

26. Wife of Dr. Joseph Benson, physician, who lived on Sixth Street in Louisville; see *Louisville Directory and Business Advertiser, 1859–60.*

Mrs. Smith and I took a long walk this morning—way down to Broadway, passing the whole length of it from Central St. to First St.

I'd really like to make my home in some of those proud old mansions. They are grand and their fine arched doors look as if they should open to none but those having happy hearts. But, ah, *don't* they? Under the rich folds of the rustling silks that clothe the many fair forms that pass in and out them are there not painfully throbbing pulses and griefs that grow all the sadder for the mask of smiles they wear? Ah, how much of this world's pomp and pride, and seeming pleasure are mockery, *very* mockery!

As we passed along the streets we saw before most of these mansions the colored servants busy at their morning task—rubbing bright the silver door knobs, dusting the paved walks, or scrubbing the dirty pavements.

Some had cheerful faces, and were humming snatches of melody of old songs that were full of the wild, sad music of these Ethiopian measures, or the low, sweet burden of joyousness. Others worked busily, as if a world of never-ending toil was before them, and not a gleam of gladness could you trace in the dark eyes or on the sombre face. Poor things!

A parrot, a real chatterbox sat in its cage before one of the large buildings on Fourth Street, I think it was, and a little Negro boy was having a nice time with it. It spoke very plainly, and seemed inclined to become acquainted. Wondrous pleased the little fellow looked with his bird companion.

SATURDAY, JANUARY 21. [1860]

Attended the Opera this afternoon. Concert given for the benefit of the Lawrence sufferers by the *New Orleans* Opera Troupe. The large Hall in the Masonic Temple was crowded, and many were unable to obtain seats.

The music, much of it, was very fine, Music such as sends its echoes along through the soul, so wondrous sweet was it.

Two beautiful little girls came out and danced upon the stage. They looked more like wax dolls than human beings however, so highly painted were they.

SUNDAY, JANUARY 22. [1860]

The Sabbath seems to have come to Nature as well as to man. It has come to it in floods of golden sunshine; in gentle, balm-breathing winds; in clear, soft, warm skies and sacred stillness.

Harry and I were not up early, and did not attend church in the morning, but the evening found us there listening to the Rev. Mr. Hoyt who discoursed from the text, "What think ye of Christ?" For the morning he had considered Him, he said, in His Divine Nature, and in the evening he sought to present Him to us in His human nature, as man; as one of us, like us, wrestling with anguish, battling with temptation, racked with pain; bowed with care, and burdened with *our* sins and infirmities.

Then he spoke of Him as our glorified and risen Savior; as our Mediator with the Father, through whom we could approach into the awful and mysterious Presence of the Invisible.

The discourse was full of interest, full of instruction.

MONDAY, JANUARY 23. [1860]

Another glorious day—a January May-day, and I've enjoyed it too.

Took a pleasant walk this morning, and on my return called at the Post Office; found letters there from Sisters Jennie and Sarah.[27] I love to hear from them.

It's past nine o'clock and I'm waiting impatiently for Harry to come home from the office.

Such constant toil! Ah, hasn't life something better in store for him? something more befitting the aspirations of that noble heart? Ah, there *must* be!

TUESDAY, JANUARY 24. [1860]

Still warm! I forget almost daily that it is the wintertime. The season thus far has had hardly a feature like our New England winters.

I've spent the day in dreaming—dreaming of what I could be and do. Ah, why dont I act—*act*—that would be better.

Harry brought me home some nice tempting oranges today. My *heart* thanks him for all his generous, kind remembrances. I hope my life may offer some fit return for all his love to me.

There are more ways than one in which a wife can lighten the burden of her Husband's life, and I would study them all, *practice* them all. Heaven, help me do it!

27. Sarah was not part of the Wetherby family; she may have been Harrison Otis's sister.

WEDNESDAY, JANUARY 25. [1860]

Passed the day with Mrs. Hull. She gave me something of her life's history. It had some sad scenes in its drama. If it had not—would it be *life*?

I'm not in a hopeful mood tonight. The shadow of the outer world I seem to feel in my heart.

O earth, *earth*, *where* is thy rest?

Fainting heart thy rest is not here; look for it only in Heaven. "Earth hath no sorrows which Heaven cannot heal."

THURSDAY, JANUARY 26. [1860]

It has been cloudy and dark today, and the light went out from my heart as well as from the sky.

I wonder what makes me have such gloomy days now and then, when my life should be love-crammed and beautiful. Ah, I *could* tell, but I'll hush the thought and wrap it in silence, and lay it away deep in my heart, where no one but God and I can watch over it.

Went out to the Catholic Cathedral tonight in company with Mr. Churchill, Harry's business being such that he could not accompany us.

Those dim old aisles, with their high carved arches, and their stillness broken only by the echo of our footsteps, wake in me a feeling akin to awe.[28]

28. A new fascination with Catholic ceremony and architecture developed among many Victorian Protestants, as their bond to Protestant theology loosened. See Rose, *Victorian America and the Civil War*, 50–51, and T. J. Jackson Lears, *No Place of Grace: Antimodernism and the Transformation of American Culture, 1880–1920* (New York: Pantheon Books, 1981), 183–216.

Roman Catholic Cathedral, Louisville. Eliza visited this grand place of worship in 1860. Its granite carvings, stained-glass windows, and many statues made her long to write a description of it. (Filson Society, Louisville, Kentucky)

High overhead was the picture of the Virgin Mary ascending into Heaven. In the faint light I could not see it clearly, but I should judge it to be a beautiful thing, a sweet, holy face, touched even before earth was lost sight of, with the light and glory of the upper skies.

On one side of the altar was a sculptured image of Jesus nailed to the cross. Down his wounded side the red drops had fallen—those drops of mercy for a ruined world.

On the opposite side of the church was an art painting representing, I inferred, the embalming of His body for burial. Mary Magdalene bends over Him tenderly, and looks into the cold, dead face of Him whom she had worshipped as her God.

I have often thought of the beautiful face of her who was last at the cross and first at the tomb.

The prophesies relative to her Savior were dim and mysterious to her. She with the Israel of God had looked for a temporal Prince and Saviour, one who should redeem them from Roman oppression and conquer all their enemies. The necessity of His death, as yet they did not see and the agonies of Calvary, the dying struggles of their God, were to his hitherto believing disciples the knell of hope that ushered in a night time of despairing awe.

But early on the morning of the third day *Mary* lingers at the tomb. The stone is rolled away from the door of the sepulchre, and her Savior is not there. The heart of the sorrowing, loving woman is heavy with its grief as she murmurs—"They have taken away my Lord, and I know not where they have laid Him." She knows not that He is to rise again, yet she loves Him still. She cannot forget his Holy teachings, nor the sacred hours of sweet communion passed with Him, and so she stands there weeping. Ah who can fancy with what startling sweetness that familiar voice breaks upon her ear as it utters her name! Mary!, and she turns and sees her risen God.

Blessed servant for love like thine! Joy, joy to the heart that has sought the Savior sorrowing!

There are numerous other pictures upon the walls, but I could not distinguish what they were.

I'd like to write a description of the grand old Cathedral, with its beautiful altar, its granite carvings, its high windows, through the stained glass of which the daylight pours with such a mellow lustre, but no, I mustn't start now. I've had too long a talk with my journal already. I mustn't gossip with it too much. If I do maybe we shall be separated altogether.

CHAPTER 2

"The Embodied Thought of God"

FRIDAY, JANUARY 27. [1860]

Called in company with Harry at Dr. Benson's this evening. On our return stopped at Mr. Churchill's, and remained there right about ten o'clock. Were entertained (?)[1] by the rehearsal of dialogues, and stage pieces, by four young gentlemen from Mrs. Lee's and elsewhere.

I don't think we'll find a stranger drama than our real life is, in all its scenes. It is incomprehensible, vast, and mysterious—threefold in its nature, taking into itself the past, present, and future, making us live in stress daily. They are blended like the colors upon a landscape—and over them all alike, the cloud and sunshine, passes.

SATURDAY, JANUARY 28. [1860]

Golden, dreamy days, balmy, fresh and beautiful, how my soul loves you! Soft, sunny skies, lighted with your mellow radiance, my spirit feels something within that answers to you, that is

1. The question mark is in the text, suggesting Eliza was not amused.

kindred with ye. Silent nature speaks to the silent world within, and the spirit *feels* and understands its language. Nature, the embodied thought of God is to God's creatures but a manifestation of Himself—a medium of communication with the Invisible.

A part of His works but standing at the head, the Crown and glory of his creations, man surveys them all, and through them may draw nearer to His God.

I often wonder how there can be in a world of so much beauty, so much of sin. But I need only to look into the deeps of depravity within my own heart to find a solution of the mystery.

I've been at home all day in my quiet room, but I've not lost sight of the beauty of the sunshine, nor the brightness of the sky.

SUNDAY, JANUARY 29. [1860]

My heart is full of solemn thoughts tonight—big, throbbing with the great mystery of life.

On the telegraphic system of the universe what words are my actions writing? On the vast picture gallery of immensity what portraits have my life-deeds painted? To what is my influence tending—to the weal or woe of those with whom I am intimately associated?

Ah, my soul, *well* may you shudder to hear the reply which conscience returns to these questionings.

Harry and I attended church to night, and listened to a solemn discourse from the Rev. Mr. Lorimer,[2] who is at present

2. George Claude Lorimer (1838–1904), a Baptist clergyman at several churches in Kentucky, Albany, and Boston, was noted for his popular preaching style. *Dictionary of American Biography*, s.v.

holding a protracted meeting in the Baptist Church on Jefferson Street. Text from Hebrews 11.4.—the last clause was more particularly dwelt upon. "And by it he being dead yet speaketh." The speaker sought to impress upon our minds the great truth that *all* exert an influence upon the world. No matter how circumscribed our sphere may be; no matter how humble our lot in life, an influence goes out from our actions that will be felt to the remotest period of time. Even when dead we shall speak. We shall speak by the impressions we made when living upon the minds of others, and through them we shall also speak by the impressions which they make upon other minds by the acts which they were influenced to do by our example.

"The voices of the dead—the voices of the dead! we feel them in our souls; they are all about us everywhere, and they speak to us. Abel speaks to us tonight—Through the lapse of the thousands of years which have passed since he died, his voice comes down to us, and "tho' dead he yet speaketh."

All nature is but a thought of God. The house in which we worship tonight is a thought of man. You find his thoughts embodied everywhere and they, in this form, will speak to you of him when he is gone.

Niagara with its voice of thunder is a thought of God. The telegraph with its iron chain linking together the continents is a thought of man. Ah, man lives and speaks to us—his influence is felt when his body is rolling in the grave, and his flesh is food for worms.

And this is one argument for the necessity for a general judgment; for then only, when time is ended, can the influence of a man be estimated, his work for weal or woe, be summed up for reward or punishment.

I feel the truthfulness of the above remarks of the [words left

Walnut Street Baptist Church, Louisville. This is a fine example of the Gothic Revival architecture that was popular in the United States before the Civil War. (Filson Society, Louisville, Kentucky)

out]. They come home with a power to my heart, as if they had been spoken only to me. My influence, circling far out into vast eternity, its circles ever widening, widening on that shoreless ocean. How shall I meet it in the future? How can I live so carelessly, as if each dying day left behind it no record, no impress for good or ill? I wonder at myself; at the world, living as we are on the confines of two worlds, with such vast, untold interests at stake, that we can act as though *today* was *all* of being, as though no limitless future was outstretched before us.

MONDAY, JANUARY 30. [1860]

Attended a prayer meeting this morning at eight o'clock. Went out to church this evening. Discourse from Rev. Mr. Lorimer from the words, "I that speak in righteousness, mighty to save."

"It requires might," said the speaker, "to save the sinner." Angels could not do it. Were the highest called upon they would feel their inability to save. Even Michael would exclaim, My arm is *too short*, and Gabriel if called upon would plead, My wings are too weak to bear one down so low, the attempt would bring upon one irretrievable stress.

I can fancy Satan going into the presence of God and saying, this sinner has given himself to my service, and I demand that he be with me through eternity.

Ah, it requireth might to save the soul from him who goeth about as a soaring lion seeking whom he may devour. It requireth *might* to overcome the opposition of the sinner's heart —to make it willing to be saved.

Christ will not save us unless we look to Him. Suppose that you were crossing a vast desert. Weary, weak and suffering you at length lie down upon its burning sands feeling that you must die. You cannot go further, and there is none to help you. But by and by you espy in the distance a cloud of dust rising, and soon you see a horseman coming towards you. You could not say to yourself, the Arab will save me whether I call to him or not, I'll lay still here and let him rescue me. No, *no*: but you'd cry aloud. Arab, *Arab*, *Arab*, come to me, I'm dying, I'm dying. Then he would come to you, and take you to a green oasis, where pure waters were flowing, and where you could refresh yourself, and feel that you were saved. And after a while, when you have eaten and drank, and are ready to go on your journey, you ask him to direct you to the city where you wish to go, and tell him that you thank him for his kindness, but that you will now go on alone. But he says to you: O no, you mustn't do it, for there are robbers in the way, and many snares and dangers will beset your path. I will go with you, and protect you.

And he goes with you, and as he meets the travelling hordes of robbers he gives them the password for himself, and the poor struggling traveller who is with him, and so he guides you on until the walls, and the high minarets and spires of the city are full in view, and you feel that you are saved, *saved*.

Poor sinner, you are out in the desert of life, hungry, starving, dying. But Christ will save you if you call to Him, and He will lead you to the green oasis of Conversion. But you mustn't let Him leave you then. He must go with you through all your life—journey till the jasper walls, and the sapphire gates, and the golden minarets of the city of our God shall burst full upon your mind.

Ah, sinner, poor sinner, Christ is *mighty* to save. He is God as well as man. I can fancy His ascension to Heaven, His garments dyed with blood, and as he nears those heavenly courts, angels are heard inquiring—"Who is this that cometh from Edom,[3] with dyed garments from Bazruh,[4] that is glorious in his apparel travelling in the greatness of his strength? And Christ answers, I that speak in righteousness, mighty to save." Then from within is heard the sound "Lift up your heads O ye gates, and be ye lift up ye everlasting doors; and the king of glory shall come in. Who is this King of glory? And the attendant angels answer: "The Lord strong and mighty, the Lord mighty in battle." And all Heaven rings with the glad cry, "Lift up your heads O ye gates, even lift them up ye everlasting doors, and the King of Glory shall come in. Who is this King of Glory? The Lord of Hosts, He is the King of Glory."

TUESDAY, JANUARY 31. [1860]

One month of the New Year goes out to night. It has brought us glorious, golden days, most of the time, days full of sunshine, and breezes such as spring breathes out so softly upon the opening flowers, and mellow, hazy skies, almost like those which hang over the world when the glory of the Indian summer-time is flooding it; when the soft October light seems to have bathed its wings in the mellowest tinges of beauty.

But today old Winter has been blustering round as if fearful that he had forgotten his duty to the world, and the wind is blowing and puffing most busily. Seems to me that January might have afforded us a more agreeable leavetaking.

But, what care I for cold or snow in my pleasant room, with

3. A region south of the Dead Sea.

4. Bazruh, a river port, was part of the Fertile Crescent in ancient times and is part of Iraq now; usually referred to as Al Bazrah or Basra.

the cheerful fire singing its song of warmth and comfort? Nothing, only as I think of the houseless, homeless, fireless ones who shrink from the pitiless blast, and with cold, numb fingers pressed to their blue lips think only of the *bitter* cold, and wonder if they *must* die; God, pity them!

I wrote to Jennie tonight. Speaking of my journal I said—It will be pleasant to recur to it when I am old. It will be a sort of landmark by which I can steer my way straight backward to that present—to its joys, its sunshine, and its gladness.

It's a pleasant thing to embody life thus; to give it a form that you may look upon in after years when the past itself has vanished.

WEDNESDAY, FEBRUARY 1. [1860]

Clear and cold. Went out to church tonight. Text—Job 35, 10—"But none saith where is God My Maker who giveth songs in the night?"

These words were addressed to Job while he was in affliction. Christians should look at all times to God, and to God alone.

It is true of sinners that "none sayeth where is God, my Maker!" Even here, where Christianity abounds, where we have the Gospel preached to us in its earnestness and purity; where we have all the blessed privileges of religion, and religious institutions, the natural man seeketh not God.

Every being having insulted God it is his imperative duty to seek Him. Good men everywhere in the Bible seek to impress upon our minds that they *sought* God and found Him.

And He will be found of us if we go unto Him. "Whomsoever cometh unto me I will in no wise cast out."

It is not the duty of God to seek us, as He in mercy does, but we, *we*, poor sinners should go to Him.

How should we seek God! We should seek Him as our Maker, our Preserver and our bountiful Benefactor. We should seek Him *in our hearts*. We should seek to be identified in the promises of hope. We must seek Him with the head, the heart and the whole man. To seek God is to seek to ourselves the imputation of Christ's righteousness. The sinner must be convinced that he *needs* God; that he is lost and ruined without Him, justly deserving of death, and under condemnation.

Being convinced of sin you must pray—pray that God will help you to come to Him.

But prayer will be of but little avail unless accompanied by repentance—by a practical life of holiness. It must not be the repentance of a Pharaoh which was past as soon as the judgments of Heaven were removed. It must not be the repentance of fear or despair, that vanishes as soon as all sense of danger is removed; but in a word, it must be a repentance that needeth not to be repented.

And as you turn from sin you must lay hold upon Christ, have confidence in Him, not so much as the Savior of the world, but as *your* Savior. Mine, *my savior*, that is the way you should feel.

You should have *faith* in Him. Faith is confidence, a full and perfect trust.

Supposing further that as you go home from meeting tonight your little girl, with her bright eyes and happy face, rushed to the door to meet you. You take her in your arms and as you sit down you say to her, My little girl, I'm going to buy you a nice doll, and it shall have large bright eyes, and wings made from the plumage of the most beautiful birds, and it shall be fixed in some way so that it can talk to you. The little girl would clap her hands in delight, and run to her mother and say, O mother, *mother*, papa is going to buy me such a *beautiful* doll! Now that little one has *faith*; she takes you at your word, and that is all you have to do, sinner, to have faith in Christ—you need only to *trust* Him—to feel that He *will* do as He has promised. Then may you have "songs in the night—*songs in the night!*"

By "songs" I understand is meant God's promises. We call them "songs" because they make us cheerful.

In the hour of trial and darkness we can sing "The Lord is my Helper in Him do I trust." We can sing His promise, "I will not leave you Comfortless," and in the hour of death, when the world recedes, and we are called to bid adieu to friends we have loved, we can sing the *sweet* song Yea though I walk thru' the valley of the shadow of death I will fear no evil, for thou, O Lord art with me, thy rod and thy staff they comfort me, O death, where is the sting, O grave where is thy victory?

You have heard of the statue of Memnon,[5] which as the first rays of the morning fall upon it, discourses sweet music. So on all the Providences of God his promises fall, and they waken music in the heart, a full and perfect harmony.

But the sinner may say, I too have songs. But sinner they are not "songs in the night." They are songs in the daytime, when all about you is bright and clear, and calm; when no danger threatens, and the loved of earth are around you. But when the night with its solemn and impressive silence is about you, when the tempest of God's wrath thunders, you have no songs, unless it be like that of the cold, fearful shriek of the Egyptians which rose on the air as the waters of the Red Sea closed over them.

5. In Greek mythology Memnon was the son of Eos and Tithonus. He was killed by Achilles during the Trojan War. The Greeks gave his name to the two colossi remaining from the great temple of Thebes built by Amenhotep III. One

THURSDAY, FEBRUARY 2. [1860]

Attended church again this evening, and listened to a discourse from the words—"Behold now is the accepted time, behold now is the day of salvation." The speaker commenced his remarks by saying, "It was a common saying among the drunkards of Israel. 'Tomorrow shall be as this day, only much more abundant.'" And this is the language of the sinner's heart when he is urged to come to Christ—*now*. "Tomorrow, tomorrow!" We all admit that we intend to be Christians *sometime* and this very admission proves that we admit the claims which God has upon us. Ah then what daring presumption to delay to put off what we know is our duty *now* until some future time. How insulting to God is such indifference—How presumptuous when we know not but tomorrow we may be in eternity.

There are only two ways which we can go. We are either going nearer to God, or further from Him, and the further we go from Him, the more difficult and doubtful is our return.

Time writes its record of changes in Nature. The seasons come and go; the summer is gone, then comes the autumn, then the winter, and next the spring-time, and then the summer again. Thus we feel that the years come and go, and we who a few days ago were little children, are tonight young men and women, and soon middle age will come, and then old age, and mostly we shall be hurried to the tomb, Time's bankrupts.

The speaker alluded to Rome, once the pride and glory of the world; to Nineveh, that once great city which is now sitting in silent desolation; "they are," said he, "the monuments of time."

---

of the colossi emitted a musical note at sunrise, said to be Memnon's greeting to his mother.

"And what is time? It is that portion of eternity which God has set apart in which to mark out his great purposes in regard to man." Beyond it our probation does not extend, for "there is no work, no knowledge, no desire in the grave to which we are hastening." We must be saved here or not at all. God's mercy will not be offered us beyond the tomb. O sinner behold then *today*, "Now is the accepted time, behold *now* is the day of salvation."

FRIDAY, FEBRUARY 3. [1860]

Clear, bright, beautiful morning. The light snow which fell on Tuesday is fast disappearing, vanishing in the warmth of the pleasant sunshine.

Attended a funeral this morning at St. John's Church on Jefferson St.[6]

The deceased was a young man, Superintendent of the Sabbath School, and an earnest, devoted Christian. His end was Peace. His young, beautiful wife seemed almost broken hearted. Her low groans of anguish were like the sound of desolation to our hearts, and many, *many* a one wept with her. I thought of my own Husband and O God, the thought of the agony which his death would bring made my heart bleed for her.

God of the Widow, *comfort* her!

The minister said he well knew how inadequate any effort at consolation would be. "I was once riding in the carriage," said he, with the chief mourner on an occasion like this. He was an imminent divine of our order, and has, many years since, gone home to Glory. I was trying to administer consolation to him,

6. A Baptist church.

when he exclaimed—"O it isn't this, it isn't this. Time is the great consoler, and it will bring consolation, I fear, all too soon. But what I want is *sanctification*." And this is what *we* want, my friends. We want our sorrows sanctified in order that they may answer the end designed. But the trouble often is, our griefs are healed too soon, before sanctification takes place."

I did not attend church this evening. I was too sad. I shrank from companionship. My spirit felt itself out in the rayless, starless darkness.

SATURDAY, FEBRUARY 4. [1860]

At home all this pleasant day. Thought was busy, and my heart felt the thrill of concrete purposes.

There's pleasure in life, *real life*. I don't mean a dreamy, aimless life. No matter how full of bright fantasies it may be, the heart isn't satisfied with them; it wants something more tangible, more progressive.

SUNDAY, FEBRUARY 5. [1860]

Raining this morning, but this afternoon the clear, soft sky was seen through the wafted cloudlets, and the wind kissed us only gently, and with a balmy breath.

Attended church with Mrs. Churchill. Witnessed the baptism of seven individuals—one a boy of not more than twelve summers, I should judge. It is pleasant to see those, such as of old Jesus took in His arms and blessed, coming to the Savior.

My head is aching tonight, and my heart keeps time with it. O my life needs purifying, and my heart cleansing!

MONDAY, FEBRUARY 6. [1860]

Just returned from evening service at the Baptist Church. Rev. Mr. Lorimer preached as usual. His discourse was from the words of Elijah to the people of Israel, assembled on Mount Carmel. And Elijah came unto all the people and said how long halt ye between two opinions? If the Lord be God, follow Him, but if Baal, follow him. 1st Kings, 18, 21.

The speaker after some extended remarks spoke of the *hopes* which the Christian enjoys. "He has the hope of being forever in the presence of his Savior; the hope of a glorious crown, a harp of praise, and the psalm of victory—of immortal life and endless glory. When the sun shines before you, your shadow is cast behind, and, so it is with the Christian. The Sun of Righteousness shines before him, and the shadows, all the cares, the griefs and sorrows of this life are cast behind him as he leaves this world. The brightness of his beams irradiates all his future. But, poor sinner this Sun is behind you, and therefore the shadows fall before you, and darken all your pathway in the future." The coming is one of still, calm, starlit beauty. I feel its influence within my heart away up over that starry pathway my soul heads its way to God. Ah, would that I could worship him aright.

TUESDAY, FEBRUARY 7. [1860]

Weary heart, would that there were use for thee! Aching, throbbing pulses how long will ye beat this drumming march of agony! My mother, my own angel mother, I wish I could leave my head on your bosom to night—could hear your voice say once again, "My Daughter, I love you," and feel your warm kisses upon my lips, for I can live only in love; without it I die evermore.

Harry, *dear* Harry, my soul's wedded self, fold me in *your* arms tonight—let me feel the beating of your strong, loving heart—let the sense, the voice of its unuttered tenderness speak peace to these troubled waves of feeling.

In fancy, Darling, I'll kiss you, and fold you closely, and more closely within my inner life.

Mrs. Holmes, Mrs. McCready, and Mrs. McIntire, with Mr. Knowlton have just left me after a very pleasant call.

WEDNESDAY, FEBRUARY 8. [1860]

Charming sunshine and clear skies again today, and I've opened my heart to them. Rev. Mr. Osborne called upon me this morning. Had rather a pleasant interview.

Took a short walk with my Husband after dinner; enjoyed it greatly. I wish that I could be with him more—could have more pleasant strolls with him. I'm so delightfully (!) organized that there's not much of the matter of fact in my composition. I believe if a competence was ours I should live a sort of a bird life—one of song and gladness.

I'm not really as it is, a child of Discontent, though. I can be happy with him I love *anywhere.*

I've been drawing off embroidery patterns today for future use.

Will little forms ever wear the tiny things which I shall fashion from them? What a wonderful thing is this giving life to life. God superintends all the wondrous formation, and it makes Him seem very near to me sometimes. I'm trembling tonight as

I think of it. I never realized it so fully before; it seems as if His Presence was all about one—me so sinful and He so holy. But He is *love.*

THURSDAY, FEBRUARY 9. [1860]

What a world is that within us! Greater and more wonderful even than the outer one, and far, *far*, more enduring!

What a story my thoughts of today would make if they were written out—a story, such as those who know me best, little dream of as mine.

I wonder if our thoughts do indeed leave their impress upon the atmosphere, and that higher intelligences, can with their expanded vision read them outwritten there!

O eternity—the *future*, isn't it mysterious? and ain't we so ourselves? I ask myself strange questions sometimes as I think of these things—questions so strange that I cannot answer them.

I believe there's nobody just like me—but there may be—because I don't know anybody, and there don't anybody know me—not even my own Harry. Some of my thoughts would perhaps make him love me better if he knew them, and others perhaps would make him pity me. I wish I could get away from them; shut myself out from them where I couldn't feel them; nor God see them.

I went out with Mrs. Smith this morning. The sun shone bright and warm; and our walk was pleasant.

On Main Street we met a poor little beggar boy (I suppose it was) his clothes were ragged and dirty, his face unwashed and his hands thrust into the pockets of his filthy pants.

He had just stopped a pleasant fine looking young man, as we passed him, and was telling him something, his tale of want, I suppose, and the young man's face was bent down close to his, and a real kindly smile was on it, that humanity must have sent up from the heart. I don't know whether he gave the little fellow anything or not, but I'm sure if he had no money for him, that kind words, and generous sympathy would be freely imparted.

As we turned back in our walk we met the sad little boy again, and he looked about him eagerly, wistfully into the thronging faces about him, as if in search of one that spoke of a kind heart and generous spirit. Ah, better than we can those little eyes read the soul as it is mirrored in the face—better than we can they judge where their sweet trust will not be betrayed or scorned.

FRIDAY, FEBRUARY 10. [1860]

Clear and somewhat cold today. The air is very fresh and pure. The brown earth looks up to the sky, with almost a smile upon her wrinkled face, for the sunshine seems to warm her old chilled heart.

I was not up this morning until eleven. I thought it best for me to keep quiet, and so when Harry was gone to the office, I got up and took a book from the table and went back to bed, and composed myself comfortably to its perusal.

"Lancton Parsonage" is its title. It's a story in three volumes and is really very interesting and instructive.

Nine o'clock, and here I am waiting for my husband.

They are busy in moving the office today into the new building on Green Street, and this is probably what detains him so late.

Darling, you are a patient worker. May God smile upon your efforts and open to you a broader path of prosperity, one in which you may realize far more fully your high and noble aspirations.

But above all may He make you *His*, an heir to that heavenly inheritance which passeth not away.

SATURDAY, FEBRUARY 11. [1860]

My hands have been wondrous idle, my thoughts wondrous busy today.

Not feeling well in the morning. I laid in bed and read "Falkland" until ten, then arose, washed and dressed for dinner, and read until I had completed the sad tale of sin, and woe, and death.

It's true to life, I think. It shows how when we have *once* yielded to temptation we are led on step by step in sin, till at last we yield to that from which at first we should have shrank in horror.

Mrs. Churchill and Smith spent the afternoon with me; Mr. Guilford, the evening.[7]

Mr. Guilford claims my sympathy. Life I should judge has been to him a disappointment, and in the future he says it will be to him he supposes, "but a bread and butter struggle."

There's one thing that I joy in for him—he has the hope of a better life beyond life: of a mansion such as "Our Father" prepares for those who love him.

7. Both Mrs. Smith and Mr. Guilford boarded at the Churchills', and Eliza saw them frequently.

SABBATH, FEBRUARY 12. [1860]

Harry and I attended service this morning at the Walnut Street Baptist Church. Sermon by Rev. Mr. Lorimer from John 4, 29, last clause of the verse—"Is not this the Christ?"

The object of the discourse was to prove the Messiahship of Christ, which he established by the fulfilment in Him, of the prophecies which related to the Messiah.

The evidence which he adduced from the Old Testament Scriptures was clear and conclusive, showing that Christ, our Savior, was the Messiah that should come. He is "The Scion of the tribe of Judah," ["]the Emmanuel which is God with us."

The Jews looked for in Him a temporal Prince and Ruler for a King. And He *will* come at this second advent as their King, when He comes in the clouds of Heaven, accompanied by his holy angels.

"In all our prayers do we ever pray for the poor Jews?" Never, or seldom ever. Our prayers go out for the heathen, but the Jew, the despised and persecuted Israelite is seldom remembered.

Whenever we see one of the seed of Abraham, we read in every line of care upon his face a testimony to the truth that Messiah has indeed come; for it is written, "The Sceptre shall not depart from Judah, nor a lawgiver from between his feet until Shiloh come." But the Sceptre has departed, and the Jews are no longer a nation, but are scattered everywhere, wandering outcasts, therefore this prophecy must have been fulfilled in Shiloh's coming.

MONDAY, FEBRUARY 13. [1860]

Warm and rainy today. Have just finished a letter to Mrs. Lindner. Speaking of her just professed belief in universal salvation, I wrote: The Scriptures are the source of all wisdom, the one great fountain of knowledge, the only source of that truth "which is able to make us wise unto salvation." Yet with the views which I entertain of its teachings you will permit me as *your friend* to say, I can but regret the conclusion at which you have arrived. From my earliest childhood I have been familiar with the word of God. I learned to lisp its sacred truths at my mother's knee, and in the soft twilight hour I used to kneel down with her and say "Our Father." But ever have I been taught to look upon Him not only as a God of *love*, of infinite, all boundless, measureless love and mercy, but as a God of justice too, a Being who "cannot look upon sin with any degree of allowance," and who has said, "For behold the day cometh that shall be as an oven, and all the proud, yea and all that do wickedly shall be stubble, and the day that cometh shall burn them up, saith the Lord of Hosts, that it shall leave them neither root nor branch." "When the Lord Jesus shall be revealed from Heaven with his mighty Angels, in flaming fire, taking vengeance on them that know not God, and that obey not the Gospel of our Lord Jesus Christ, *who shall be punished with everlasting destruction from the presence of the Lord,* and from the glory of his Power?" Mal 4,1–2 Thes 1 chap. 7–9.

Ah dear Mrs. Lindner the Bible is full of these solemn teachings, and all along upon its sacred pages is taught the fearful truth, "The soul that sinneth, it shall die;" shall be cast out from the presence of its God, into the eternal death of darkness and despair.

Ones sees and hears lots of pleasant things here in Louisville. Lectures, musical soirees, etc. for the intellectual, and works of art, splendid architecture, and grand, flowing paintings; artificial fruits and flowers, that make the mouth water, and the senses long to inhale their odorous sweetness, all these and more, are here to charm the lovers of the beautiful. And who doesn't love the beautiful, however embodied?

TUESDAY, FEBRUARY 14. [1860]

Valentine's Day, and our darling Etta's birthday. It is a dark gloomy one to us, but bright to her, for she spends it in Heaven.

The spring is coming and it will bring such flowers, beautiful birds and blossoms to shed their fragrance around her far off resting place; but even now, in that better land is the better resting place of her spirit, fadeless amaranth,[8] and sweet perfumes, crystal streamlets and "green pastures" make glad her life, and the Son of Righteousness makes radiant all her heavenly day.

This evening we had a musical entertainment at Mr. Churchill's. There a pathos, a sweetness, and touching sense of goodness in many of these Ethiopian melodies that thrills sometimes every fibre in our emotional being, and awakens echoes that are long in dying; *very long*.

WEDNESDAY, FEBRUARY 15. [1860]

It is raining today, although it is still cloudy and dark.

I'm in a dreary mood today, in a state of mental inactivity. I'm

8. An imaginary flower supposed never to fade, brilliant reddish in color, red-blue in hue.

trying to study a little, but the very effort makes me drowsy. O dear, what am I to do!

THURSDAY, FEBRUARY 16. [1860]

Busy with my books today. I'm really in a studious mood. Hope it will last. I'm thinking of going home soon, but the thought really pains me. Not that I do not love the dear friends there just as well as ever; O no, *that's* not it, but there's one here who is dearer even than they, and my poor heart aches at the thought of leaving him. But it's for the best, so be still my heart and strong.[9]

FRIDAY, FEBRUARY 17. [1860]

Eleven o'clock finds me but just returned to my room from the exercises at Mrs. Churchill's. They were not entertaining in the least—all that was pleasant was the refreshment afterwards, and that was about as satisfactory as sugar plums generally are.

SATURDAY, FEBRUARY 18. [1860]

Not well today and so took refuge in the bed this afternoon.

I was in at Mrs. Churchill's today, and there came in a poor, miserable, feeble old beggar woman, who held out her shrivelled hands, and in a faint voice uttered the one word "*money.*"

9. The journal does not reveal why Eliza and Harry thought it necessary to separate at this point. It may have been sparked by Elroy Churchill's decision to sell his house (see EAO journal entry for April 6, 1861). Richard Miller adds that Harry was concerned about the possibility of war breaking out in Kentucky and sent his wife back to Lowell while he removed to Wheeling, West Virginia; see Miller, "Otis and His *Times*," 13.

In her eye was a wild vacant stare, that showed at once that reason was dethroned and the poor mind was a wreck, tossed on the dark, terrible, muddy waters of idiocy. Her face was full of deep furrows, in every one of which was written a long story of care, and want, and misery, and perhaps of crime.

Life is a terrible thing when it comes to this, when its bright morning ends in such a long, long blank night. But perhaps the poor spirit looks out—from what seems to us its mental muck into the clear light and sunshine of God's love.

Though through the medium of the shattered bodily organization it may find no way of communication with the outer world of humanity, yet perhaps to what chaos of darkened spirit God may speak, and daily through mysterious, unseen inlets hold converse with the soul. Mrs. Churchill gave the poor woman a generous supper, and her muttered "God bless you" made me think that all thought of the Infinite had not yet finished.

CHAPTER 3

"I'm Going Away from Harry for a Little While"

FEBRUARY 19. [1860]

I did not go out to church today—felt unable to be up until afternoon.

My Sabbaths are very pleasant with *Harry* with me all day. God bless his noble heart. His love makes my life one sweet psalm; one long, rich refrain; one glad, happy melody, with the music of which every heart-string trembles, and the silent lips of the soul whisper ever in their gladness, "Husband, *darling husband, God bless you.*"

We've sold our little furniture here, and I'm going away from Harry for a little while. I don't like to think of it, yet I'll try and go cheerfully, for his sake, and when away we'll each be cheered, as he said, "by the thought of how dear and true we are to each other when we are together, and of our happy meeting again."

There'll be gladness, joy ever in these thoughts.

MONDAY, FEBRUARY 20. [1860]

I love such calm, sweet days as this has been; full of soft air and sunshine.

I've been busy in my room today, mending Harry's things before I leave him.

Mrs. Smith spent the afternoon with me. We passed it rather quietly for I was in too thoughtful a mood to be very sociable.

My head is aching, so I'll bid good night to my journal.

TUESDAY, FEBRUARY 21. [1860]

Warm and springlike. Mrs. Mercer, Mrs. Smith and myself went out shopping this afternoon. Life was busy and stirring as ever on Main Street. I noticed nothing new, only new faces and new goods. The faces, many of them, as well as the goods were in *market*—I suppose, and will be turned over to the highest bidder.[1]

WEDNESDAY, FEBRUARY 22. [1860]

Gloriously beautiful today. All the morning my window was open to let in the soft, balmy air, and I breathed it in with a sense of delicious gladness.

Mr. Guilford is to be married this evening. My own bridal day is not far back in the past; only just a *little* way, as far back as the eleventh of sunny September.

I remember the beauty of that evening. It was just such a

1. Eliza's sarcastic tone, plus the emphasis on faces, suggests she is referring to prostitutes, although they could be female slaves.

night as should come to all *who love* when they are first wedded. The moon shed the soft lustre of her full form upon the world, and the stars looked down, tremulous with gladness, and my own heart answered their look.

And I've been happy since then, and my Husband is *dearer*, and every day of our wedded life makes me more fully *his*.

The love of earth! There's something of Eden in it yet, I own.

THURSDAY, FEBRUARY 23. [1860]

There's a little of a sombre hue to my feelings to night. Our room, minus our bright carpet looks hardly homelike—it *seems lonely*.

I've written three letters today. For my letter to father, the first part of which was dated yesterday, I said—It's been a glorious, glowing day today. The air was soft and balmy, the sky clear, and the sunshine almost summerlike.

And the night is beautiful, with its clear, silvery starlight, unshadowed by mist or cloud, and there's stillness here where I am, right in the heart of this great city, as if the beauty of the day, and of the night had spoken to the surging, throbbing, restless tide of human passion, bidding it to be still.

This beauty speaks to my soul, in a way that ought to make me better. But, I'm afraid my good resolves are more the children of *Impulse*, than firm, fixed unwavering Determination. If they are they will die.

FRIDAY, FEBRUARY 24. [1860]

The morning was very pleasant, taking little Charlie Mercer with me I went out first to the Post-Office, then down bustling

Fourth, called on Mr. Minor, and after a few minutes chat, left and returned home.

Spent the afternoon with Mrs. Smith rather pleasantly. This evening there are a few soft, fleecy flakes of snow falling, dropping down silently and still, and resting desolate-like, upon the bare brown earth.

I used to watch the snow flakes falling when I was a child. How I used to wonder at them, and wish they could talk to me, could tell me something of the mysteries which seemed brooding in the still, solemn sky from which they fell.

But still they fell, fell, never heeding the wishes of my child heart, and so I still sat nursing my wild fancies.

SATURDAY, FEBRUARY 25. [1860]

In company with Mrs. Smith attended service this morning at the Jewish Synagogue in this city.[2] The services, with the exception of a single prayer, were in Hebrew, and consisted almost wholly of chants—the sweet psalms of David, I supposed the words to be.

The chief Priest was dressed in a long, flowing robe of black silk or satin, and over his shoulders he wore a white scarf or mantle of a very fine texture. There were six other priests who assisted him, chanting separately, or in concert with him. They, as well as all of the gentlemen in the congregation kept their hats on during the whole time of worship.

As a congregation they were neither devout nor attentive. The whole service seemed like a farce, and it saddened me as I

2. The synagogue, built in 1848, was located on Fourth Street between Walnut and Green; see *Louisville Directory and Business Advertiser, 1859–60*.

looked upon them, for I could but feel that "the veil is upon their hearts."

There were some beautiful faces among them—dark Jewish faces, with the light olive tint, glowing with the rich mantling blush, and smiling upon you thro' the sweet cherry lips. Dark curling locks were pushed back from delicately formed brows, and eyes dark as the shadows which fall upon Judea's plains in the still midnight, looked around with their gleaming glances upon us. But, ah

"the cedars wave on Lebanon,
But Judah's statelier maids are gone."

SABBATH, FEBRUARY 26. [1860]

Wrote to Cousin E. A. Towne. My soul goes out after the future life yearningly sometimes, and my heart waits reverently for it. Death has in it nothing terrible with the bright vision of that beyond it; and time's sorrows when sanctified are but the rounds of that ladder on which we climb to bliss.

The day has been very lovely, just as all days are now.

MONDAY, FEBRUARY 27. [1860]

Harry took a holiday today, because I'm going away; and we have visited various places of interest in the city.

We first went out to several of the daguerrian galleries on Main Street. In one of them we saw a large oil painting—one of the finest I ever saw. In the background rose the high, heaven-reaching hills, shrouded in their soft mantle of misty blue, and between them, far down in the green, silent valley flowed the clear, crystal waters of a beautiful river.

In the foreground was a mansion, and round its marble pillars were twined the numberless tendrils of the clustering vines, from among the thick leaves of which peeped out many a bright, red blossom.

Over the roof, the long, sheltering arms of a giant tree were cast, and standing in its leafy shade was a beautiful young girl, of perhaps sixteen summers, large as living life, and seemingly as real.

Her dress was of rich white silk, falling low from her fair shoulders, and sweeping with its elegant trail the marble floor upon which she stood.

Back from her high, beautiful temples were pushed the tresses of her brown hair, and her great, dark eyes looked earnestly out into the distance, with a glance as if the soul was in them, bathing in their liquid depths, and looking thro' their light into the unseen lying beyond the present.

Visited the Artesian well in the afternoon. Old Uncle Charlie is the greatest curiosity to be met with there—he's a perfect walking vocabulary of long, ponderous words, which he pronounces together in the most ludicrous and meaningless way possible.

He's a jolly Ethiopian, and seems to have acted pretty freely upon the maxim "Laugh and grow fat." I'm in debt to him for a right, merry laugh, which I enjoyed that afternoon, the merriest, the fullest of irrepressible mirth of any enjoyed in Louisville.

Long life to Uncle Charlie.

The water of the well is not pleasant to the taste. It has the odor and taste of sulphur.

Called upon Mrs. McCready this evening.

TUESDAY, FEBRUARY 28. [1860]

Beautiful day. Visited Mr. Brown's saloon and took my first lesson in Italian Portrait Painting.[3]

WEDNESDAY, FEBRUARY 29. [1860]

Dark, raining all day. Went to the picture gallery at eleven o'clock; painted until nearly dark. Portrait of "Little Nellie."[4]

THURSDAY, MARCH 1. [1860]

Painted all day. I'd love an artist's life. Love its power of delineating the glowing fancies that spring to life within the spirit. The beautiful pictures that are painted daily within the soul.

FRIDAY, MARCH 2. [1860]

March comes to us with smiles and sunshine.

> "The winds are hushed, nor dare to breathe aloud.
> The sky seems never to have borne a cloud."

At the gallery all day. The hours passed pleasantly. Light, sparkling conversation gave them a charmed flight.

3. There are two picture galleries mentioned in the *Louisville Directory and Business Advertiser, 1859–60*, but not Mr. Brown's, which may mean he was an itinerant artist, picking up some extra money by giving painting lessons.

4. Presumably the pathetic "Little Nell" from Charles Dickens's *The Old Curiosity Shop* (1841).

SATURDAY, MARCH 3. [1860]

Cloudy all day, and a slight rain, yet very warm. Finished my two pictures today, "Little Nellie" and the "Old Mill at Sleepy Hollow."[5] Harry called for me at about four o'clock and we came home by way of Third Street, where we saw some beautiful pictures.

One was an oil portrait, the sweet, womanly face of Lola Montez.[6] Eyes of deep, liquid blue, soft brown hair, and beautiful arched brow. Her features are fine, and bright with the intellectual light within.

SUNDAY, MARCH 4. [1860]

Harry and I attended church this morning on Brook Street and listened to a fine discourse from Rev. Mr. Parsons.

As we returned from evening service on Seventh St. we went for a few moments into the African church on Centre.

The house was full of sable faces, and all were listening with their native earnestness to the words of their noisy speaker.

The church was a real Babel—responses, fervent amens, shouting and leaping—all filled up the measure of their devotional exercises.

After stopping for a few moments, we were glad enough to make our egress.

5. The latter title derives from Washington Irving's famous tale "The Legend of Sleepy Hollow" in *The Sketch Book* (1819–20).

6. Montez, a famous European dancer and courtesan, was exiled from Bavaria in the Revolution of 1848 and spent her final days in America. One suspects Eliza was unaware of her flamboyant life.

MONDAY, MARCH 5. [1860]

Passed the day at the picture gallery. It was sunny without and within doors; in the outer world and in my heart.

TUESDAY, MARCH 6. [1860]

A real fine day. Summer breezes came softly from the south, and the warm sunshine lingers among the dead branches of the trees as if to kiss them back to life and leafy greenness again.

I did not paint any until afternoon. The charms of Nature irresistibly won me from the charms of art, out into the open beauty of the golden sunlight; into the wide world's picture gallery of tall, bare trees, and green, springing grass, and timid, first opening flowers.

WEDNESDAY, MARCH 7. [1860]

Busy as ever—my pictures are progressing finely.

March is still clothing herself with April charms, and if she continues as smiling we must love her as well as her usually more sunny sister.

THURSDAY, MARCH 8. [1860]

How quickly the clouds follow the sunshine. Our April weather is vanishing and March is appearing without any hypocrisy, the blustery, fitful thing she is—her face full of frowns.

FRIDAY, MARCH 9. [1860]

Cold and windy today. Went with Harry down to Main Street, where we were treated to a perfect cloud of dust. We were glad enough to beat a retreat homeward without going further.

SATURDAY, MARCH 10. [1860]

The sun looks out from a rent in the clouds with a bright smile now and then, which is really cheering, and its not quite as cold today.

SUNDAY, MARCH 11. [1860]

Six months today since we were married, and six months of real earnest happiness have they been—"joy mad" have I been sometimes in them, and sometimes I fear that earthly love has claimed all my heart—all its thoughts.

MONDAY, MARCH 12. [1860]

Wrote to Satie White today. Speaking of my paintings I said: I've got some beautiful pictures—some faces that look into my eyes almost like living things, and if I were lonely I believe I should talk to them, almost hoping that they would answer me.

And the landscapes, to look at them, Satie, they bring up visions of pleasant things, and you dream of green woods, and fresh, sparkling streams, and cool shady nooks, and soft, flowery banks, and gushes of bird music, and all the wondrous beautiful things that we find in God's world, but never get a

Downtown Louisville. (Filson Society, Louisville, Kentucky)

glimpse of in the great world that man has made—the crowded, dusty town.

It's a real March day, windy and blustering. Went to walk this morning, but it was so breezy I was glad to turn back when I reached the Post-Office.

TUESDAY, MARCH 13. [1860]

The weather is delightful again—real springlike. Mrs. Guilford and I took a long walk this morning—up Chestnut and away out to the quiet Hospital. The grounds about the building are quite extensive, and adorned with shrubbery and trees. It's a pleasant beautiful spot for the sick. Its very beauty would almost charm them back to health again. It reminded me of my old Seminary Home,[7] the building being something like it in form and style of architecture.

WEDNESDAY, MARCH 14. [1860]

Mrs. Smith and myself visited Preston Woods today. How delightful the fresh country breezes seemed to us—so pure and invigorating.

Ah, the grand old woods, rightly are they styled "God's first Temples." One of the choir which sings in them was there this morning, and he warbled forth his native hymn in notes of the richest melody.

7. The Castleton Seminary in Vermont, where Eliza attended secondary school.

THURSDAY, MARCH 15. [1860]

Sunny and bright today. I've been out to Broadway this afternoon with Mrs. Smith. Our walk was very pleasant.

Poor little Ida Churchill is very ill today. I'm afraid that bright little head will be laid under the green sod ere many days.

Poor little one, aint you afraid of the dark grave? Wouldn't you want momma if you should be laid there? Ah, no, He who loves the little Children will care for you. Jesus will take "the lambs in His arms and carry them in His Bosom." He will watch tenderly the darlings of our household if we will leave them to His keeping.

FRIDAY, MARCH 16. [1860]

One gets a pretty good glimpse of life in walking through the crowded streets of a city. They see it in its several phases. The rich and poor you meet everywhere—the gay and the heavy hearted, the young and the old—and those who are beautiful and those who are not.

We went down Jefferson Street in our walk today—down as far as the old cemetery opposite St. John's Church, and returned by way of Green.

There are many fine residences upon the former street, but I didn't notice them as much as I did, the sweet, just budding flowers, and fresh springing grass. The heart loves them better than all the piled monuments of wealth.

Little Ida's sickness saddened me—it darkened even the sunshine to my sight. Everything earthly seems painfully uncertain."Don't you wish there were no such thing as death, Mrs. Smith," said I. "I don't know as I do," she replied. "I don't dread it much." "But the future is so uncertain," I answered. "We don't know what is before us—the Christian expects to be happy, and yet he can form no really just conceptions as to that happiness—not even the faintest idea of the scenes which are to open before him as he makes an exchange of worlds."

"I know it, we don't know anything about it," Mrs. Smith replied in answer to what I was saying.

"But then Mrs. Smith," said I, "I believe that the Christian is sustained when he is called to die—all fear is gone—But then don't we shrink from it as we see it in others? As we watch their battling with the King of Terrors, doesn't there naturally arise a feeling of dread, a wish to escape the struggle?"

"Yes, I suppose there does," she answered. "I've always hoped that I should have the consumption when I die. That is the death that I should choose—One drops away without much suffering."

"Yes, I replied, "it's a dying day by day—one doesn't go all at once as in other diseases. My mother died of consumption, and she went at last just as calmly as if she had been going to sleep. I almost envied her rest. O there's nothing to fear in death if the spirit is ready. We die to win a better life."

"Yes, that is true"—and thinking thus we walked thoughtfully homeward.

SATURDAY, MARCH 17. [1860]

"Will you go walking with me this morning, Mrs. Smith?" I asked as I looked into her pleasant room just after breakfast.

"Yes, I'll be ready about nine, and you call for me in the parlor."

A few minutes past nine and we were tripping along in the

bright sunshine past little ragged dirty children, with faces all unwashed, and hair laying in tangled masses on their once bare heads; then by well dressed little cherubs, the darlings of fond mamas, and the pride of doating fathers—past richly draped ladies, some with sweet faces just such as God had given them, others with faces of their own make—a sort of second edition of the same, daubed with rouge and carmine, and the sallow complextion made of almost pearly whiteness by the free use of "Meen Fun"[8] or "Lilly White,"—"so beneficial (?) for beautifying the complexion."

We saw a real genuinely happy couple away at the upper end of Market Street.

They were seated on something by the side of the old Market building, talking soft words to each other I [illegible], and their feet dressed in coarse cowhide shoes, they kept swinging to and fro, with the glad beatings of their happy hearts.

The only gown the girl had on was a bright yellow flannel petticoat, and over that a long apron which covered her waist and arms.

Yet, she sat, seemingly just as contentedly as if the richest silks had been thrown with their soft folds about her, looking with a real joyous smile into the upturned face of the boy whose eager, earnest gaze met her own.

I was somewhat wearied with my long walk as I came home at eleven, but I was soon rested. I'm sitting without a fire—have had none since last night its so warm today.

8. Obviously a facial cosmetic, which Eliza, as a proper Victorian woman, would not wear. Eliza's spelling of the product's name may not be correct.

SUNDAY, MARCH 18. [1860]

Very pleasant and springlike today—but the night has spread a soft curtain of clouds over the sleeping world.

MONDAY, MARCH 19. [1860]

I wish sometimes that I could look into the future—could unwrap its hidden mysteries. I often indulge in speculative questionings as to the future of our country. Seems to me that she is now drifting out into a troublous, stormy sea, where there are many shoals and quick sands.

Monsieur Buchanan,[9] you are not the man to sit at the helm. We want some one with keener sense of sight, of justice and of duty.

The next Presidential campaign will doubtless be one of intense, exciting interest. I never looked forwards to an election with so much anxiety.

Shall Freedom triumph, or the proud mermidons of slavery sit in the high places of power? Greece and Rome, those great lights of the past have gone out in darkness, and with us, as with them shall the light of Liberty perish? Shall we sit calmly down and see the vestal flame go out upon her altars? Ah, there is an "irrepressible conflict" waging, a conflict between the mighty hosts of evil, and the opposing battalions of freedom and of right.

9. James Buchanan, president of the United States and the Democratic candidate for reelection in 1860. The Otises, of course, favored the Republican candidate, Abraham Lincoln. In fact, Harrison attended the Chicago convention that nominated Lincoln.

TUESDAY, MARCH 20. [1860]

Glorious, cheering news comes to us from the old Granite State,[10] that dear old home of my earlier years. She has taken a noble stand in favor of freedom, and her great heart is throbbing and warm with its love of Republicanism and Liberty.

WEDNESDAY, MARCH 21. [1860]

Pleasant and springlike today. March must be playing the hypocrite; it's surely not her nature to be so sunny and bright.

THURSDAY, MARCH 22. [1860]

Harry has gone out to attend a Republican Convention tonight. A new thing in Kentucky I fancy. Yet I believe that there are many in this state, who, if they acted upon their honest convictions, would advocate the principles of the Republican party. Men at the present day, and at the present crisis of political interests *must think*, and earnest, honest thought, will lead to noble action. I have faith to believe that Kentucky will yet throw off her shackles and let the oppressed go free. Seems as though, even now, there were here and there, indications of good, a few faint glimmering beams of light—as if the day were breaking.[11]

10. New Hampshire.

11. Eliza proved prophetic. Although the state struggled to remain neutral in view of its sharply divided population, by September 1861 Kentucky had formally joined the Union cause.

FRIDAY, MARCH 23. [1860]

Last night the sky threatened rain, but the morning today brought the sweet sunshine and the deep, clear blue of heaven. It's cooler tonight than yesterday, and maybe there will be rain tomorrow.

Harry came home last night full of enthusiasm at the result of the Repub. meeting. There are true, earnest spirits in "our old Kentucky home" that will dare to do and suffer for the right. "A little leaven leaveneth the whole lump," and the leaven is at work, all ready to be mixed up with the great "lump" of popular feeling and to change it so that it shall nourish and strengthen every freedom loving impulse, every philanthropic movement that may arise to throw a protecting arm around the interest of the oppressed—the poor dark browed children of toil. God speed them ever in the right.

SATURDAY, MARCH 24. [1860]

Cold and chilly today. Spent the day at Mr. Wilson's picture gallery.

SUNDAY, MARCH 25. [1860]

Little Ida Churchill went to rest this morning. As beautifully her life went out as a star fades in the light of morning. The little prattling lips are singing sweeter than earth's songs now, and the cherub face is bright with immortal beauty.

Sleep on in thy beauty, sweet innocent sleep,
While angels, above thee their blest vigils keep

Bright cherubs are guarding the spot of thy rest
And angel toned whispers float over thy breast.[12]

MONDAY, MARCH 26. [1860]

Cold and chilly today. We followed little Ida to her last resting place this afternoon. It is a beautiful spot where we laid her—a lovely resting place for the dead. The stars will watch above her and the dew distill its pearly showers.

TUESDAY, MARCH 27. [1860]

Life seems like weariness and desolation to me today. Somehow I feel *alone*: as if my heart was shut out from every other heart in the wide, wide world. I wish that I could hush some of its unanswered yearnings—but they wont be still, and so I walk on and try to crush them, but they only fall back like a heavy weight upon my heart, making it ache, while their great cry goes up still, always, never ceasingly.

WEDNESDAY, MARCH 28. [1860]

Very lovely out today. The night is here with its starry softness—and I welcome its quiet for I want rest and slumber.

THURSDAY. MARCH 29. [1860]

"One day, nearer home." The heart loves to whisper that sometimes even when earth is bright to it. "Nearer home"—the thought has in it the earnest of immortality.

12. Though the poet is not identified, these lines do sound like Eliza's work.

FRIDAY, MARCH 30. [1860]

Mrs. Churchill and I are busy painting today. Bright forest trees, and little tiny forms, with sweet childish faces all of these seem to spring into real life at the touch of our pencil.

Wonderful this imaging upon dull canvass the numberless forms of life and beauty which are found in the outer world.

SATURDAY, MARCH 31. [1860]

The thunder is clapping its hands tonight, and the red lightning darts along the clouds, while the rain falls thick and fast—patter, patter on the paved street.

But, I'm sleepy, so I'll bid good night to it all and go to bed.

SUNDAY, APRIL 1. [1860]

The sky was dark and frowning this morning, but the evening brought out the deep calm blue of heaven and the soft light of the stars.

Harry and I attended service tonight at the First Presbyterian Church. Discourse by Rev. Mr. Hoyt. It was addressed to young men, but was full of interest to all. He commenced by saying "Supposing we stood, upon a high hilltop and from our elevated position looked down upon the plain below. It is covered with peaceful villages, nestled in the beautiful foliage, and all of the plain is smiling with greenness and verdure. As you look down upon it, the prospect seems to you very delightful—all brightness.

["]But let us descend. Here in this village you enter a lovely cottage, beautiful without, covered with lovely vines, and

First Presbyterian Church, Louisville. This is another example of the Gothic Revival style. Eliza and Harry attended many churches in the city, drawn usually by reports of a good preacher.
(Filson Society, Louisville, Kentucky)

sleeping in the sunshine, and you find a mother bending over the dying form of a darling child. You pass into the street and you see a long procession returning from the burial of one of the principal citizens of the place—one who was generally beloved, and whose death has cast a gloom over many a heart. You enter another home—the fair young mother is alone, with her fatherless ones—the strong arm on which she leaned, death has palsied, and the faithful heart she loved is lying silent under the sod. You find sorrow everywhere and you turn away, sick at heart from the sorrows of that place which looked so charming, so desirable to you from the hilltop.

[“]Young men you are standing upon this eminence and life, like the bright valley of which I have spoken, lies outspread before you. From the height on which you now stand, it seems to you very desirable, full of brightness and of beauty. But as you descend to a more intimate acquaintance with it, you will find the prospect changed. Unseen sorrows will unfold themselves everywhere, and the illusions which now cheat you will all vanish.”

The speaker here proceeded to show the various evils that we have to battle with as we come upon the stage of being. There is sickness, there is death; there is war with all its mighty forces of ill; there is famine, and pestilence, and all the unconquered powers of sin which are raging within our own hearts. We are constantly at war with ourselves—and this life is at best but a scene of strife, a wearisome burden of sorrow and of sin.

Yet it is noble in that, if rightly improved it enables us to pass on to immortality.

I cannot do justice to Mr. Hoyt’s remarks as I have but a few moments in which to write. His view of life is one which I wish that all could take, a picture that I would that all could be familiar with.

MONDAY, APRIL 2. [1860]

Mrs. Churchill finished her first piece in painting today. It is very pretty, very pretty. A scene in olden time—the Sabbath has come and young and old are going to the house of God. Through the thick boughs of the tall trees the church spire gleams, pointing with its slender finger to the sky—the green grass is on the hillside, and the flowers have opened their petals to the Sabbath air and sunshine. I'd love to steal away to such a spot.

TUESDAY, APRIL 3. [1860]

Busy in preparations to go home. I'll take all my things with me, and yet not that which makes this home to me here. My husband is not going with me, so I turn from the thought of leaving with dread.

WEDNESDAY, APRIL 4. [1860]

I am almost ready to go. My room looks anything but homelike. I'll go to bed and when asleep perhaps I can forget this confusion and disorder.

THURSDAY, APRIL 5. [1860]

Harry is not well this morning, so I brought him up his breakfast, which he took in bed. We have passed this morning pleasantly. There is not less sunshine in our hearts than in the outer world—there's only a little shadow which the thought of separation brings.

FRIDAY, APRIL 6. [1860]

Today leave for Ohio. Harry and I staid last night alone in the house which Mr. Churchill has just vacated. We took tea with Mrs. Lee, after which we went out to walk. It was a beautiful moonlight night—as bright as could be. On our return we called at Mrs. Williams and stopped with her until past nine, then we came to our room. Harry made the bed while I undressed, and we went to sleep in this deserted house caring nothing for its loneliness. Our *hearts* couldn't feel it while they were beating so warmly side by side. The day is very bright, and it's as warm as a June day. Harry has gone for a hackman, and so I stay with Mrs. Williams until he returns.

CHAPTER 4

"I'm a Mother!"

APRIL 24. [1860] [LOWELL]

It is long since my journal and I have met. In the quiet of Jennie's home I sit down to write this morning, but my thoughts, and my *heart* the while are away with the loved One whom I left behind in my Southern home—with *My Husband*.

My passage from Louisville to Cincinnati was very pleasant. I made some agreeable acquaintances. Mr. Connell of Cin. was a noble, friendly man—a widower, of about forty years. And Abby Eastman, I shall remember her this many a day. One of New England's daughters, and a graduate of noble, old Mt. Holyoke Seminary. That institution has done a great deal for our Country—for the World, for Woman. It lays broad, and deep, and solid the foundations for woman's mental enlargement, and intellectual growth. It has fully demonstrated the fact that the female mind is capable of grasping abstruse sciences and attaining intellectual eminences hardly inferior to the loftiest which the giant powers of man have enabled him to attain.[1]

1. Mary Kelly makes a powerful case for the positive effect of advanced education on women like Eliza, education that endowed them with new powers of

I remember noble women who graduated there, and came out into the world eminently fitted for usefulness. Some of them now have gone to their quiet rest, their work early done, and others still working—solving the great problem of a noble life.

Dear Lydia Abbott, she was young when she died, but she illustrated the truth of the poet's words:

"They live longest who live noblest.
Set the best."

And Hattie Haile—Mt. Holyoke was her Alma Mater—and she was a jewel of a woman—worthy of such a fostering mother. May her life be long, and bright and full of sunshine.

APRIL 25. [1860]

It's cold and windy. More like March weather than sunny April days.

APRIL 26. [1860]

I've been reading Mr. Lovejoy's[2] speech, of Illinois, today. It is strong in its description of slavery and earnest in its detestation of this crying sin.

---

expression and greater access to the world, see "Reading Women/Women Reading: The Making of Learned Women in Antebellum America," *Journal of American History*, no. 83 (1996): 401–24.

2. Owen Lovejoy (1811–64), member of the House of Representatives from Illinois, was a radical abolitionist and founder of the Republican Party in his state. *Dictionary of American Biography*, s.v.

He speaks of the plea that is so often made by its southern supports, that it's a *Christianizing* institution, and asks if a system which violates all domestic and conjugal relations and tramples in the dust the sacred institution of marriage can be *Christianizing* in its influence—A system which robs men of *homes* can that elevate and ennoble?

For my own part I've seen enough of this *Christianizing*. Not long before I left Louisville, I went one Sabbath evening with Harry, after our return from service, into an African church.

One woman with her little dark browed baby presented herself for baptism.

After the ceremony had been performed the preacher, a venerable looking old man, who made me think of good old Uncle Tom, remarked "That all others who were desirous of receiving baptism, he would baptize the next Sabbath *provided the consent of their masters could be obtained, but without their consent he should not dare to perform the rite.*"

And *this* is the way they *Christianize*. They are not left free to act for themselves even in the great concerns of immortality. Not free to obey this plain and simple precept of Him who has redeemed them *unless they first obtain the consent of their owners*, and yet talk of the *missionary* work that *slavery* is doing. Such talk seems hardly less than heaven daring blasphemy.

FRIDAY, APRIL 27. [1860]

It is very beautiful today. Warm, balmy April weather. Wrote to Harry and Satie White, and commenced a letter to Mrs. Denny today. My heart is yearning for My Husband. Time seems very long without him. I wish I was at "home where the heart is."

SATURDAY, APRIL 28. [1860]

Thinking of Harry my heart sings—

"Such mortal meaning my love begets
For things which else were dumb
That I kiss the ears of the violets
As they turn the way you'll come."[3]

We find wonderful companionship in Nature sometimes—we find sympathy in her voiceless things when we turn away from human hearts, that have met us coldly.

SUNDAY, APRIL 29. [1860]

Bright and beautiful as a dream of Hope, today. Attended church in the morning and spent the evening and night with sister Sarah.

MONDAY, APRIL 30. [1860]

A long, sweet letter from Harry today. It cheered my lonely heart wonderfully.

My life shall be the answer to its tenderness.

TUESDAY, MAY 1. [1860]

May morning is ushered in with a cloudless sky and bright sunshine.

3. These lines were almost certainly Eliza's.

It makes me think of the Mayday long ago in my glad childhood, when my lighthearted friend, Lucia Lathrop, was our queen, and all the morning we wandered in the woods, and gathered the sweet smelling May-flowers, and wove them in crowns and garlands.

Ah, but I am mistaken—This morning wasn't full of sunshine—it was cloudy and wet. Well it rains in the *inner* world too sometimes. Clouds of doubt and distrust gather there sometimes and they weep great tears that fill the *heart* as well as the eyes.

O dear! I say it like a tired child—like one who has broken a cherished plaything, and is weeping over its loss, which is all its little heart can bear. What *meaning* there is then in this childish voice of exclamation, o dear! It is the voice of numberless griefs, or the outer form of one that is all absorbing.

WEDNESDAY, MAY 2. [1860]

It's a little cool today. A day that seems somewhat in keeping with stoicism and misanthropy—if ever days are in keeping with such feelings. I'm inclined to think, I will confess, on sober second thought that they are not. Nature dont shake hands, I guess after all, with any such feelings, so on the whole I guess I'd better not.

THURSDAY, MAY 3. [1860]

Sarah and I went to Marietta today. The birds furnished us with a full choir of songsters, and my heart felt like chiming in with their melody.

THURSDAY, MAY 4. [1860]

I'm lady housekeeper today, Jennie having gone to Marietta and left me alone. May is out with a clear sky, and a sunny smile today.

SATURDAY, MAY 5. [1860]

Wrote Harry and Nell Shafer today. To Nell I wrote, Speaking of the plea of slave holders generally that "slavery on the whole is a blessing to the black race—Can you look for any enobling, elevating influences to go out from a system that tramples upon and *annihilates* the sacredness of the marriage relation—that denies the slave the endearments of home, and the delights that spring from the sunlight of happy little faces, and innocent prattlings around the dear home hearth? No, *never*!"

The solemn Past lifts up her voice and says that in all her domain it has never been. Experience, in the present speaks with her deep toned utterance, and asserts the truthfulness of what the great Past affirms, and all the host of Freedom and of right thunder forth the declaration that it cannot be.

SUNDAY, MAY 6. [1860]

Wrote Mary Williams this morning, I told her of my journey home on the *Jacob Strader*, the fine mail packet from Louisville to Cincinnati.

There was a sweet little mulatto girl on board; a bright eyed little darling, with sprightly winning ways, and a charming, dark little face.

I did wish that I could take the poor lamb to my heart and

shelter her. I trembled as I thought of her future, belonging as she did to a wronged and outraged race.

The soul, bright with its native intelligence, looked out of those dark eyes and you could look down depth on depth and yet not fathom the world of feeling which lay mirrored in them.

But, poor little one! The iron hand of tyranny will fetter your spirit! It may flutter and throw itself ever so wildly against its prison bars, but it will be all in vain. Darkness and Ignorance will chain it down and hold it there forever. And yet *not* forever! Thank God, *Death* will set it free. He is a bold Deliverer and up into the sunlight of eternal truth out into the freedom of immortality and endless being his strong arm shall bear you and *then* you shall be free.

MONDAY, MAY 7. [1860]

I am not a very good journalist now-a-days, I believe. The fact is that I find nothing here to chronicle—only the golden days; I might speak of *them*—they are full of beauty.

TUESDAY, MAY 8. [1860]

Sunny and bright. The day is a real sunbeam of itself. A letter from Harry—and that was a sunbeam to my heart.

WEDNESDAY, MAY 9. [1860]

Cloudy and dark today, and a little cool. I'm writing to Harry. I find his letters together with the pleasure of answering them, the greatest solace I have in my absence from him.

THURSDAY, MAY 10. [1860]

Cloudy and frowning still. Storms gather in the natural and in the political world. The horizon of our national affairs looks dark and threatening—full of gloom. But Right shall yet triumph, and the dark clouds of human oppression be dispersed, and give place to the clear sunlight of freedom's new born day.

FRIDAY, MAY 11. [1860]

Eight months ago tonight since Harry made me his *Wife*. They have been full of gladness, of deep quiet joy. There's nothing in the world that makes life so beautiful as Love. I was almost a stranger to love after my mother and Mary died, till Harry came.

AUGUST 15—WEDNESDAY. [1860]

It's wonderful, isn't it, how intimate the connection between dull senseless clay and the thinking, active, living spirit! How interlocked their sympathies; how inseparable their sufferings. The throwing off of the mortal will be to the sanctified, but a divorce from suffering, a sweet release from pain.

Death looks more and more pleasant to me, as daily I draw nearer to it. It is only a sweet releasing, a pleasant going home unto "Our Father." The struggle, the pain, the ghastliness, the pallor, the shroud and the narrow house, are nothing; I see nothing but the life beyond.

This life seems to me sometimes like some old story that I've read over and over again so often that its novelty is all gone, and I wonder how it ever could have charmed me so. Yet I dream once in a while, just as I used to; build up the same old castles, with foundations something like that of a rainbow's, but somehow the castles melt away like the glory of a summer's sunset, into the darkness.

Yet after all we may make life what we will. On every page we may draw pictures of beauty, and on every leaf write something of fresh interest so that if the story is old, it will be beautiful still. It will be my fault alone if I do not color it rightly. I have all the beautiful tints to work with. God has given me enough to make the sunset scene of my picture cloudless—to make the heavens bright with a golden radiance that shall melt with a glory into the clear starry radiance of an happy immortality.

I hope I may prove a good artist, reason being that I'm not only painting for all time, but for endless being a picture which cannot die.

1861

MARCH 28. [1861] [LOWELL]

I'm a mother! A little life born of my own blesses me with its presence. I've a baby boy. The tiny little thing, I'm almost afraid to touch him, lest I should harm him.

MARCH 29. [1861]

I'm very comfortable today, and happy too, with this little helpless thing lying in my bosom. It was half past eleven last night when I first heard his little feeble, wailing cry. Harry watches him with real fatherly pride—and takes him carefully in his arms. I love him for it.

MARCH 30. [1861]

My Darling is doing finely. How I love to kiss the soft velvet cheeks, and feel that this beautiful, tiny, helpless thing is mine! But—what a solemn trust! God help me to fulfill it and train this little one for His Kingdom.

APRIL 1. [1861]

I'll call my baby, Harry. He shall have his father's name, for there's no other name I love so well, and his father tells me I may call him what I please.

APRIL [?]. [1861]

Baby Harry is three weeks old, and his father has left me for Wheeling. I don't get strong yet I miss my good Husband more than if I was well. I've cried more than my Baby today.

SUNDAY, APRIL [?]. [1861]

Harrison is back again and I am happy. I hope that I'll get strong soon so that I shant be as babyish as I have been.

Everything in our national life looks dark and frowning. Could I give up my Husband if my Country should need him? God help me to do my Duty![4]

4. A long break in the journal follows, during which Harry enlists in the Twelfth Regiment, Ohio Volunteers, as a private.

DECEMBER 24. [1861]

Tonight My Husband is with me. He came this morning, taking me quite by surprise. I was delighted to see him after his long absence of six months. During that absence he has been in two battles—those of Scary[5] and Carnifex Ferry[6] in Western Virginia. Numberless perils have been about him, but God has brought him to me again in health and safety, for which I thank Him.

Dear Baby Harry was sitting on the carpet when his papa came, and looked up with wondering eyes at the stranger—I took up the little boy in my arms, and he looked up with a pleased smile into his father's face, with no sign of fear such as he has sometimes evinced in the presence of strangers.

The little boy has grown very beautiful, and his mental life is unfolding rapidly.

DECEMBER 25. [1861]

This is "Merry Christmas" to me; with My Husband and baby boy.

My little one seems to be troubled with a pneuma.[7] I don't

5. A brief battle was fought at Scary Creek, West Virginia, on 17 July 1861, with the Confederates claiming victory. See Tim McKinney, *The Civil War in Fayette County, West Virginia* (Charleston, West Virginia: Pictorial Histories Publishing Co., 1988), 27, 37.

6. This was the site of a successful ambush of Southern cavalrymen by Union soldiers on August 25, 1861, and later a more serious battle on September 18 in which both sides claimed victory. Ibid., 44–5, 58–9.

7. A vague term indicating breathing difficulties, the "pneuma" was probably the onset of pneumonia.

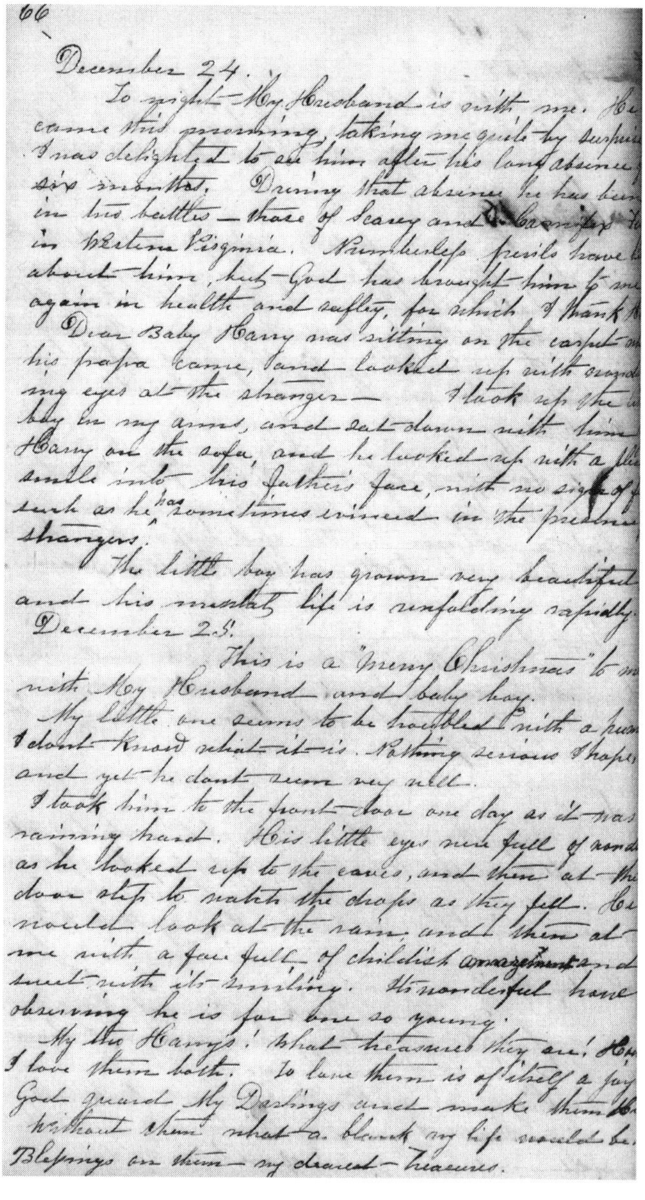
66

December 24.

To night My Husband is with me. He came this morning, taking me quite by surpri[se]. I was delighted to see him after his long absence [of] six months. During that absence he has been in two battles — those of Scarey and Carnifex [Fe-] in Western Virginia. Numberless perils have [been] about him, but God has brought him to me again in health and safety, for which I thank [Him].

Dear Baby Harry was sitting on the carpet [when] his papa came, and looked up with wonder[-]ing eyes at the stranger — I took up the li[ttle] boy in my arms, and sat down with him Harry on the sofa, and he looked up with a [...] smile into his father's face, with no sign of f[ear] such as he has sometimes evinced in the presen[ce of] strangers.

The little boy has grown very beautiful and his mental life is unfolding rapidly.

December 25.

This is a "merry Christmas" to m[e] with My Husband and baby boy.

My little one seems to be troubled with a [...] I dont know what it is. Nothing serious I hope, and yet he dont seem very well.

I took him to the front door one day as it was raining hard. His little eyes were full of wonde[r] as he looked up to the eaves, and then at the door step to watch the drops as they fell. He would look at the rain, and then at me with a face full of childish amazement and sweet with its smiling. Its wonderful how observing he is for one so young.

My two Harrys! What treasures they are! How I love them both. To have them is of itself a joy. God guard My Darlings and make them [...] Without them what a blank my life would be. Blessings on them — my dearest treasures.

Journal entries for December 24 and 25, 1861, the only Christmas Eliza and Harry spent with Harry, Jr., their firstborn child. (Huntington Library) know what it is. Nothing serious I hope, and yet he dont seem very well.

I took him to the front door one day as it was raining hard. His little eyes were full of wonder as he looked up to the eaves, and then at the door step to watch the drops as they fell. He would look at the rain, and then at me with a face full of childish amazement and sweet with its smiling. It's wonderful how observing he is for one so young.

My two Harrys! What treasures they are! How I love them both. To love them is of itself a joy. God guard My Darlings and make them His. Without them what a blank my life would be. Blessings on them my dearest treasures.

1862

MONDAY, FEBRUARY 17. [1862]

Little Harry—My Darling, *Precious Baby Boy*, his little life went out at ten minutes past eleven this morning, after just one short week of suffering.

SUNDAY, MARCH 2. [1862]

Dear Little Harry's second Sabbath in Heaven! How I miss him! The hours seem long and silent with Sorrow. The Little One had entwined himself with every fibre of my heart—every tendril was twined around my Baby. My arms are aching to hold him again. All day long I miss his sweet prattle, his happy laugh, his glad smile; his baby kiss, and childish caresses. I miss the soft touch of the dimpled hand—the look of the bright, dark

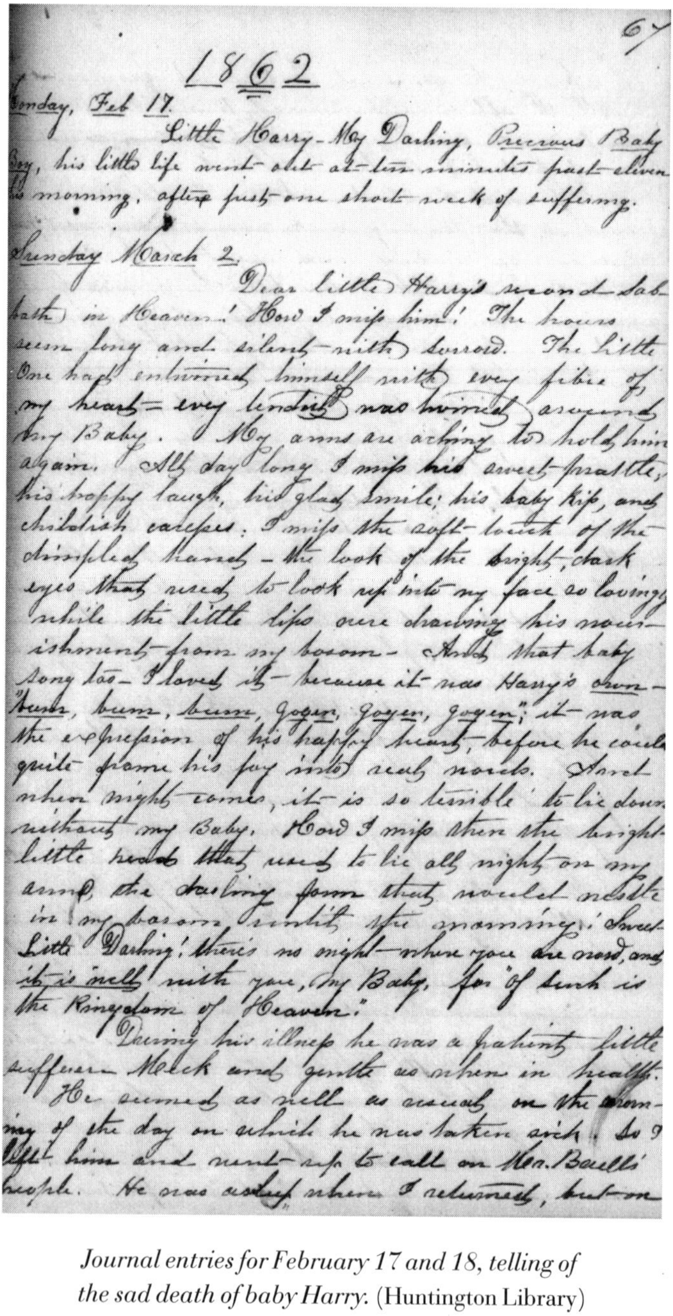
67

1862

[S]unday, Feb 17.

Little Harry - My Darling, Precious Baby Boy, his little life went out at ten minutes past eleven this morning, after just one short week of suffering.

Sunday March 2.

Dear little Harry's second Sabbath in Heaven! How I miss him! The hours seem long and silent with sorrow. The Little One had entwined himself with every fibre of my heart - every tendril was twined around my Baby. My arms are aching to hold him again. All day long I miss his sweet prattle, his happy laugh, his glad smile; his baby kiss, and childish caresses. I miss the soft touch of the dimpled hands - the look of the bright, dark eyes that used to look up into my face so lovingly while the little lips were drawing his nourishment from my bosom - And that baby song too - I loved it - because it was Harry's own - "bum, bum, bum, goyer, goyer, goyen"; it was the expression of his happy heart, before he could quite frame his joy into real words. And when night comes, it is so terrible to lie down without my Baby. How I miss then the bright little head that used to lie all night on my arm, the darling form that would nestle in my bosom until the morning! Sweet Little Darling! there's no night where you are now, and it is well with you, my Baby, for "of such is the Kingdom of Heaven."

During his illness he was a patient little sufferer. Meek and gentle as when in health. He seemed as well as usual on the morning of the day on which he was taken sick. So I left him and went up to call on Mr. Beall's people. He was asleep when I returned, but on

Journal entries for February 17 and 18, telling of the sad death of baby Harry. (Huntington Library)

eyes that used to look up into my face so lovingly, while the little lips were drawing the nourishment from my bosom—And that baby song too—I loved it—because it was Harry's *own*—"*bum, bum, bum, gogen, gogen, gogen,*" it was the expression of his happy heart, before he could quite frame his joy into real words. And when night comes, it is so terrible to lie down without my Baby. How I miss then the bright little head that used to lie all night on my arm, the darling form that would nestle in my bosom until the morning: Sweet Little Darling! there's no night where you are now, and *it is well* with you, my Baby, for "of Such is the Kingdom of Heaven."

During his illness he was a patient little sufferer—Meek and gentle as when in health.

He seemed as well as usual on the morning of the day on which he was taken sick. So I left him and went up to call on Mr. Beull's people. He was asleep when I returned, but on awaking he seemed hot and feverish. All the afternoon he seemed to want, "mama," but in the evening I undressed him as usual and put him in his little crib. He soon fell asleep, and I sat down to write to Harrison.

But, the Darling woke about nine so I put away my writing and went to bed with him. I noticed his breathing was bad, and he was more restless than usual, but only once in the night did he cry, and then as if he was in great pain.

Tuesday morning dressed him as usual, and during the day he slept a great deal. When I held him he would lean his little head ever so wearily on my bosom. I sat him in his crib about tea time and bolstered him up with pillows, but I saw he was too weak to sit so, and he cried for me to take him up, and I could not deny his pleadings. Rapidly he grew worse and about nine I sent for Dr. Clark.

He came and told me the Darling was very ill. All night long I watched by his crib, bathed his little head, and wet his fevered lips, but the morning found him no better. Evening father came over to see him, and he pulled pa's face down to his with his little hot hands, and seemed full of joy to see him. All through his sickness he seemed to rouse up at father's coming, and he'd work his little shoulders and ask him in his baby way to take him.

I think the last time that the little One recognized me fully and clearly was on Sabbath morning. All day Saturday his eyes had been closed so that he couldn't open them. Sunday morning, Jennie washed them, and picked apart the long dark lashes, then he turned around and saw me, and cried at once for his mama to take him. I thought him better, and my heart grew strong with the hope that my Baby would be spared me—but before noon a change for the worse took place, and in the midst of most intense suffering on Monday morning his little life ebbed out.

He was very beautiful in death—and it almost broke my heart to lay him away in the cold grave. I wished his father could have looked on the sweet, pale face of his Darling, but he was too late for that. But he comforted me when he did come by the sweet reminder that we had not lost our Treasure for "we have a Baby Boy in Heaven."

MONDAY, MARCH 3. [1862]

Stormy and dark today—Nature, as well as my heart, seems filled with sorrow. The clouds drop down their tears in heavy showers, and the winds are sobbing fitfully, and shaking the naked arms of the old trees.

It's two weeks today since *My Darling* went *home*. Precious Baby, he doesn't need his mother now. But, I can't feel that I don't need him. Why are such Treasures given us for such a little while, and then snatched from us? It seems mysterious, yet I doubt not but it is *well.* "Will not the Judge of all the earth do right?"

TUESDAY, MARCH 4. [1862]

Still dark and cloudy—Not much of spring in these cold, blustering March days. But the future will have its sunshine, and its genial warmth and dead Nature shall waken to new life and beauty.

And so will the little one, for whom I weep today. My little Harry shall live again thro' the long, beautiful summertime of endless being.

WEDNESDAY, MARCH 5. [1862]

Two weeks today since Harry was laid in his little grave on the hillside.

Mr. Gibbs made some remarks at his funeral from the words —"Is it well with thee? is it well with thy husband? is it well with the child? And she answered. It is well." 2 Kings, 4th chap, and 26th verse. He also read the 14th chapter of Job. Man that is born of woman is of few days and full of trouble. He cometh forth as a flower, and is cut down; he fleeth also as a shadow, and continueth not." &c. The sweet hymn commencing—

Unveil thy bosom faithful tomb,
Take this new treasure to thy trust,

And give these sacred relics room
To slumber in the silent dust—

was sung; while my heart sobbed in its sorrow. How I wish that dear Harrison could have been with me then. It would have been a comfort to him and to me.

He came the morning after we had laid his baby and mine to rest. It was a comfort to me—his coming.

We went up together to little Harry's grave, and he smoothed off the sods above it, and placed some fresh ones over our Darling's head. His loving presence comforted me, and I felt that I could live for him, and I was thankful that God had spared me my Husband while He had taken my child.

There can be no tenderer tie than that which binds a mother to her child—but there is a stronger one. I felt it as I stood beside my Husband and thanked God that Death had spared him still. God keep him and me until we can enter with our Baby Harry into His own eternal rest.[8]

MAY 3. [1862] [CHARLESTON]

Today the Twelfth moved from Charleston, and I bid Harrison a tearful goodby. It seemed as though I *could not* part with him so soon after our little Harry had gone.

He didn't quite understand my feelings, and thought it was weakness that made me feel as I did—but it wasn't that.

I've spent a pleasant five weeks with him here in Mrs New-

8. One page was cut out of the journal at this point, presumably because it contained material that even she did not want to remember. Eliza later wrote that she was "very sick after this." See entry for March 28, 1863.

Tombstone of baby Harry.

ton's home, and the memory of these weeks will go with me while memory lasts.

As I went out this morning the long line of ambulances filled the streets, and the soldiers were hurrying to and fro busy in their final preparations for departure.

It was one of the saddest mornings of my life. One realizes something about war here.

Mrs. Walls called to see me today, but I was feeling too lonely to see her, so I sent down an excuse.

I received a little note from Harry after he went to camp. It was kind, generous and noble just like himself. My heart goes with him, and blesses him always. But it's hard to do without him. And yet I would as soon lay my head upon the block, and throw away forever my hopes of immortality, as to say one word to dissuade him from duty, or lead him to seek a life of inglorious ease at home, in this hour of our Nation's imminent peril.

His Country has higher claims upon him now than I have, and I yield him to her praying our Father to keep him safe from any danger.

I'll go back to Lowell soon. It matters little how soon. I've a home beside my Baby Harry's grave. I'm going to try and be cheerful. It's a duty and I must fulfil it. It would pain little Harry, I know, to see his "mama" so sad.

Why can't I realize that he is blessed—that he doesn't need me now. I will try and look beyond the valley of Shadows, to the land of light and glory where his pure Spirit reposes.

Earth holds no charms for him now, and Heaven should have new charms for me for it is his home.

I believe that I am selfish. As I look into my own heart, I find that it is everything that is evil. Would I take angel robes from my boy to give him the poor, perishable ones that my own hands have fashioned? Would I take from him a Savior's smile for my own look of earthly love? Would I take from him the melody of Heaven for the sake of the low, loving words, which my poor lips could whisper? No, no! Rest, my Darling, and your mother will patiently strive to walk the thorny path that shall yet lead her to you—and will yet learn to rejoice that her Darling is in Heaven.

It's very warm today. Summer is fairly here. Mrs. Newton and I are going to the woods soon to gather materials for picture frames. We have already made some pretty ones. Nature is generous with her materials.

The woods about here are full of riches. Beautiful cones and shells and mosses and other things too numerous to mention. God has manifested his love in everything and because He has afflicted me I will not doubt his goodness. It is ever sweet to feel that,

"Earth hath no sorrow which Heaven cannot heal."

SUNDAY, MAY 30. [1862] [LOWELL]

The day is bright and sunny, full of beauty, and gladness. Received a letter from Mrs. Newton, and Mr. Lutz[9] today, the first ever received from either of them. They were kind, friendly letters, such as are always welcome. Not being able to work today, I've responded at once to Mr. L., and I'll copy a part, if not all of my reply.

Mr. L, My Kind Friend: Your very welcome letter was received today and I hasten to respond to all its kindly utterances. My heart goes out as to old friends to the brave, noble, "boys" of

9. Peter Lutz, musician, was a member of the Twelfth Regiment. See *Roster*, vol. 2, 361.

the Twelfth whose acquaintance I made while in Charleston. I expect I feel only as every true American woman feels, that *all* who have taken up arms in this hour of our Country's need and peril, who taking their lives in their hands have gone forth to strike for the defence of Freedom and all the sacred rights of man, have a *claim* upon our sympathies, and should be loved and cherished by every loyal heart in the land. And so I sit down and write you just as I would a dear, absent brother, and would cheer you by the remembrance that not only at home are thoughts of you kept fresh and warm, but there's not a home in the free North where beats a woman's heart true to the old stars and stripes, but in that heart our soldiers, *one and all*, are cherished with prayers and blessings, and sacred benedictions.

You mentioned a death in the fever ward. Was it one of the poor men that was lying so very ill the last time I called there? There were two whom I noticed particularly, their countenances looked so palid and deathly. I was greatly pleased with the arrangements of your Hospital, with the general order and neatness which prevailed, and with the kind attention and care which your sick received, yet I felt, as you remarked in your letter "that is was sad to die there." Some one has said, I do not remember whom, "There are no words in the English language so sad as these, '*He died away from home.*'" And they *are* full of meaning, ain't they? No mother to bend over her boy, and with gentle, loving fingers to push back the damp hair from the cold brow of her loved one, and whisper words of hope and faith to the parting spirit—No sister to soothe the aching head or smoothe your pillow gently, softly so that the movement shall not weary you,—No Father, no Wife, no Child, all these dear ones away, and the dying one struggles with thoughts of the hearts at home that are breaking for him. But over all these sad thoughts comes one of gladness. The remembrance of an Infinite Father, a pitying Savior whose love encircles you like the atmosphere, and whose everlasting arms enfold you, if you trust in Him, and bear you to a better, holier, happier life of endless being.

And when the spirit has gone, and you carry out the cold, coffined form to its last resting place among strangers the hearts of the Nation follow it throbbing with the thought—He died for freedom for me.

There has been in this vicinity a prompt response to the call for fifty thousand more volunteers. Our college at Marietta has opened its door wide, and twenty or thirty of its best students have gone out from the cherishing care of their Alma Mater to meet unthinkingly the perils and dangers of this crisis hour. Between one and two hundred of our citizens have left within three days.

I hear from Mr. Otis often. His last letter was dated May sixteenth, and was written from their camp near East River. They were very near the outposts of the Rebel Army, and some shots had been exchanged. All were in good health & spirits.

I had a pleasant trip on my return from Charleston. The Capt. of the boat which I took at Galipolis was just from Pittsburg Landing. The description which he gave of that battle field after the dreadful struggle was over was fearfully thrilling.[10] The account of that battle will fill one of the bloodiest pages of

10. Known more typically as the Battle of Shiloh, it was the first of the monumental confrontations of the Civil War, producing 23,000 dead and wounded and a decisive Union victory. Shiloh gave the North control of the Mississippi Valley. See McPherson, *Battle Cry of Freedom: The Civil War Era*, 400–415.

Old School House, Lowell, Ohio, built in 1854 and photographed in 1895. This school was not connected with Wetherby's Academy where Eliza and her father taught, although it may have replaced it. (Ohio Historical Society)

History. What a long, black, criminal record will be the story of this Rebellion which the Future will write. The world will stand appalled and horror stricken at the Heaven-daring treason that has lifted its parricidal hands against the Government to which it owes all that is best and noblest in the life of a free people.

But I am writing you a long letter. If you dislike long letters as much as some do, I have wearied you, for which I ask your pardon. My kindest regards to Mr. Newton's people when you see them. Please remember me to Major Stone[11] also. My respects to Dr. Bell and others with whom I am acquainted. Let me hear from you again. Your letters will always be welcome.

And now I must close. With my best wishes going out to you, and my heart echoing the hopes and prayers of a grateful people, that you, and all of our brave, noble soldiers may receive the blessings of "Our Father," and be permitted to soon return to your homes crowned with the fadeless laurels of victorious peace, I am

Yours truly—

E. A. W. Otis

SATURDAY, MAY 31. [1862]

My heart is palpitating with anxiety to hear from our armies. I've not seen the daily newspapers for several days. I've buried myself a little while today in writing to Frank[12] and I copy what I've written.

11. Major Mortimer A. Stone, Twelfth Regiment, was a drum major later promoted to Field Staff. See *Roster*, vol. 2, 355.

12. Private Frank Fornshell, Twelfth Regiment. He was appointed sergeant in 1863, wounded at South Mountain, and reduced in rank at own request. See *Roster*, vol. 2, 368.

Mr. Fornshell—My Dear Friend:

Your very kind letter was forwarded me some days ago from Charleston, and I should have given it earlier attention had I been able to do so. But I've been on the invalid list for a week past, and unable to write.

I need not tell you how my heart follows you and all of the brave "boys" of the Twelfth with whom I became acquainted at Charleston. To be a *soldier*, Frank, is to have a claim upon the sympathies, the prayers, the blessings of every loyal heart in the land. There's not a home-altar in the free North where the voice is not lifted night and morning to the God of armies that He will *bless* you who have gone forth from home, and friends, and all that you hold dear, to protect our firesides, and strike for the defence of humanity and Freedom. There's not a closet where the humblest Christian kneels in prayer, where you, one and all, are not remembered, and the soul's best warmest utterances are poured out in your behalf. God be with our soldiers and guard and bless them, and give them victory, is our morning and our evening supplication. So you see that in going out from the hearts and the homes which you have held dear from childhood, you have only gone into the inmost sanctuaries of other hearts, and into the "Holy of Holies" of every loyal, Christian home. And may the prayers that shall go up from them all, be to you a bulwark of safety, a sure defence in time of danger and of battle.

You must find a rare delight in the beauty of some of these wild mountain fastnesses of Virginia. You love Nature, as I do, in all her varied forms, and she has a language full of impressive teachings, and sublime truths, which make the heart better, and gladder, if heeded.

I wish that I could stray off in some way, and find myself in your midst. When I think of home now-a-days, I find myself thinking of the place where my Husband is,[13] and when away from there I get homesick, just a little.

I had a nice, long letter from Mrs. Newton yesterday. She gets lonely without her "soldier boys," and she misses the soldier's wife a little too, she says. She's a noble woman, isn't she? I wish that you could find just such a friend wherever you go. There's nothing she wouldn't share with you cheerfully, gladly. Mrs. Newton has told you, I suppose that she accompanied me as far as Galipolis on my way home. We had a pleasant trip, though not much of romance in it. I fought over your battle of Scarrey again as I came past, and how I made the rebels *run*.

Mrs. Newton told me in her letter how narrowly you escaped the aim of a rebel bushwacker. I am thankful that a kind Providence spared you from such a cowardly foe. I hope that the policy pursued (towards such traitors) wont be a milk and water one, but one of utter and entire extermination.

You see Mr. Otis often, don't you? I am glad that he has so good a friend as you with him. And wont you let me ask a favor of you, just such an one as I would ask of a dear brother? I am *sure* you will. I know as well as any one all the dangers of the battlefield, and all that may possibly happen to my Husband, and you'll let me ask you, Frank, to care for him, if he should be wounded, and to send me word; and if he should fall in the strife you would take him up *tenderly*, wouldn't you and send all that death would leave to earth, home to me? Promise me *this*, and I will *bless* you always.

Keep us a strong, brave heart, my Friend. The crisis hour

13. That home is where the other is becomes a key theme in the writings of both Eliza and Harrison.

seems to be near at hand, and we know where the triumph will rest.

I've not written you a very cheerful or interesting letter, but I'll try and do better when I write again. I am not quite well yet, and this must be my excuse for it.

My love to Mr. Clevenger.[14] I have not heard from him yet. Please remember me also to Mr. Stevens,[15] and to all with whom I am acquainted.

Hoping to hear from you again I'll bid you good bye now, but friendship's best and warmest wishes shall follow you, and my heart always be glad to hear of your prosperity and happiness.

Yours truly—

E. A. W. Otis

SATURDAY, MAY 31. [1862]

Dear Mr. Masten: I've only a few brief moments before mail time in which to write you this morning, but I did not feel like sending Mrs. Newton's letter without adding one word to you, whose kind attentions I remember so gratefully, and with so much pleasure. I don't expect that I shall be entertaining at all, for it's a gloomy, dark morning, and my feelings appear to have taken their coloring from the clouds. The shadows in the sky seem to have fallen upon my heart. I'm inclined to think, though, that I am hardly honest in charging my despondency upon Nature. I expect that anxiety for My Husband has as much to do with it as anything.

14. Corporal Issac J. Clevenger, Twelfth Regiment. See *Roster*, vol. 2, 370.

15. This probably refers to Daniel Stevens, principal musician of the Twelfth Regiment, later transferred to Field Staff. See *Roster*, vol. 2, 34.

The situation of a portion of our Mountain Department is exceedingly dark and perilous, if I understand it rightly—threatened on all sides by large forces of the enemy, with no reinforcements ready upon which they can fall back for succor. And every day makes me realize more fully what a deadly foe they have to deal with. So base, so inhuman, so barbarous, so recreant to every principle of humanity; so dead to pity, so malignant in their hatred to those whose only crime is a love for that glorious lesson which has nourished and perpetuated every blessing which we have enjoyed as a free and enlightened people. Our poor wounded soldiers, taken from the field of battle to be conveyed to the shelter of the Hospital, writhing in mortal anguish, and struggling already with the King of Terrors, are on their way thither fired upon—helpless, weak, fallen, bleeding and dying, yet not exempt from the assaults of their *chivalrous foes*! I do wonder that the Arm of Divine justice is stayed; that the thunderbolts of God's wrath are not hurled upon them overwhelming them in a worse destruction than that which covered the hosts of Pharaoh when the waters of the Red Sea rolled over them. I live on indignation as I read the papers. I can't help it. Every feeling of my soul revolts at the record of southern barbarity, and human outrages.—But you read not less than I do, and it's not a pleasant theme to dwell upon. People in our vicinity have responded promptly to the call of our President for fifty thousand more volunteers.

Every day impresses more deeply upon the minds of the people the fact that treason can't be dealt with lightly—that it must be met with iron agreements, and bombshell conclusions.

It seems very quiet in my home here among the green hills of Ohio. Our town wears nothing of the military aspect of your own.

I've not yet visited the hills since my return. I've been unable to. I wish we had a Horse Shoe Falls[16] like your own—so full of wild, romantic beauty, so sweet with the melody of soft, clear, falling waters, so grand with its vast rock ribbed, tree crowned, hilly sentinels. I shall remember our visits there till I grow old. I cannot tell you how much I enjoyed it, and I shall remember always too, the friends that were with me there.

But now, Mr. Masten, I must close. You will excuse my brevity and dullness and when I write you again I'll try and be more sociable. Permit the expression of my best wishes for your happiness, and the hope that your life may be full of peace, full of sunshine—Respectfully and truly yours

E. A. W. Otis

TUESDAY, JUNE 17. [1862]

This is a real June day—full of warmth and brightness, and the sweet fragrance of flowers.

It's just four months today since my Baby Boy went to his rest. I've been up to his little grave today, and I tried to look up from it, and remember that he was not there. Sweet one: how I miss him. Not less than when he died. There's no thought more than that I may [go] up to him sometime. God help me to live so that I shall be meet to enter into the same eternal rest.

WEDNESDAY, JUNE 18. [1862]

No letter from Harrison today. This anxious waiting makes life a little dark.—It's summerlike and sunny out of doors; and I

16. These falls, at an especially scenic spot in West Virginia in the Appalachian Mountains, empty into the Kanawha River.

suppose that it ought to be all the same in the world within one. Life's trials should all prove a blessing, and would if their design was answered.

JULY I. MONDAY. [1862]

News of a battle near Richmond reached us today,[17] but no particulars as to the result have been received. We wait in almost breathless suspense for the tidings, such vast interests seem to be depending upon the result of the engagement there. If our forces are not successful we have much to fear from foreign intervention, as well as other evils resulting from defeat.

I've been writing Frank today, I believe that I will copy what I've written—Frank, My Dear Friend:

I am glad to have the pleasure of writing you again, but before I say anything to you let me thank you for your last long and welcome letter. I love long letters from my friends when they are so full of friendliness and familiar talk. Letters in which I can almost feel the heart throbbing in every word, and in the outgoings of the soul in its love of the beautiful, and its appreciation of all that is good, or great, or holy in life.

I wish with you that these "mellow summer Sabbath mornings["] could find you where you could worship "Our Father" among your friends in Ohio, & I hope that the time will not be long before it may be so. I think that in some respects the

17. This is a reference to the "Seven Days Battles" in Virginia between the forces of Generals George B. McClellan and Robert E. Lee, June 25–July 1, 1862. McClellan was within four miles of Richmond, the Confederate capital, before opting to retreat. The casualties were appalling: thirty thousand dead, wounded, or missing. See McPherson, *Battle Cry of Freedom*, 463–71.

prospects of Peace are brightening, though we all know that there is a vast deal to be accomplished yet before our triumph shall be final, and complete.

Don't you all feel badly on account of Fremont's resignation?[18] He's a persecuted man, isn't he?

Frank, I judge from your letter that you are a little sceptical in regard to the sincerity of those who write you "of how much of their hearts you occupy," and if you were here I should scold you a little for it, but as you are so far away out among those old mountains where one would be likely to be gloomy and a little misanthropic if anywhere, I'll only be sorry that you feel so, and wont find a bit of fault with you; I'll only tell you that I think you've got into Doubting Castle, so don't see things as they are. I believe, my Friend, that if there's anything will open the heart to you, and awaken its strongest sympathies its best and purest emotions it is your sacrifices for the cause which we all love. Our soldiers walk just as naturally into our warm loving remembrance, into our prayers, as they would walk into the door of their own homes if they were there. I don't see how any really intelligent, loyal heart can forget them, and I don't believe they do. "*He's a soldier*" is the key which unlocks all our sympathies, which awakens all our gratitude, and makes [us] remember those whom we have scarcely met as if they had grown up with us by our father's hearth stone.

I am glad to know that your regiment has been taken under

18. John C. Frémont, the famous "Pathfinder" and Republican nominee for president in 1856, served as a general in the Union army in the early years of the war but created great controversy by repeatedly exceeding his orders. He resigned in 1862 when Lincoln made a junior officer Frémont's superior. Eliza would have admired his extreme antislavery sentiments. Ibid., 352–8.

Gen. Cox's[19] "special care," & so will have better fare than otherwise.

I don't think, Frank, that you eulogize Mrs. Newton any too highly. Her goodness of heart exalts her far above most of her sex. She is the embodiment of all that is best and noblest in women. God bless her and hers, and reward her for all that she has so freely done for our Country's defenders.

I'll tell you what I am going to do when the war is over, I'm going to invite Mr. Otis to let me meet him at Mrs. Newton's and you'll be there too, and we'll have a glad reunion there, and be happier than ever we were in her home before, for there'll be no fear of future perils or bloody strife. You don't know how impatiently I wait for that time to come. I almost wish that I could grasp hold of the nearest future, and write on it victory and peace, and loved ones at home again. But that isn't for *Human* hands to do.

I *thank* you for your promise, My Kind Friend, in regard to Mr. Otis; I begin to have faith now, however, to hope that it will never need a fulfilment, but should it I should hold it sacred.

And I was *ever so glad* to learn that "Frank, *your Frank*, was getting along all right," and I thank you for telling me of it too.

And before I close let me bid you look hopefully out into the future. There are bright days in store for you in it. Let me see! I believe that I get a glimpse of it now. Shall I tell you *what* I see? "Yes," you say. Well, I see a pleasant home; the soft summer light is falling on it, and the glories of the golden sunset shine in at the open window. There's the breath of flowers about it, and

19. General Jacob D. Cox, an Ohioan and commander in charge of the vital Kanawha Valley. See McKinney, *The Civil War in Fayette County*, 23.

the good night song of birds, and it looks so pleasant I step a little nearer, and saucily just steal a look in at the open window. (I beg pardon) I see the glad, happy face there of the young wife, and can it be?—why yes, he who sits by her side, her Husband, is none other than yourself, looking just as of old, only there's a look of deep, quiet joy in your eyes, and I hear you say, "The world doesn't know, Frank much of the glad fruition which Peace has brought me, and"—but no I won't listen any longer, but I go away feeling sure that mine is not the only happy home that I can find. But I must close now. Mr. Otis and I will have a home not very far from yours, I guess when we get *that office*,[20] and then we'll come and see you and Frank every day.

Till then write often, and believe me ever,

Truly Your Friend

EAW Otis

20. An obvious reference to a postwar dream including an office for Harry to conduct business or publish a newspaper.

CHAPTER 5

"This Unnatural Strife"

AUG 21. [1862] [LOWELL]

Nellie Van Clief is with me. Tonight we take the boat for Parkersburg. I'll see Harry tomorrow I hope. What joy! How I wish I could have received his dispatch sooner.

FRIDAY, AUG 22. [1862]

Met Harrison at Parkersburg, as he was on his way to Washington. He was looking well and hearty, but sunburnt, as all of our soldiers are. God bless him, My noble Husband!

I was with him but about four hours and they passed away very quickly. I met him in his tent, under the shadow of the forest trees, that seemed to wave their long arms above us in silent benediction.

Dear Husband! God keep you in safety amid all the perils of the battle fields to which you go.

AUG 31. [1862]

The twenty seventh was a day of battle to our brave Twelfth.[1] How anxious I am to hear from Harry, and yet there seems to be a something within me that tells me he is safe.

OCTOBER 24. [1862]

I've just sent a box of things to Harry, which I trust will reach him. He's back with his regiment in Western Virginia again, after two months hard service in the eastern part of the state. The regiment has been in three severe engagements, the battles of Bull Run, on the 27th, and South Mountain and Antietam,[2] still later, and my dear Husband has been preserved through them all, unharmed save a slight wound in the shoulder. How can I be as thankful as I ought to that infinite Love which has preserved him.

I hope that I may see him now this coming winter. I'll meet him at Mrs. Newton's perhaps—How happy my heart will be when it's beating against his arm.

He is good and true, and the wrong that others do me shall never make me distrust him.[3] Life has nothing dearer to me than Harry.

1. The Battle of Second Manassas, or Bull Run, took place July 14–August 27, 1862. See Harrison Otis diary entry for August 27, 1862. See also McPherson, *Battle Cry of Freedom*, 526–44.

2. All were exceptionally fierce encounters. Ibid., 525–44.

3. This is the first reference Eliza makes to her family feud. See Introduction.

1863

MARCH 28, 1863. [CHARLESTON]

This is the anniversary of dear little Harry's birth. He would have been two years old today, had he lived. I can but feel sad on anniversary days like this, but then I don't feel like repining for I know that our Baby is happier than we could make him. I wouldn't be so selfish as to wish him back again. He left the world before the taint of sin could sully his infant purity, and "of Such is the Kingdom of Heaven."

There's something so sweet in the memory of such little ones. No unpleasant remembrances of disobedience, and numberless naughty ways that children have when they are a few years older; nothing but smiles and innocent prattlings, and fond lisping words. How I treasure them all! I'm so glad that I've been a Mother. I believe that it has made me better. Little Harry has made life seem broader, and more beautiful. Our Angel Harry opened my heart to little children, and enlarged it so that there is a sense of emptiness without them. Dear boy! what a beautiful mirror of love his was! I bless him for it, and love him today not less than when he was with me. What cunning words and ways he would have cheered us with had he lived until now. His sweet baby talk should have been so beautiful to me. But then it is better as it is. The Darling is blessed now! Harry isn't dear to me any more than when he was in my arms. He will always be *my own Baby Boy*, and no others can ever make me forget my first born Darling!

Two years ago tonight, how ill I was! I remember it as though it were but yesterday, and I remember too how when the struggle was over My Husband bent over me, and in his earnest loving tones murmured "God bless you Lizzie."

Won't I hear the same dear voice again soon that said then, "God bless you Lizzie?" I hope so. I wait for you, Dear One!

WEDNESDAY, APRIL 1. [1863]

As I was sitting in my chamber this afternoon, feeling a little lonely, and thinking I'd give anything in the world if Harry was here, I heard the front door open, and then someone looked into the parlor, and then the footsteps came up stairs, and as my door opened I looked up there stood My Husband, his dear face full of joy, and smiling on me just as of old.

How glad I was to see him, and to be clasped to his heart again. We talked over that evening all the *trial* that I had passed through since our last meeting, and Harry said that I shouldn't go back again to Lowell where everything is so unpleasant.

This evening he folded me to his heart and said kissing me. "Lizzie you are my love," and with that assurance I am content and forget all sorrow.

THURSDAY, APRIL 2. [1863]

How delightful to be with Harry again. I live in the sunshine.

SATURDAY, APRIL 4. [1863]

Harry and I visited Horse Shoe Falls this morning. The morning was very beautiful. The sky clear and cloudless, the air fresh and pure, but a little cold.

We went up in the direction of Colonel White's,[4] and then out through the fields to the hills. We passed over some low, marshy ground, and came out to the camping ground of the cavalry, and from then went out past the former residence of the rebel, Colonel Clarkson. It's a fine brick building, two stories high, with a piazza along the front and side, and stands upon a beautiful eminence back from town, with fine grounds in front, descending in a gentle slope towards the South, and at its base runs a little brook, laughing and dancing along with the merriest song in the world.

The fine old house is now occupied by a company of our Cavalry, and they find in it the most commodious quarters.

We climbed up over the high hill back of the house and stood a while by the high monument on its top, which is sacred to the memory of the dead. Here we had a fine view of town, and of the camp of the Twenty Third Ohio, which is on the opposite bank of the Kanawha, and whose numerous tents looked clear and white in the bright sunshine.

Back from us on the hill where we stood were the vestiges of an old rebel camp. Heaps of rubbish were scattered about, and a cooking stove rusty from exposure was standing where our enemies had left it a year ago.

While we stood by the monument Harry asked me how I would feel about his enlisting in the regular army when the war is over. The thought chilled me. I told him that I never could consent to it, that I wouldn't feel as if there was any brightness in the future for me if he would do that. That while his Country

4. Colonel Carr B. White was brigade commander of the Twelfth Regiment. See *Roster*, vol. 2, 353.

Col. Carr B. White, commander of the Twelfth Regiment and the official host when Eliza and other wives visited the troops in camp. It was White who urged Harrison to join Capt. Richard Blazer's Independent Scouts, a behind-the-lines operation dedicated to rooting out the Confederate forces lurking in the West Virginia mountains. Harry served as a scout from 1863 to July 1864 and suffered a severe leg wound toward the end of his tour.
(United States Army Military History Institute, Carlisle, Pennsylvania)

needed him in this great strife for Freedom, and National existence I would not say one word to keep him from the field, but when this war was over, I should feel that I had some claim upon him, and with him I should want a home. I hope he has no intention of entering the Army. He only wanted to sound me a little I guess.[5]

Our walk to the falls was very pleasant. We sat down for a little while under the shadow of those old rocks, and talked of a thousand things, and then came home by way of Front Street.

SABBATH, APRIL 5. [1863]

Harrison and I attended church today. Rev. Mr. Stevens preached. His discourse was not very edifying. Came home and Harry slept a part of the afternoon.

Evening there was service at the Hospital, but I did not attend as Harry did not feel like going out—There are several cases of small pox among the soldiers there.

MONDAY, APRIL 6. [1863]

Harry and I were having a pleasant and sociable time, when Maria came up to tell me there was a gentlemen below who wished to see me. Went down to the parlor and found our good friend Mr. Clevenger. Was glad to see him. He stopped to tea with us.

5. See Introduction, footnote 49 for the later history of Harry's proposal to join the regular Army.

TUESDAY, APRIL 7. [1863]

Captain Williams[6] and Lieutenant Palmer took dinner with us today. We enjoyed it all by ourselves, and had the table set in the parlor. They were all very sociable, and the hours passed quickly and pleasantly.

Captain Williams thought it would not be surprising if the rebels made an attack upon their fortifications soon. Said it would be an easy matter for the enemy to concentrate a force of ten or twelve thousand against them.

God guard and watch over our little band of patriots there, and shield them from all dangers.

WEDNESDAY, APRIL 8. [1863]

The day is pleasant. This afternoon Harry and I went up to call on Mrs. White.[7] Was disappointed in finding that she had returned to Ohio. Went in however and sat a few moments with her landlady Mrs. Young. Found her a good Union woman. Came back and spent the remainder of the afternoon with Mrs. Robinson, Found Lieutenants Stevens and Naughton[8] there and had a pleasant chat with them. Took tea with them, and then went back to Mrs. Newton's. Harry went down town to get his mule on board the boat which he had taken passage for Loup Creek. Came back about nine o'clock and said he would stay all night with me. Sat up until about ten reading the pa-

6. Captain Rigdon Williams was a member of the Twelfth Regiment. *Roster*, vol. 2, 359.

7. She was the wife of Colonel Carr B. White.

8. Possibly Lieutenant James Naughton of the Twenty-third Regiment. See *Roster*, vol. 3, 71.

pers. The thought that he must leave me in the morning would not let me sleep, so I lay awake and let him sleep in my arms.

I woke him at four o'clock in the morning. He got up at half past four, and was soon dressed and kissed him good bye. I tried to bid him good bye cheerfully, but I felt lonely enough when he was gone.

APRIL 9. [1863]

I didn't know that I should miss My Husband so much, but I've felt all alone today. When will this war be over, and our Separation ended; God grant that it may be soon.

FRIDAY, APRIL 10. [1863]

Today is as warm and sunny as a June day. Jennie Robinson and I went out walking this morning. Went nearly up to the old camping ground of the Twelfth—Camp Warren. I wished that the regiment were still there. This afternoon in company with Mr. Clevenger, Missus Dallas, Missus Agen, Missus Rand,[9] and others went to Horse Shoe Falls. Took dinner at Mrs. Robinson's, and started from there. Had a most delightful time—enjoyed it as I rarely do such trips.

Heard this evening that a demand to surrender had been sent into our forces at Fayette under a flag of truce. If so dear Harry will doubtless be engaged in bloody conflict to-morrow. May Our Father Shield him My Beloved Husband.

9. These were presumably Charleston acquaintances, perhaps all from the Newtons' boardinghouse.

SATURDAY, APRIL 11. [1863]

The day is very beautiful. Soft, smoky and warm, the air having the deliciousness of an Indian summer's day. How forcibly I'm reminded as I look on this loveliness of Nature of the truth of the Poet's words—

"And only man is vile."[10]

Received a letter from dear Harry this evening, just a little brief one written from the camp of the 91st. I miss his presence, yet I will try and be cheerful. I ought to be since it is Duty alone that keeps him from me. God bless him and all of the Brave who are battling for Freedom. May His Angels encamp round about them.

SUNDAY, APRIL 12. [1863]

The morning was wet and rainy, but the afternoon bright with pleasant sunshine. Another letter from Harrison which speaks to my heart. He is back in camp at Fayette again and on duty. I wish that I was with him there.

Our newspapers bring the intelligence of great want at the South. At Richmond, the rebel Capitol, there was recently a fearful bread riot. Three thousand women armed themselves with clubs, guns and stones, determined to have food if it cost them their lives. The cry of famishing little ones they could not resist, and they went to the Government Store Houses, and rolled out their hoarded stores into the streets. The military

10. Bishop Reginald Heber, "Missionary Hymn," *From Greenland's Icy Mountains* (1819).

were unable to disperse them until the august Jeff[11] made his appearance, and promised that their wants should be cared for.

It appears that the Confederate Government had impressed all of the flour for sale in the city, and other provisions, and stored them away for the use of the Army, forbidding their sale to the starving citizens, and gaunt hunger, and Want and Famine pressed wretched mothers, and sisters, and wives to deeds of desperation and violence.

When will this unnatural strife end, and Prosperity and Plenty brood once more over our great sisterhood of States?

Like riots it seems are occurring in other Southern cities. The fruits of secession are being tasted and they are full of bitterness.

Mr. Clevenger has been sitting with me today. I was glad to see him for I was feeling lonely. I prize him, and friendship will always hold him in remembrance.

I feel dull and sleepy. Haven't felt much mental activity today. I must write to Harry before I retire.

MONDAY, APRIL 13. [1863]

It's been very pleasant today. Went out walking this afternoon with Jennie Robinson.

Lieutenant Sherwood,[12] of the Twelfth Ohio called on me this evening. I liked him much.

Later received a letter from Aunt Susan, and Uncle Martin Thompson, which bro't me the sad intelligence of dear Cousin

11. Sarcastic reference to Jefferson Davis, president of the Confederacy.

12. Lieutenant Henry L. Sherwood, Twelfth Regiment. See *Roster*, vol. 2, 360, 371.

Abbie's death.[13] May God comfort them in their great sorrow. How well I know the bitterness of such grief.

TUESDAY, APRIL 14. [1863]

Wrote to Pa today, and commenced a letter to Aunt Susan. Been at work on a picture frame. It's cloudy this evening and raining. Waiting anxiously for intelligence from our armies. Hope soon for the cheering intelligence that Vicksburg is in possession of our forces.[14] If that stronghold could be taken, it would be a blow at which Treason would recoil and tremble.

WEDNESDAY, APRIL 15. [1863]

The day has been rainy and dark, but a letter from Harry of the thirteenth brought sunshine to my soul. A thousand blessings on his dear head! God help me to be worthy of the love of his great heart.

Been writing to Aunt Susan today. In speaking of Cousin Abbie's death, said to her—"Earth can afford no consolation in trials like these. We must look up beyond the grave, away from its darkness to the better life—to *Our Father.* I remember a beautiful thought of some writer which comforted me, and which I hope may comfort you in your sorrow. Let me quote it. "A

13. Susan B. Wetherby was the sister of Eliza's father, Charles Wetherby. The text suggests that Uncle Martin Thompson was her husband and cousin Abbie her daughter, but the available genealogical records are not specific.

14. Vicksburg, "the Gibraltar of the West," was repeatedly assaulted by Union forces under General Ulysses S. Grant over a period of seven months and finally captured on July 4, 1863. James McPherson has called it "the most important strategic victory of the war," confirming Eliza's opinion. See *Battle Cry of Freedom*, 437.

Shepherd lost a sheep with its lamb. He went in pursuit of them. He found them far off in a lonely valley. He tried to drive them home but was not able. At length he picked up and carried off the lamb, and the mother followed. Thus the Savior brings the mother to Himself by taking away the little child from her bosom." And isn't it so, dear friends? Don't these sorrows—if rightly improved lead us nearer to the Savior? I know that since *my* little lamb has been taken I have felt as though the Savior was nearer to me because He had my Darling, and I have more earnestly desired to live so that I might follow the little angel feet of my baby Harry into the Kingdom of God; and in the loss of your dear Abbie may you feel that you walk nearer the shining shore, nearer that gentle Shepherd who has taken her to Himself.

Wrote Harry this evening. I love to write him and he shall hear from me often.

Received intelligence today of the bombardment of Charleston, South Carolina by our ironclads. Nothing decisive was the result. Several large breaches were made in the walls of Fort Sumpter, and one of our monitors was sunk, and several impressed so that they could not operate effectively. Our fleet withdrew, and at latest advices the attack had not been resumed.

WEDNESDAY, APRIL 16. [1863]

Still raining, but Nature is looking beautifully. The grass looks green and velvety, and the peach trees are blushing pink with blooms. Spring comes tardily on, almost as if she felt herself an intruder, but she'll gather courage by and by I hope, and come to us a little more in earnest.

FRIDAY, APRIL 17. [1863]

Wrote Harry today but received no letter from him. I'll have one tomorrow.

The sun looked out gloriously this afternoon, and I could not withstand the inducements to go out of doors. Took a walk down Front Street, and on my way home called at Mrs. Robinson's.

Papers bring us the intelligence of the renewal of the attack upon Charlestons, South Carolina—result not yet known.[15]

SATURDAY, APRIL 18. [1863]

How the days and months glide away, out into that vast, unseen, ever grasping Past, and the tide rolls onward, and we go nearer down to the great River, *Death*. Happy are they who see the shining shores beyond it, and whose barks are safely piloted out into "the still waters."

The day is one of Spring's most beautiful ones. The air breathes balm, and there's beauty everywhere.

Writing to Harry again this morning. Told him of Mrs. Cotton's arrest for treason. She was sent beyond our lines today. Glad that Government has begun to deal with these female traitors. If they will indulge in rampant treason, then sex should not shield them from punishment. Justice shouldn't deal with the grammatical distinctions of gender, and make treason either masculine or feminine, and I'm glad that they are not doing it.

I wouldn't call my Husband from the field for anything in the

15. Despite repeated attempts by land and by sea, Union forces were unsuccessful in their efforts to conquer "the Citadel of Secession." See McPherson, *Battle Cry of Freedom*, 646.

wide world, but yet I can't but wish now and then that I was with him. Our hearts will drift us away sometimes, from life's stern, fierce realities into the quiet, still beauty that they love, where there's only music, and gentle words. We toil in the desert and *rest* on the green oasis.

Went to the woods again in company with Mr. Clevenger, the Missus Agen, and Jennie Robinson. Visited the cemetery where so many of our brave soldiers are buried.

It seemed sad to see them lying so far from home with none near who loved them!—But, let them rest our immortal, heroic dead.

Their deeds the Present's gift to Future time.

A long letter from Harry today, such an one as he only can write. I bless him for all his noble, loving words, and may God bless him too. I wish that my heart could palpitate its reply—I'll write him in the morning, though I feel the poverty of language when it seeks to be the heart's interpreter.

SUNDAY, APRIL 19. [1863]

It was pleasant this morning, Went to the Sabbath School, and was appointed as teacher to a class of young ladies. The school just organized. Mr. Newton superintendent.

April showers this afternoon, and the earth looks up and smiles for the refreshing which they bring. This evening attended service at the Hospital. A good many soldiers present. The ward in which service was held was pleasant, and all the beds looked clean and nice. The lamp which hung in the centre of the room was tastefully trimmed with evergreens, and gave it a fresh, cheerful look.

There was a sick soldier in the room who was very feeble. I

spoke with him, and said a few, friendly words to him, and he seemed glad to talk with me. Poor man, I'm fearful that he'll never see home anymore.

MONDAY, APRIL 20. [1863]

Been busy completing a little picture frame for Harry to present to Lieutenant Palmer.

Another letter from my good Husband today, and I've finished a long letter to him, which I will send by Sergeant Clevenger tomorrow.

No news tonight. Waiting anxiously to hear from Charleston. May that foul birth place of Treason be laid in the dust, and perish like its guilty child.

Received a letter from Sergeant Fornshell this morning.

TUESDAY, APRIL 21. [1863]

The day has been lovely—but the night threatens rain. This evening Grandpa Newton gave me a little account of the effect of secession in the domestic circle.

There is a gentleman and his wife here in Charleston, who here-to-fore have always lived happily. He is loyal to the old flag, while she longs for the [illegible] of the "stars and bars" floating over the Southern Confederacy, and as a conclusion and *feeling* argument in support of her advocacy of treason she made use of the broom stick, till he, becoming enraged and excited, seized it from her, and inflicted a blow the effect of which was so serious that he was compelled to call in a physician.

Ah this *viper* of treason, how it crawls into the home-circle and like the Serpent of old destroys all that is bright in Eden.

WEDNESDAY, APRIL 22. [1863]

Rainy and dark today.—No news of importance from any source, save a detailed account of a great union meeting in Hamilton, Butler Co. Ohio. Twenty thousand people present, and the most earnest, and enthusiastic devotion expressed to Our Old Flag and the cause of Freedom.

THURSDAY, APRIL 23. [1863]

No news of any importance from our armies. Our last papers state that the Czar of Russia has the prospect of new difficulties on hand. The Tartars have caught the spirit of revolution, and have risen up against the Government, and are striking for Freedom.[16]

It makes one thoughtful to witness these great national convulsions—these world wide revolutionary movements. One can but wonder if these are not the days which the far-reaching visions of prophecy foresaw, in which there should be "wars and rumors of war," and "men's hearts failing them because of fear."[17]

FRIDAY, APRIL 24. [1863]

Rainy today with occasional gleams of sunshine. A letter from Harry brought sunshine to my heart. My life, with all its sorrows is more than blessed in his love.

16. There was a very serious revolt in Poland against the czar in 1863, but the standard texts do not report an uprising by the Tartars.

17. Matt. 24: 6,7.

I feel light hearted tonight—My soul revels in its hopes of *our* golden days to come.

The buds are just peeping out from the tree in front of my window—the "Tree of Heaven" with its broad, beautiful leaves just beginning to swell in the bud with their new life which the Spring has brought.

How beautiful this awakening of Nature after the death sleep of winter has passed. More beautiful will be our awakening in the springtime of eternal being.

SATURDAY, APRIL 25. [1863]

Nature is unfolding in loveliness. Winter no longer "lingers in the lap of spring"—but the sunshine is warm, the air balmy, and everything speaks of freshness and newborn life.

MAY 18—MONDAY. [1863]

A long time has passed since my last entry in my journal. Mr. Newton's illness has prevented my writing, but Mrs. Newton is at home once more, and now my time is all at my command.

Tonight dear Harry came. How my heart bounded with joy at his coming. I was sitting by my pleasant chamber window watching and waiting for him, when Jennie Stephens came running out and said to me. "Mr. Otis is coming."—I went out to meet him, and kissed him the welcome that my glad heart gave him. We spent the evening in my little room and I was happy as only his dear presence can make me.

TUESDAY, MAY 19. [1863]

Went with Mrs. Newton, Mr. McClain,[18] Harry and others to visit the fortifications on the hill. Harry and I outwalked the others, and we had a quiet walk together, and I felt the joy of being alone with my Husband. It's a deep joy—one that I love, and one that I wish could be oftener mine.

The fortifications are upon a high eminence, on the opposite banks of the Kanawha, and command the country for miles up and down the river.

The view is beautiful and extensive. The Kanawha lay at our feet, and rolled on in the majesty of its silent flow—smiling to the bending trees on its banks—and seeming proud like a thing of life of the green fields that lay around it like the setting of a pearl.

Nearly opposite the fort the Elk empties its waters into those of the Kanawha, where they mingle like the sunlight in the air. As we returned stopped at Mrs. Robinson's, and Harry and I took tea there.

Returned to Mrs. Newton's about eight o'clock. Great excitement in town on account of the rumored approach of the rebel army.

Harry left me this morning about half past eight. It was hard to part with him, but my heart blessed him and bid him good bye. May God keep him, my Precious Husband in safety. He's dearer to me every day—my life grows to his more and more closely. I hope that I'll go to Fayette soon and spend a week or two with him.

18. A fellow boarder at the Newtons'.

THURSDAY, MAY 21. [1863]

The weather is warm and beautiful. Nature has put on her most charming face. Sometimes I enjoy this beauty and sometimes it makes me feel lonely. My heart cries out now and then "Harry, Harry." God bless my Only Darling.

FRIDAY, MAY 22. [1863]

Poor old "Grandma Newton" is failing day by day. How near Death comes sometimes. We see those about us dying; but, yet it is difficult for us to realize that we must die.

It's hard to realize that every day brings us nearer to that *last hour*. But if we are ready for it is laden with richer gladness than all the busy ones of life. It lies on the threshold of immortality—it's the Beulah where we halt before we cross the river—where the fragrance of its odors is wafted to us, and the echo of its music is borne to our ears.

SATURDAY, MAY 23. [1863]

I hoped to hear from Harry today, but no letter came. The reports from Fayette are very conflicting, but I seem to have an inner assurance of Harry's safety, and with that I am thankful, and content.

SUNDAY, MAY 24. [1863]

Went to church this morning, and this evening wrote a letter to Harry. After tea Misses Somers and Kelly called. Miss Somers gave me a most beautiful bouquet of flowers. They fill my room with fragrance, and smile upon me like a friend.

MONDAY, MAY 25. [1863]

A letter from Harry today. 'Twas written on Saturday, and he had just returned with his Brigade from a long chase after the enemy, under McCauslin.[19] He writes that our troops at Fayette were attacked by the Rebels on Tuesday of last week, and the firing was continued at intervals until Wednesday noon, when the rebels, finding that the Twelfth had been reinforced, set their faces towards Princeton, and shortly Col. White with his Brigade followed in pursuit.

Harry left Charleston about nine o'clock on Wednesday (the day following the one on which the attack was first made) and on Thursday night reached the advance of his regiment, having in the mean time travelled seventy five miles, twenty seven of which he walked. All honor to my soldier Husband! Our bleeding Country has not a truer son. Liberty will never die with such defenders. The blessing of the Most High be poured upon his Beloved head.

TUESDAY, MAY 26. [1863]

News comes to us today of the evacuation of Vicksburg by the rebels, and the taking of seventeen thousand prisoners by our forces, together with a large number of canon.

I hope that this may not prove to be simply Rumor, like the

19. General John McCauslin was commander of Confederate forces in the Kanawha Valley. See McKinney, *The Civil War in Fayette County*, 183–7.

recently reported taking of the Rebel Capitol, but we must wait for further intelligence, before we can rely implicitly upon tidings which if true will thrill my loyal heart with excellent gladness.

Writing to Frank today of the Rumor I said "If these tidings prove true, won't we begin to have visions of Peace again, and Loved Ones coming home? I almost tremble at the thought of such deep, *deep* joy."

Charleston was last week in a state of most intense excitement on account of the approach of the rebels. I kept delightfully cool though, did not feel half as much excited as I would now to know that my Husband would take tea with me tonight.

Writing to Mr. Clevenger I said "The view from the hill-top (where the fortifications of the Twenty Third are built) was glorious and extensive. It made my heart throb faster, for the *voice* of the beautiful reached it, and the green valley at our feet with its sentinel mountains spoke eloquently to my soul, as though it was instinct with human life, and underneath the green grass was a great heart throbbing in sympathy with my own. I'm a child of Nature, and what I feel when in communion with her words cannot utter.

½ past nine P.M. The evening has passed very pleasantly. Mr. McClain and Mrs. Newton have been with me in my little room, and we've chatted and gossiped to our heart's content. Mr. McClain is one of my Uncle Sam's best boys—one of the best of my soldier cousins.

WEDNESDAY, MAY 27. [1863]

A letter from Harry tonight containing an account of the late attack upon Fayette. He is kind to write me so often. I sit up tonight with old Mrs. Newton, We think she cannot live until morning. The evening is lovely—clear, bright moonlight, and air soft as the breath of summer.

THURSDAY, MAY 28. [1863]

How times flies! Summer will soon be here. June, the month of roses, is almost blushing into being.

I feel weary and dull after my night's watching, although with my pleasant company the night did not seem long. Miss Irene Estill sat up with me. She is a good girl, even though her heart is with the enemies of her Country.

I'd be glad to hear from Harry again today, though I do not dare to hope that I shall. He has been more prompt that I have in writing since he left me last. God bless him ever.

FRIDAY, MAY 29. [1863]

A letter from Harry today which gladdened me. I love him for his promptness in writing as well as all of his other kindness.

Mr. McClain spent the evening with us. Had a pleasant visit with him.

The news by telegraph this evening is indeed glorious, heart-cheering. It comes to us like the lifting up of a shadow, and we can but hope for complete and final triumph. The dispatch stated that Banks[20] reported to be on his way to reinforce Grant.

20. General Nathaniel P. Banks of the Union army.

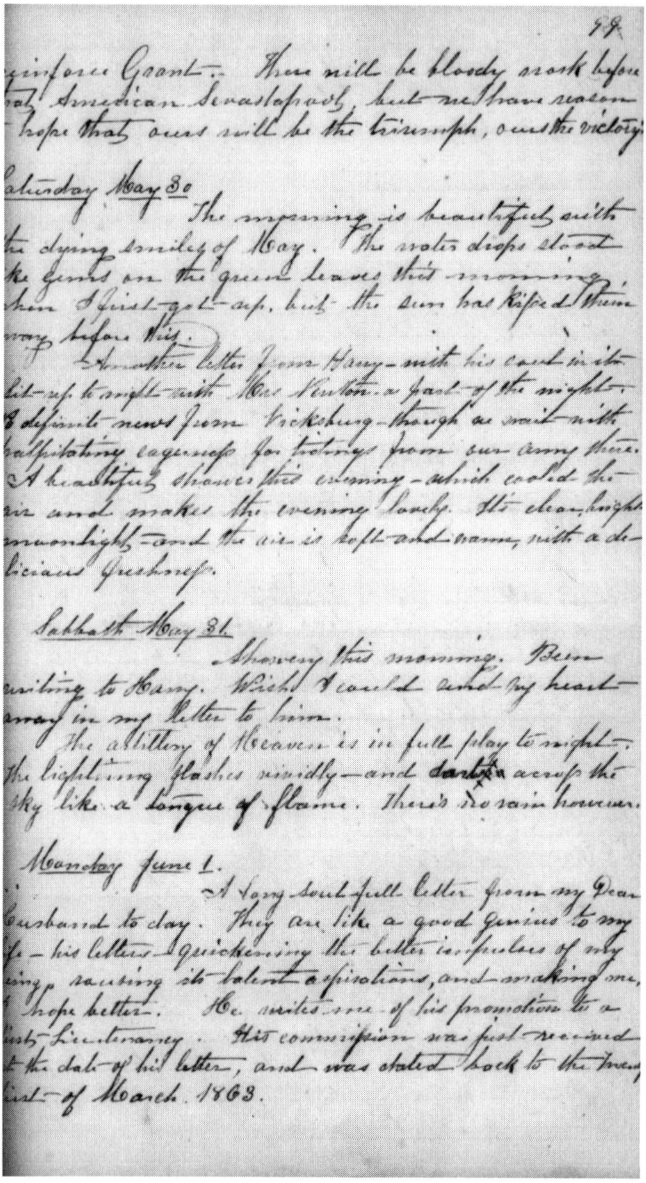

98

reinforce Grant. There will be bloody work before that American Sevastopol, but we have reason to hope that ours will be the triumph, ours the victory.

Saturday May 30

The morning is beautiful with the dying smile of May. The water drops stood like gems on the green leaves this morning when I first got up, but the sun has kissed them away before this.

Another letter from Harry – with his card in it. Sat up to night with Mrs Newton a part of the night. No definite news from Vicksburg – though we wait with palpitating eagerness for tidings from our army there. A beautiful shower this evening – which cooled the air and makes the evening lovely. Its clear, bright moonlight – and the air is soft and warm, with a delicious freshness.

Sabbath May 31.

Showery this morning. Been writing to Harry. Wish I could send my heart away in my letter to him.

The artillery of Heaven is in full play to night. The lightning flashes vividly – and darts across the sky like a tongue of flame. There's no rain however.

Monday June 1.

A long soul-full letter from my Dear Husband to day. They are like a good Genius to my life – his letters – quickening the better impulses of my being, rousing its latent aspirations, and making me hope better. He writes me of his promotion to a First Lieutenancy. His commission was just received at the date of his letter, and was dated back to the very first of March. 1863.

Journal entries for May 30 through June 1, 1863, in which Eliza comments on the war and the absent Harry, now a soldier fighting in West Virginia. (Huntington Library)

There will be bloody work before that American Sevastopol;[21] but we have reason to hope that ours will be the triumph, ours the victory.

SATURDAY, MAY 30. [1863]

The morning is beautiful with the dying smiles of May. The water drops stood like gems on the green leaves this morning, when I first got up, but the sun has kissed them away before this.

Another letter from Harry—with his soul in it. Sit up tonight with Mrs. Newton—a part of the night. No definite news from Vicksburg—though we wait with palpitating eagerness for tidings from our army there.

A beautiful shower this evening—which cooled the air and makes the evening lovely. It's clear, bright moonlight and the air is soft and warm, with a delicious freshness.

SABBATH, MAY 31. [1863]

Showery this morning. Been writing to Harry. Wish I could send my heart away in my letter to him.

The artillery of Heaven is in full play tonight. The lightning flashes vividly—and darts across the sky like a tongue of flame. There's no rain however.

21. The bloodiest battle of the Crimean War, fought between England, France, Russia, and Turkey. Eliza's comparison with Vicksburg is quite apt.

MONDAY, JUNE 1. [1863]

A long soul-full letter from my Dear Husband today. They are like a good genius to my life—his letters—quickening the better impulses of my being, rousing its latent aspirations, and making me, I hope better. He writes me of his promotion to a first Lieutenant. His commission was just received at the date of his letter, and was dated back to the twenty first of March, 1863.

CHAPTER 6

Life with Uncle Sam's Boys

SATURDAY, JUNE 6, 1863.

We left Charleston this morning at ten o'clock. The ambulance called for me at Mrs. Newton's and with a feeling of zest for new enterprises, and an eager desire to see my Husband, I stepped into it, and commenced my tour of Kanawha Valley.

The day was bright and sunny, full of the fresh beauty of June, but the roads were dry and dusty, it having been some weeks since any rain had fallen.

Malden, the first town through which we passed after leaving Charleston, is rather a pretty little place, with fine old hills about it, which look down with a sort of fatherly air upon it—the place owes its importance to the salt works in the vicinity, which are among the finest in the country.

We only came as far as Mrs. Tompkin's today, where we have been kindly received and entertained. It's a pretty place. The house is embowered in trees and roses, and the river flows along in front, making with the high hills and valley, a beautiful picture. The young ladies entertained us in the evening with music

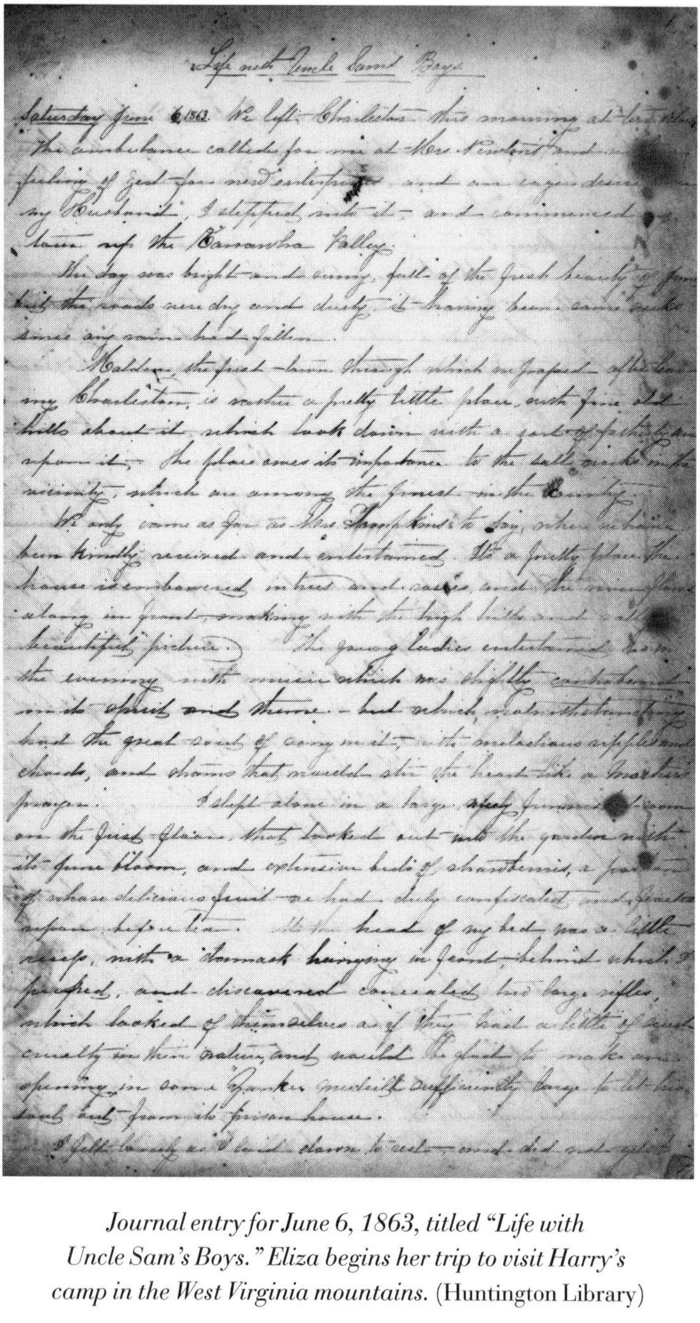
Life with Uncle Sam's Boys

Saturday June 6 1863. We left Charleston this morning at [illegible]. The ambulance called for me at Mrs. Newton's and with feeling of zest for new enterprise and an eager desire [illegible] my Husband, I stepped into it and commenced my [illegible] up the Kanawha Valley.

The day was bright and sunny, full of the fresh beauty of June but the roads were dry and dusty, it having been some weeks since any rain had fallen.

Malden, the first town through which we passed after leaving Charleston, is rather a pretty little place, with fine old hills about it, which look down with a sort of fatherly air upon it. The place owes its importance to the salt works in the vicinity, which are among the finest in the County.

We only came as far as Mrs. Thompkins' to-day, where we have been kindly received and entertained. It's a pretty place, the house is embowered in trees and vines, and the river flows along in front, making with the high hills and valley a beautiful picture. The young ladies entertained us in the evening with music which was slightly contraband in its spirit and theme — but which notwithstanding had the great soul of song in it, with melodious ripples and chords, and strains that would stir the heart like a Mother's prayer. I slept alone in a large airy furnished room on the first floor, that looked out into the garden with its fine bloom, and extensive beds of strawberries, a portion of whose delicious fruit we had duly confiscated and feasted upon before tea. At the head of my bed was a little recess, with a damask hanging in front, behind which I peeped, and discovered concealed two large rifles, which looked of themselves as if they had a little of Secesh cruelty in their nature, and would [illegible] to make an opening in some Yankee [illegible] sufficiently large to let his soul out from its prison house.

I felt lonely as I laid down to rest, and did not get

Journal entry for June 6, 1863, titled "Life with Uncle Sam's Boys." Eliza begins her trip to visit Harry's camp in the West Virginia mountains. (Huntington Library) which was slightly *contraband*[1] in its spirit and theme—but which notwithstanding had the great soul of song on it, with melodious ripples and chords, and strains that would stir the heart like a mother's prayer. I slept alone in a large, nicely furnished room on the first floor, that looked out into the garden with its June bloom, and extensive beds of strawberries, a portion of whose delicious fruit we had duly confiscated and feasted upon before tea. At the head of my bed was a little recess, with a damask hanging in front, behind which I peeked, and discovered concealed two large rifles, which looked of themselves as if they had a little of such cruelty in their nature, and would be glad to make an opening in some Yankee mudsill sufficiently large to let his soul out from its prison house.

I felt lonely as I laid down to rest, and did not get to sleep until about twelve o'clock. The shadow that is on our land seemed to be crawling in and mingling with the midnight darkness and my spirit seemed to feel the chill of war and its desolation.

SUNDAY, JUNE 7. [1863]

The Sabbath could hardly have dawned more beautifully in Eden, than it dawned upon the world this morning. There was a whole choir of birds singing as I woke and the cool, fresh air stole in at my open window fragrant with flowery incense.

I was up and dressed early, and went into the parlor before Lieutenant Sherwood and Lady came down.

There was a large photograph album upon the table, filled with pictures. Among them was that of the rebel General

1. Eliza uses the word, technically a Northern term referring to escaped slaves, more loosely to refer to Southern culture and to blacks.

"Stonewall Jackson."[2] It was a fine face—one of rare manly beauty—a high massive forehead—large, full, pleasant eyes, hair finely cut—withal a sort of hero face, such as we long remember. Mrs. Sherwood tells me that the portrait more than does him justice, she thinks; but of that I cannot judge.

About nine o'clock the ambulance was brought to the door, and bidding the family good bye we set out again on our journey. There was nothing to remind us of the seriousness of the day. No Sabbath bell, nor house of God where the people could go up to worship. Just above the house a few soldiers were camped, and we could hear them singing—they were not sacred songs though—not songs that they had learned at home—but such as came into being in camp with loud strains in them which have no melody.

As we passed up the valley the scenery above Mrs. Tompkin's (which is nineteen miles above Charleston) increased in its wildness and beauty. The mountains were suggestive of Alpine heights—vast, frowning, and majestic—just the place where mythologists might dream, and people their caverns, and rock-ribbed, heaven-reaching cliffs with Gods and demons—and the Druids that lived in the forests of old. My life seemed to freshen amid the freshness of nature, and grow gladder amid its greenness and beauty. I wish that I could tell something how I felt as my eye took in this vast panorama, with its grand magnificence of mountains, their tops kissing the clouds and the blue sky touching them softly like a mother's hand, while they stood, as

2. Thomas J. ("Stonewall") Jackson, easily the most feared Confederate general, noted for his courage and his fanaticism, was killed mistakenly by his own troops at Chancellorsville in 1863. See McPherson, *Battle Cry of Freedom*, 524–38, 642.

if a tired world might lean itself against them and rest. But words won't do it—such emotions lie too deep in the soul to admit of word painting.

The scenery in the vicinity of the falls is particularly fine. The hills here are higher than at any point below. They are mostly covered with trees, but now and then a line of rocks juts out like the frowning battlements of a castle, or the rocky fortress of some old storm demon—whose breath sweeps along like a tempest, when the clouds burst their rain upon the world.

We enjoyed our ride over Cotton Mountain. The road winds along the side of the mountain, and in places is very narrow. Mrs. Sherwood and I were very quiet as we rode up the long ascent. The wild beauty of the view made us dumb—those giant mountain sentinels—preaching with their silent voices, with an eloquence old as time, their echoes sounding far back into the eternity of years—and coming up to us from the old Past talked to me more impressively of the *Power* that formed them, and the wide world, than any voice that I have listened to for years.

A part of the way we could look down into deep valleys that seemed almost fathomless—the tops of the tallest trees far, far below us—and we looking down upon them as the stars look down upon the world.

From the top of the mountain the view is broad and extensive. Two rivers lie at our feet—and the Valley stretched out for miles green with verdure, and grounded by eternal hills. The whole scene spoke of the power of Him who "spoke and it was done."

We reached our stopping place about seven o'clock on this Sabbath evening. It's a country farm house about a mile and a half on the west side of camp. The location is pleasant—woods on all sides.

Here we are *rusticating* in the most primitive style imaginable. If I was only good at word painting, I'd picture our *quarters*. The house was occupied about two years ago, at the time of Floyd's retreat, as a rebel hospital, and Headquarters—and now it's hardly anything but a shell.

The family who occupied it were compelled to leave—and they went out from their home leaving everything—all their household goods, at the mercy of the rebel soldiery, and returned after the army had retreated to find almost everything either stolen or destroyed.

There are great cracks in the sides of the house through which the daylight looks at us most familiarly, and the wind comes in, in a dancing, saucy way as if it had all the privileges of an old acquaintance.

There are two large, square chambers in the front of the house, with a wide, grim hall between them, in which is stored barrels, and trunks, and boxes, and various etcetera pertaining to domestic institutions. Lieutenant Sherwood and his wife occupy one room, and Harry and I the other. The walls of both rooms are roughly oiled, and the floors were bare and unpainted. But we extemporized some carpets for them. Lieutenant S. found an old rag carpet in camp which he has appropriated, and for our own room floor we have some tent awnings or flys, and I walk over it as lightly as I would over the most velvety Persian or Brussels. Then I have a table in my room, my trunk, a long wooden bench, and a bedstead which totters terribly—like the Southern Confederacy is ready to fall. We don't venture to sleep on it, but at night lay feathers and straw upon the floor, and sleep soundly, with never a dream of bushwhacking rebels.

Undated letter to Mrs. Newton

Dear Mrs. Newton,

I'll write you a word today for my heart is with you, though my bodily self is up away among these mountain fastnesses, and "soldier boys."

We had a charming trip up here in our jolting ambulance, and my life seemed to freshen amid the freshness of Nature, and grow gladder amid its greenness and beauty.

I was not disappointed in the scenery as we came up the valley. I wish I could tell you something how I felt as my eye took in the grand panorama—with its vast magnificence of mountains—their tops kissing the cloud and the blue sky touching them softly like a mother's hand, while they stood as if a tired world might lean itself against them and rest, but words wont do it—such emotions lie too deep in the soul to admit of word painting. They are fathomless by language.

We only reached Mrs. Tompkins on Saturday where we were kindly received and entertained. It's a pretty place. The house is embowered in trees and roses, and the river flows along in front making with the high hills and the valley a beautiful picture.

We reached Fayette about seven o'clock on Sabbath evening, and are stopping at a country house about a mile and a half this side of camp.

Here we are rusticating in the most primitive style imaginable. I wish that I could picture our "quarters" to you fairly. If I was only good at word painting, I'd do it. The house was occupied at the time of Floyd's retreat as a rebel hospital, and General Headquarters during his brief stay, and now it's hardly anything but a shell, and thru the great cracks in its sides the daylight looks through at us most familiarly, and the wind

View between Tompkins Farm and Gauley Bridge. Eliza stayed overnight at Mrs. Tompkins' farm. The two women found conversation difficult, since Mrs. Tompkins was a strong supporter of the Southern cause, the wife of a Confederate colonel and a relative of General Thomas J. "Stonewall" Jackson. The photograph shows the dense, rocky terrain of West Virginia that made soldiering so difficult. (West Virginia State Archives, William Forbes Collection)

comes in, in a jolly dancing way as if it had all the privileges of an old acquaintance.

There are two large, spare chambers in the front of the house, with a wide grim hall between them, and Lieutenant Sherwood and his wife occupy one, and Mr. Otis and I the other. The walls of both rooms are roughly oiled, and the floor was bare and unpainted. Yesterday we extemporized some carpets. We had some tent awnings, or flys brought down from camp, and now they grace the floor of my chamber, and I walk over it as lightly as I would over the most velvety Persian or Brussels. Then I have a table in my room, my trunk, a long wooden bench and a bedstead which totters terribly and I expect one of these nights I'll hear something drop and will look around to see what it was and will find that [unfinished]

MONDAY, JUNE 8. [1863]

Mrs. Sherwood and myself reconnoitered a little distance towards camp this morning. Went as far as the first picket—post, and then returned.

Harry came down late last evening after I had abandoned the hope of his coming. He was on guard duty or he would have met me at the foot of Cotton Mountain. He gave me a welcome that made me glad to be here. He is with me again tonight, and so I feel *at home*.

TUESDAY, JUNE 9. [1863]

Went up to camp this morning, and passed the day there. Felt sadly disappointed to learn on my arrival there that Harry had been sent out on a scouting expedition, and would be absent three or four days.

Mrs. Captain Hill[3] was along with us. She's a quiet, pleasant lady, though not much of a *soldier*. This pioneer life doesn't quite suit her. We took dinner in camp, at Capt. Hill's and Harry's quarters, and the table was spread bountifully. Boiled ham, nice biscuit, eggs, nice pudding, doughnuts, apple and peach pie, butter, preserves, coffee, tea, together with a feast of wit and a flow of soul which was charming. We visited the Hospital, met some pleasant gentlemen there—among them Chaplain Allen[4] of the Twelfth, and Dr. Graham.[5] There were but few patients in the different wards but those who were there seemed well cared for. There were two who were wounded in the late skirmish here—one who was shot in the arm who was suffering greatly and another who had his leg broken. I said a few words to both of them, telling them how wholly our sympathies were with our brave martyrs to Liberty, and they seemed to be cheered by them, as we came away they begged us to come often, which we promised to do.

In the afternoon we took an ambulance and went out some three or four miles on the Raleigh Road. Mr. Fornshell with other gentlemen accompanied us, and pointed out numerous places of interest—where the rebels had laid an ambuscade, and where most of the fighting was done.

At one point we could see away off in the distance the long range of the Alleghenies, among them Big Sewell Mountain,

3. Wife of Captain Thomas F. Hill, Twelfth Regiment. *Roster*, vol. 2, 374.

4. Charles L. Allen, chaplain of the Twelfth Regiment, was also a member of the Field Staff. *Roster*, vol. 2, 353.

5. Dr. N. F. Graham was a surgeon. See Whitelaw Reid, *Ohio in the War: Her Statesmen, Her Generals, and Soldiers*, vol. 2 (New York: Moore, Wilstach, and Baldwin, 1868), 87.

their blue and hazy outlines stretching like a thread against the sky.

We also visited one of the forts, and I got lodged within my cranium for the first time a clear and correct idea of an *abbatis*—how it is formed. It is constructed of the tops of trees—a part of the trunk is cut off, and they are laid down in a line, their branches facing the enemy, and reaching out in every direction, and forming no very slight barrier to a rapid advance.

Towards evening we called at Headquarters, on Col. White, from whom we received a most cordial welcome. He showed us all over his establishment, and treated us to some most delicious currant pie, which was "gotten up" by his colored boy. The *boy* was peeping at us around the corners, and flushing his soul on the Colonel's and our praises of his culinary powers, when Lieutenant Sherwood came in. *Africa* could keep quiet no longer—and taking the Lieutenant aside he asked, pointing to us, the whites of his eyes dilated, and every white tooth on exhibition, "Lieutenant, is one of them yours?" "Yes," was the response—"Mighty pretty women them are" was the response.

The Colonel is anxious that we should come up nearer camp, and showed us two large spare rooms, in a little building back from the one which he occupies in which he is anxious that we should establish ourselves.

WEDNESDAY, JUNE 10. [1863]

Yesterday I received the gift of a late number of *Harper's Weekly* with its usual number of fine engravings. This morning I proceeded to dissect it—and the pictures [illegible] adorn the walls of my chamber as gracefully as would the paintings of the world's old Artists. I look up and fancy them the work of Michael Angelo, and imagine that I can see the ideality of his great soul shaping itself in them, and taking form, and color, and life under the magic touch of his pencil, and I dream as quaint reveries over them as ever "I K Marvel"[6] dreamed over the smoke and ashes on the hearthstone of his bachelor dominions. By the way, he dreamed just as all bachelors do of the nice little wife that met him with her smile when he came home at night, and if he was tired her soft hand on his brow would make him forget how his head ached, and how wearily the great world went with him. But I don't have any unpleasant awakenings as "I K" did, for after all these pleasant imaginings he used to come to himself and find that he was all alone, and the fire gone out—and nothing but the *might have been* of his dreams left him.

I miss H. tonight. I wish that he was here. He will be back tomorrow I hope.

THURSDAY, JUNE 11. [1863]

Harry is back again, after having been in full view of the enemy's pickets near Raleigh. The rebels at that point have received reinforcements, and may possibly make another dash upon us here by and by. They'll meet with a warm reception if they do come, and find it not a very *healthy* point. It would require a large force to drive our forces from their well fortified position—and the foe is not wise if he attempts it.

6. I K Marvel was the pseudonym for the American Donald Grant Mitchell (1822–1908), a prolific and versatile author whose works include books on rural life, travel, dreams, and his bachelor existence. See *Dictionary of American Biography*, s.v.

FRIDAY, JUNE 12. [1863]

Visited camp again today, and returned in the evening. Bill of fare was excellent. *Solomon* did his best. His cheery face smiled upon us, as we went in to dinner and he made us one of his best bows, which extended about half way down his body. Capt. and Mrs. Hill, Lieutenant Sherwood and Wife, Capt. Gordy,[7] Harry and myself, and little Luke Hill comprised our dinner party.

After dinner we visited the reading rooms of the Twelfth, which had just been established, and opened by Chaplain Allen. We found quite a number of the boys there, and their faces betokened the pleasure which they felt in having this free companionship with books again. The building in which the rooms are enclosed is a rough, wooden structure without floor and it stands just on the outskirts of camp—and on the border of the woods. Its location could not have been better chosen, and its founding does honor to the Christian man that first conceived the plan for its erection.

After leaving the reading rooms we went to the picture gallery. Saw some fine portraits of the officers of the regiment, and Mrs. Sherwood sat for her picture.

From there we went to the fortifications, and were surprised at their strength and extent. They command quite an extent of country—and let their cannon thunder forth with their tongues of flame—and Death would riot in the ranks of the foe.

After leaving the forts we took Mrs. Sherwood to her husband's office, and Harry and I rode down to Mr. Platt's, a noble, loyal old man who lives about a mile from camp. His own

7. Possibly a misspelling of the name of Captain Jacob A. Yordy, Twelfth Regiment. See *Roster*, vol. 2, 537.

residence was burned at the battle of Fayetteville last September,[8] but we went past where it used to stand—a pleasant place once, but war has written desolation upon it now.

This evening after our return home, we were pleasantly surprised by a company of officers who came to call upon us. Captain Wilson,[9] Captain Gordy, Captain McKay,[10] Lieutenant Ludlum,[11] Lieutenant Glotfelter[12] comprised the party. I enjoyed the evening—was *myself* more than I often am, lighthearted and gay as in happy girlhood.

We had not chairs enough for the company, so we brought in a rude bench, on which I stowed myself, away by the side of Lieutenant Ludlum—and we talked of various, funny things, and of some that were grave and mystical. Altogether this has been one of the pleasantest days of my life. It will be a white waymark that the sun will always shine on.

SATURDAY, JUNE 13. [1863]

This morning we had an unpleasant duty to perform—but one which war necessitates often. It was the examination of the person and baggage of Mrs. Woodson, whose husband is in the Confederate Army, and who was herself, on her way to Dixie. She was sent through our lines in an ambulance, under a flag of

8. See McKinney, *The Civil War in Fayette County*, 147–70.

9. Captain Harrison Wilson, later colonel and brigadier general, Twelfth and Twentieth Regiments. See *Roster*, vol. 2, 685.

10. Captain Hiram McKay, Twelfth Regiment. See Reid, *Ohio in the War*, vol. 2, 88.

11. Lieutenant William A. Ludlum, Twelfth Regiment and Headquarters Staff. See *Roster*, vol. 2, 353–4.

12. Lieutenant William H. Glotfelter, Twelfth Regiment. *Roster*, vol. 2, 357.

truce, in charge of Major Carey[13] of the Twelfth Ohio. She had with her a large amount of Confederate money, and some few articles which were *contraband*. She submitted to the examination without any apparent reluctance. Rouge and powder were plenty, so with her beauty could hardly be called even skin deep.

In the evening, went out riding with Harry on horseback. Went nearly to camp, and visited one of the outer forts. Would have gone further but did not feel well.

The sun had gone down behind the hills as we returned and the west was hung "With crimson banner and golden pall" while a gentle breeze just attired the green forest leaves, and fanned them to rest after the heat of the day was over. I felt that Nature spoke to me and the burden of her words was "Love."

SUNDAY, JUNE 14. [1863]

We took dinner in camp today. Went with the intention of remaining to services at the chapel, but did not feel well so came home early.

This evening several of the soldiers gave us a call. We sat out in the yard, under the shadow of the fine old trees in front of the house. Nature seemed to be enjoying a Sabbath. Everything was still and lovely and seemed to whisper "Peace."

The whippoorwills were in a most musical mood, and they sat in the forest boughs in front of us, and warbled away till the stars came out in the bending sky and it was time for them to go to rest.

13. Major Edward M. Carey, Twelfth Regiment. *Roster*, vol. 2, 353.

MONDAY, JUNE 15. [1863]

Set out for camp this morning in company with Mrs. Sherwood. The morning was very warm, the sun poured down his most fervid rays upon us. I was not well when I left our boarding place, but hoped the walk would revive me. Near Mr. Harris met a troop of Government horses, who were prancing about as if they felt free to go any where in Uncle Sam's dominions. Felt a little afraid of them and climbed a high fence, and took refuge in the fields.

Reached the daguerrean saloon and fell very ill. Was taken with a severe chill which later lasted an hour or two. Sent for an ambulance, rode over to camp, where I met Harry, who took me into a tent where I could lie down.

In the evening rode home, and went at once to bed. How many phases life has. It seems weary enough when one is ill—and the fact of our mortality comes home so strongly to us. How welcome will be that better life where never a shadow falls—where all time's ills can reach us nevermore. My heart goes out to that home often, for the little voice that used to call me "*Mama*" is singing there—My darling Harry is with Him who loveth the little children, and when this life is over may I be meet to rest with him there.

TUESDAY, JUNE 16. [1863]

I've but little of interest to write today. When on the invalid list one has but little of incident or variety.

The day itself is lovely—and for some hours there's been a charming little bird singing near my window. I'd like to interpret his song. It's joyous, a real trilling melody.

WEDNESDAY, JUNE 17. [1863]

The heat is intense today—like the sultry days of July and August.

Busy this morning in preparing to leave Mrs. Jones' and to commence life in camp.

Evening—We came up to our quarters this morning in an ambulance. The house we occupy is a small frame building with two rooms, each with a door and a window. The windows open to the northeast, and from them we have a view of the Hospital of the Twelfth, a neat cottage house, with wings and broad piazza, and stately portico, and grounds that must have once been delightful. The building is painted a dark red or brown color and presents even in its neglected condition, an attractive appearance.

Still beyond the Hospital, on an eminence are the outer fortifications of our forces here. They are not yet quite complete—as since the last attack they are being extended and strengthened. Within them I can see the white tents gleaming, and about them the soldiers moving in their busy, toilsome work, shovelling up the fresh earth, or moving the heavy timbers. Everything tells of war—and its sad and terrible necessities.

Nearer rises to our view the rude humble chapel of the Twelfth. It is spireless and domeless, with no outward semblance to the proud home churches reared by wealthy and aristocratic worshippers, but does not the "Our Father" meet with the brave true hearts who gather there and pause upon them the blessing of Him who loveth the right? The chapel holds about two hundred and on Sabbath afternoon the soldiers meet there for a Bible lesson—and in the evening services are held by the Chaplain.

We have a fireplace in each of our rooms, and have filled them with fresh laurel boughs, fragrant with smiling blossoms, and on the hearth we have a *rug* of the greenest and most beautiful moss that could be found in old Dame Nature's storehouse. Our floor is covered with new clean coffee sacks, which really make quite a presentable carpet, as comfortable as those with the richest designs wrought with oriental fingers.

In one corner stands our bunk—minus feather beds and sheets—to be sure, but with plenty of hay, over which is spread two or three of the heavy army blankets which Uncle Sam bestows so freely upon his boys. They felt a little rough when I first crept into them, created sufficient friction upon the surface to keep the skin in a healthy condition, and made my sleep a little less sound than it would have been had I reposed amid the folds of fine linen that have such an inviting look at home.

My little trunk sits opposite the laurel boughs, and contains the not very extensive wardrobe that I have brought for use in camp. One black silk dress, one light, sky blue all wool wrapper, one white morning wrapper, my travelling and one calico dress. Wouldn't Mademoiselle Flora McKinsey[14] cry louder than ever "Nothing to Wear" could she behold the extent of a lady's wardrobe for a whole summer's wear bounded by five dresses?

In the corner opposite the one where stands our bunk is my little writing table, which certainly has quite a look of civilization about it notwithstanding the brown blanket that serves for a cover. On it is a charming bouquet of laurel flowers with their delicate pink buds, and full blown blossoms, mingled with roses, red and variegated, fragrant as roses always are, blushing as if conscious of their beauty, and the blush deepening in some

14. A fashion queen of the day.

Ohio troops crossing a viaduct in West Virginia. The state played a pivotal role as a transportation crossroads but was a treacherous region to defend militarily. (Ohio Historical Society)

until the leaf is crimson, and the laurel hangs over it gently as if to shield it from too eager and admiring a gaze, and the rose sends out its sweetest incense, and it mingles with that of the laurel like the breath of two lovers.

My vase is quite original. It's formed of a little glass jar which found its way to me from the suttler's through Harry's kindness, filled with delicious peach jelly, rich in color as the richest vines.

The late papers, with their "Latest by Telegraph" lie on the table, with tidings of rebel raids into the free state of Pennsylvania, and their threatened invasion of Ohio and West Virginia, and with these listings comes the call of the President for a hundred thousand more to go and strong in their love of Liberty to strike for home and Freedom.

Side by side with these is *Harper's Magazine* sent me with the "compliments" of one of my soldier friends, and *Godey's*, which I owe to the kindness of Chaplain Allen, and *Harper's Weekly*, and *Frank Leslie's Illustrated*, with their faces of heroes, and pictures of strife and bloody battlefields. Such things as these didn't find their way into the camps of olden times, did they? Newspapers and books find their way into the tented fields now-a-days though, just as naturally as do army bread and crackers.

My window curtain is not of damask, but of something a little more appropriate. It keeps out rain and sunshine when necessary, and is formed of some tenting material, and has the very desirable quality of durableness and strength, if it is minus that of beauty. The walls of our room are painted green, while the rough boards overhead look bright with whitewash, and always have a cheerful look, as everything to which we *look up* should have.

THURSDAY, JUNE 18. [1863]

We are getting settled, and accustomed a little to the novelty of our new life.

I do not feel quite well today, and Mrs. Sherwood is ill—been in bed all day.

Got up this morning when *revellie* sounded. There was a novelty in being aroused by the call of fife and drum not unpleasing.

FRIDAY, JUNE 19. [1863]

We have a wall tent pitched just outside our door which we use for an eating room. It has in it a plain unpainted wooden table, a small bench which serves the place of chairs, a water bucket, and in one corner a tin mess chest, which holds our commissary stores. We supply our table with bread at twenty cents per loaf, pies twenty cents each, fresh butter at forty cents per pound, condensed milk at fifty cents per pound and other things at the same *desirable* rates. The tent floor is covered with a fresh grassy carpet, green as an emerald, and just outside it is a long row of currant bushes, with their fruit inviting us to the act of confiscation.

Just back of our house and tent are the Headquarters of Colonel White, Commander of Second Brigade, Second Kanawha Division, Eighth Army Corps. The building which he occupies is of brick painted a lead or stone color, with a broad front two stories high, with fine portico, and a long wing extending back, with a broad verandah, from which you look out on pleasant grounds, ornamented with trees and shrubs, and flowers, inviting culture to aid in the perfecting of their beauty.

Col. Turley[15] of the Ninety First, Ohio occupies a small frame house a little above us, and on the opposite side of the street. His whole family are with him, including his oldest son, who is now a cadet in the United States Naval School, at Newport, Rhode Island.

The Colonel gave us a call this morning. He's a social, pleasant man, and a good talker. I should judge him to be not far from fifty years of age, tall and rather slim, light hair and complexion, short, light whiskers, sprinkled with gray, and a face that lights up when it smiles as if there were an illumination within, the radiance of which shines through in bright sparkles, and drifting sunbeams.

Called this afternoon in company with Harry on Mrs. Colonel White. Found her quite unwell yet sitting up. Was quite pleased with her, and had a pleasant call. The Colonel was in. He is a man whom one instinctively likes. There's something about him which makes you feel his *manhood*, although he is plain, and unpretending in his manners, wholly free from ostentation or display, and talks to you as if he had known you always.

Mrs. White is a lady of about medium size, a little above it, I should judge, with a fine, womanly face, eyes large and dark, a little of the Italian type, almost liquid in their softness; hair, black and shining, combed plainly back, over the ears, with a forehead somewhat arched, mouth expansive,—charming when it smiles,—and an easy ladylike way with her, which makes you feel at once at home and wonder if you are indeed strangers.

Her floor was covered like our own with a carpet formed of

15. John A. Turley, colonel of the Ninety-first Regiment. See *Roster*, vol. 9, 464.

grain sacks, and her furniture was peculiar to our homes in camp.

This evening Lieutenants Ludlum and Glotfelter, together with Captain McKay, called upon us. The evening passed pleasantly. In the course of conversation their campaign in Eastern Virginia was alluded to, and some of the incidents of its bloody battle fields which came under their personal observation and of which I had not before heard were related. After the battle of South Mountain the dead were piled in heaps. Army wagons rumbling along would pass over corpses lying in the sun crushing legs and arms as the Enemy's dead lay unburied.

In one place, near South Mountain, I think, they said it was, sixty dead bodies were thrown into a deep old well—that was their only sepulcher—they were those of the rebel soldiers, and were placed there by our men who were three days in burying the dead, and time and their various duties gave them no opportunity to afford to the fallen foe a better mausoleum.[16]

General Burnside offered a dollar to every citizen who would bury a dead body, but few were willing after this great harvest of Death was over.

SATURDAY, JUNE 20. [1863]

The welcome rain is pouring down today in pleasant showers. The dry earth drinks it in with a look of gladness, and the grass wears a greener look, and the flowers have a smile as sweet as a young maiden's. It's a blessed baptism for Nature, and it will

16. Daniel Wise, a farmer, was the owner of the well, and seeing that it was ruined by the number of dead bodies at the bottom, offered to take over burying the bodies from the soldiers at $1.00 per body. (Information supplied by Darl Stephenson.)

make her bud and bloom anew, and bring forth wonderful treasures of grain and fruit.

I've been quietly in the house all day, and Harry has been with me.

The sun is just struggling through the clouds, and one bright beam falls across my paper. The flies buzz about me, and the mice are nibbling away at a box of cake and other tempting things that stand in one corner of my room. These are almost the only sounds I hear in the house past noon.

The sun is setting in the West on a bright golden pavillion. The air is cool—and pure as water gushing out of a rock. Harry and Mrs. Sherwood have gone out horseback riding. I did not feel like going myself.

Mrs. Sherwood is a pleasant lady, full of life and spirit, with light, curling hair which hangs in ringlets, laughing eyes, and lips dimpling with mirth. Our life here together is a sort of a Mayday.

SUNDAY, JUNE 21. [1863]

When I woke this morning at *revellie* the rain was dashing and pattering against the window panes, but shortly the clouds began to break, and the sunshine came bursting through their rifts and chasms, and soon a real Sabbath day glory flooded the world.

Harry is officer of the Guard today, but every time that he posts his reliefs he gives us a few minutes call. Captain Wilson and Sergeant Fornshell called upon us this morning. The Captain is a native of Montreal, and all of his friends are in the Canada's, but he gave cheerfully his heart and hand to Freedom—

and he has been with the Twelfth ever since it has been in the field.

This afternoon Mrs. Sherwood and myself attended service in camp. The boys were seated upon the ground, listening devoutly and attentively to the words of their chaplain.

I was sorry to see but few of the officers present.

During the services a long train of army wagons came up from the direction of Gauley. The long line of mules tugged them along—and every now and then made the air vocal with their braying.

After the sermon the soldiers sang the beautiful song commencing, or closing rather, with the words, "I'm going home, I'm going home to die no more." Beautiful hope; Sweet assurance. The bending sky listened as on the still air of this Sabbath afternoon, swelled the music of a hundred voices "I'm going home to die no more."

MONDAY, JUNE 22. [1863]

We were wakened at *revellie* again this morning. The air was so cold a fire was very desirable—so we cleared away the laurel boughs from the fireplace, and took up our green moss rug, sent for black Peter and soon he had a blazing fire *roaring* away on our hearth, and diffusing warmth and cheerfulness through our little room. The mornings and evenings are very cool at the great elevation which we are. We are almost living among the clouds. Fayetteville is [altitude omitted] feet above Charleston, and sometimes we can see in the distance the clouds creeping up from the valleys below us, and turning themselves around the sides of the mountains like the white hair of a spirit.

Went out this afternoon in an ambulance in company with Mrs. Sherwood, Dr. Graham and Harry in search of strawberries. Found a few just beyond the second picket on the Raleigh road. We had a delightful drive, and went nearly as far as our lines extend in that direction. Our picket posts are more frequent than they have been, which looks a little as if danger were apprehended.

The road winds over hills and through pleasant dales, past old farm houses, nearly all of which are deserted.

We saw, I believe, only one field of corn, and in that the green blades had hardly more than lifted themselves above the furrows which the plow had made, and they hardly looked as if they could ever ripen and bring forth the full ear. Maybe the soil is too sacred for corn to grow well on it.

Dr. Graham pocketed a nice little ground squirrel, a tiny tumbling thing, and its bright eyes looked as if they had a wish for freedom in them.

It was almost sundown as we returned. We left the Dr. at the Hospital. Our driver is one of the funniest of Uncle Sam's boys —full of quiet drollery, and always in the best humor in the world. We call him Denis, but his name is Greenberry Sims, and he's always obliging—"always ready to do the ladies a favor." He wears a black feather in his hat which he says is his badge of office—of his Brigadier Generalship.

This evening a company of our soldier friends came to give us a Serenade. Among them Lieutenant Wilson who played the guitar—dashing out from under his fingers melody whose tumbling strains went vibrating into the soul, quivering along all its chords like the heart was full of feeling, and there were echoes that were soundless, but still not the less heard, nor the less melodious.

Our friends had also flute and violin accompaniments and before we were aware the wee small hours of the night were upon us, and the "boys" said a hurried Good night, leaving us with a pleasant remembrance of their coming that will not die out like the echoes of their songs.

TUESDAY, JUNE 23. [1863]

Today some Confederate officers came in and gave themselves up as prisoners. They may be *bona fide*, all that they represent themselves to be, but without sufficient evidence in times like these it is necessary to act a little upon the strength of suspicion.

They have been placed in the guard house, and will not be allowed to go at large until they have been examined before the Commander of the Department and taken the oath of allegiance to the United States.

Lieutenant Sherwood returned from Charleston today, bringing the intelligence that the order has been issued by General Sherman that all soldier's wives shall leave the Department forthright—Mrs. Colonel Lesley's[17] hurried departure, together with the proposed return of Mrs. Colonel White—in part prepared us for such intelligence.

We have been very happy here in our camp home—joy has come to us in earnest, and pleasure has presented itself in many a new and novel form all the more delightfully from its very strangeness.

Two weeks and a half that we have been here! How they have glided away—silently as the bubble on the bosom of a stream.

Went to camp again this evening. Visited the reading rooms

17. Wife of Colonel William Lesley, Thirteenth Regiment. *Roster*, vol. 3, 396.

Drawing etched in stone of the Union army camp at Camp Gauley, where Eliza enjoyed two visits with Harry and his comrades. (West Virginia State Archives, Nep Roesler Collection)

of the regiment. Met Captain Gordy and Chaplain Allen there, together with others whom we knew. There were three tables in the floorless room, all covered with books, papers and Magazines.

On the walls I noticed some pretty steel engravings fastened up. Among them the picture of a pretty child out in the fresh, bright morning, the little head bare, and the ringlets of dark hair clustering about the round sweet face—the shoeless feet pattering on the green, grassy way, while both of the dimpled hands were raised to brush away the "cobwebs" whose threads had been stretched out so mystically in the night—above the path where the child was passing.

I remember when I used to walk among the cobwebs—when my childish heart wondered at their formation. The wonders wrought by Aladdin's lamp would not have surprised me more than did these little thin, gauzy network of fibers. I used to brush them away from my face, and wish that I could see how the long line was stretched out and hung in the air so. Everything is a mystery to childhood, isn't it, and this is why life is so charming then. It's new and strange.

We are making arrangements to leave day after tomorrow. It's hard to go out and leave our loved ones here where fresh perils may be deepening every hour, but the necessity is unyielding and we cannot compromise with it.

God be with our dear ones, and the little band of patriots here, and shield them in the day of battle.

CHAPTER 7

"Old Time Has Cast Me, a Strong Waif on His Billows"

WEDNESDAY, JUNE 24. [1863]

Mrs. Colonel White left this morning in an ambulance in company with Major Dodridge. We are prepared to go tomorrow.

Set out for Hines Point[1] this afternoon in company with Mrs. Sherwood and Harry. The sky looked a little frowning—as though it might rain, but thinking this our last opportunity to visit that interesting point the clouds did not detain us, and the afternoon proved highly favorable. The clouds hindered the sun from shining which made it cooler and more favorable for walking.

As we passed the guard house we saw two of our own boys who had been guilty of cowardice in yielding themselves up, without a single effort at resistance, as prisoners to a rebel bushwhacker, with an old rusty, useless rifle, walking wearily back and forth with a knapsack weighing forty pounds upon their shoulders. They are compelled to do this for six hours each day. The guards were posted about watching them, guns in

1. A beautiful, treed stretch of flatland on the banks of the Kanawha.

hand, and the long bayonets gleaming threateningly at them bidding defiance to their escape.

We went on out past the camp of the Twelfth, till we came to the picket post, which was stationed at an old house, which afforded at least a shelter from the rain. Showing our pass we were permitted to go on. Our road lay in the direction of New River and at various points we found it hedged up, fences having been built directly across it. But these we scaled without difficulty, high rail fences though they were, and we went on merrily. Our path took us through an orchard where were several government horses. One poor animal had in some way caught one of his hind feet in the low branches of a tree and was struggling in vain to release himself. Harry went forward to his assistance, and soon the poor beast was free, and dashed away proudly over the green field.

Our road soon led us into the woods, and it lost its fresh, gravelly look, and narrowed and lessened until it terminated in a narrow trail of footpaths. After walking awhile we emerged from the woods into a small cleared space, in the center of which was a rude dwelling. Looking about us, and being at a loss to know what direction to take we approached the house hoping to obtain some information from its inmates.

As we came into the opening four savage looking dogs came rushing towards, growling and barking, and giving us a somewhat questionable welcome. But we duly dispersed them and made our advance to the open door. There were two windows in front, one with a white curtain parted in the center, with a narrow ruffle ornamenting it, and opposite the door we noticed a neat hair-cloth covered sofa, which was hardly in keeping with its surroundings, and we wondered how it found its way there.

As Harry entered the door a tall, grim looking woman advanced to meet him. Her face was not womanly, but was long, cadaverous and brown, just fitted to crown the unshapely form. She eyed us half suspiciously. Perhaps she had a terror of My Husband's shoulder straps—they might have created a real living assurance, in the dim, misty regions of her brain that he was one of the "invaders of sacred soil," one of the minions of tyranny who had come to destroy and desolate where they could not subjugate or subdue. Poor woman she looked like one of the many of that large class all over the South, who have been made the vassals of Slavery, and upon whose necks the iron heel of aristocrat's tyranny has been placed, until they have been made to minister to the pride and selfishness of designing leaders not less than the toiling slave in the field, with his back torn with stripes, and his future darkened by a hopeless despair.

The woman could give us no positive directions in regard to our route, so we retraced our footsteps for a short distance and entered the woods again. Finally we came to a narrow, winding footpath which we thought might lead us to the Point. Accordingly we turned into it, and followed it until it led us into the very depths of the forest. It was well defined and we made our way without difficulty, occasionally coming across a fallen tree, which had lain down as if to rest, with grand watchers all about it, clasping their green boughs away far up above its resting place, parting their fresh leaves now and then so that a glimpse of sunshine could steal through, and linger on the moss and tender buds that covered the ground. We kept on our way until our path began to lead down a steep declivity, and in the distance we could hear the roar of New River, as it dashed along in its wild freedom among the rocks that have crowded themselves into its cool bed. Away over on the other side of the river towered huge mountains, lifting their tree crowned heads some six or seven hundred feet above the bed of the river, now and then exposing to view bare, rugged cliffs, so vast and strong that it seemed as if the sky might rest on their giant columns, and yet its weight be unfelt.

Looking about us a little Harry discovered that we had taken the wrong direction and that we were not quite in the vicinity of Hines' Point. Accordingly after due deliberation we concluded to go back again hoping some propitious Fate would direct us to the right path. As we commenced climbing the steep ascent Mrs. Sherwood expressed a wish that it was in our power to press into our service, an animal of the long eared, obstinate species, to which Harry responded that he was at our service *a la mule* if we desired. Mrs. Sherwood modestly declined his condescending gallantry, but fancying the thing would afford us a little sport I accepted the offer without hesitation. I assumed a position a little novel for a lady equestrian, but still it was in *beautiful* conformity to the necessities of the occasion. I clasped my arms about Harry's neck, and with my feet dangling about his knees, my whole frame on a *charming* perpendicular, I commenced my ride up the precipitous slope. My "beast" wearied not, but I did, and begged leave to descend, which I did, with Mrs. Sherwood and Harry's merry peals of laughter echoing about me.

We soon made our way back again, and came in sight once more of the log house, where the dogs bayed at us afresh, and leaped upon us like half starved wolves till we called upon our attendant to drive them away.

A single footpath leading into the forest on the left of the house looked rather inviting to us, so we turned into it thinking that by following it, it might lead us to the desired point. But we soon found ourselves in a dense pathless thicket—crowding through underbrush, now under the branches, then over them —with fallen trees hedging up our way, and moss covered rocks over which we must climb—our veils catching on the limbs that interlaced on our front and sides, and all around us, then our hair tangling in with the brush, as we crept through it pushing it back with one hand from our faces, while the other hand was employed in gathering up refractory crinoline which fastened itself on every little twig and stick and held us fast. Finally after much pulling, and twisting, we gathered up skirts, hoops and all, and arranged them into a sort of Zouave costume, which enabled us to progress with greater ease and rapidity, while our picturesque appearance afforded our guide no little amusement, and a fine opportunity to study the physiological outlines of our feet and ankles.

No end to the underbrush. Where are we? Not a trace of human footsteps could we see in these wilds. Not a sound of life—nothing but the silence of the vast forest about us, its primeval wildness untouched by the Ages, and its magnificence stretching out whichever way we turned, green, vast and solitary.

We began to feel that not very welcome fear that we were lost creeping over us, and whether we ever saw Hines' Point or not was a matter of far greater indifference to us, than the sight of a well beaten path would have been. On, on through the dense thicket, everything deepening in wildness about us we kept [on] for about two hours, till at length we came to a place where a tree had been lately felled. With the welcome sight fresh hope sprang up in our hearts—and in a few moments we came to where another, and still another tree had been felled by the woodman's axe—and shortly our feet were following a well trod path, which led us out to the verge of this woody wildness. "We must get a glimpse of the river, at least, before we return," said

Mrs. S. "so let us go out in the direction which we just took and follow that path down until it takes us within view of it." With scarcely a thought of weariness, we turned into the same path that we had taken two or three hours before, and followed it until it began to descend to the river's bank. The murmurs of the waters came to us with a sullen roar—like the deep rich toned bass of a grand old anthem. Down, down we went till at last we came in sight of a high cliff, towering above us on our right, spreading itself over the tree tops below it, and looking as if it were monarch of the mountains. That suggested itself to us as the finest point from which to view the almost limitless perspective before us. So over rocks, and dead leaves, and decaying trees we made our way till we stood on its broad platform, and looked down over the high tree tops into the valley hundreds of feet below. We caught a glimpse of the river with its white foam, of wide stretches of cedar and pine on the opposite heights—saw mountain rising above mountain, till the clouds seemed almost to rest on them like a crown—and then we sat down for a few moments on the mossy rock, and thought of the Creative Power that had formed all this, and the very stillness about us spoke to us, and the blooming laurel smiled—and we went home subdued by Nature's impressive teaching, and with a new feeling of trust in Our Father.

Scarcely was our simple evening's meal over, when we were surprised by a company of soldier musicians who gave us a delightful entertainment of both vocal and instrumental music.

Drs. Graham and Buck[2] were also present. They are pleasant, gentlemanly men, and both are good talkers. Among other

2. Dr. Silas T. Buck, assistant surgeon, Twelfth Regiment. See Reid, *Ohio in the War*, vol. 2, 87.

things we sang "Sweet Home," and "Old Hundred," heart and soul sung them as well as lips, and the rich, melodious strains swelled out full and sweet from nearly a score of voices—the deep, musical bass, and melodious soprano, with the high clear tones of the tenor mixing and mingling in a melodious whole. It was twelve o'clock when we parted. We said our good byes to our friends feeling that perhaps never more should we meet again, and our hearts were sad at the thought of parting with those who but a few days ago were strangers, but with whom we had often met and mingled until they had grown into our hearts and our sympathies, and whose remembrance would come to us like the morning and evening of the day.

As he turned to go, Dr. Graham said to us "You shall not go tomorrow, ladies, you shall have a few days of grace extended you yet." We thanked him, but told him that we could hardly hope for the favor of a prolonged stay. We recognize our going as a "military necessity" and therefore did not complain of it, although it would be most agreeable to us to remain longer. "Never mind," he replied, "I'll assume command here tomorrow, and you shall stay. Good Night."

Bless his noble, generous heart! But the will be mightier than the deed, I fear.

How little I dreamed at first that under this roof I would ever feel so much at home. It isn't to the outward surroundings that the affections cling. They throw out their tendrils to the appreciations that cluster about the spot where Love has been, to the memories that make it hallowed. Sunny as the sunniest rays of childhood has been my stay here, and often in the future if ever life weary or sad I shall turn back to this quiet little room, with its bare walls, and rough hewn timbers overhead, and rest, and the darkness shall brighten as the beams of happy remembrances quiver through and permeate it.

It shall be the green isle to which my bark shall glide out leaving behind it the clouds and the mists, and barren masts, and the waves kissing its shores shall murmur of bright things—"Bright things which never die, E'en though they fade." Now let me sleep till the morning.

THURSDAY, JUNE 25. [1863]

Rose at a late hour this morning. Were just getting up when Dr. Graham came to our door to assure us of the fulfillment of his promise. He had seen Colonel White, and we are permitted to remain until Monday next. Mrs. Sherwood and myself felt amazingly as if we would love to get our arms about the good Doctor's neck, and cover those tempting looking bachelor lips of his with genuine, heartfelt kisses. But the thing wouldn't do you know, so we had to be content with thanking him, and telling him as we should remember him always, just as we shall be sure to do, for doesn't he deserve it? Mrs. S. and I contented ourselves by kissing our husbands, *of course*, fancying all the while that we were kissing the Doctor, which made the thing *unusually* delightful.

Our trunks are all packed, everything ready to leave, so we've nothing to do but to enjoy ourselves while we stay which we shall doubtless do to the utmost of our abilities.

Sent an invitation to the Drs. this forenoon to go out to Hines Point with us, which invitation they accepted, but the rain vetoed our arrangements, for it commenced falling just as we were about to start.

The weather still continues cool. We've had a wood fire blazing away on our hearth for several days. Heavy winter dresses are far more comfortable than the lighter summer wear. These don't seem like June days, notwithstanding Nature is blushing in roses and pinks, and the mountains are smiling with laurel bloom, and rich wild flowers that are filling the air with their fragrance.

FRIDAY, JUNE 26. [1863]

All the morning was wet and rainy, but this afternoon there was a little sunshine with the clouds.

Greenberry went out this morning and purchased us some milk. It ought to be good, for we paid the modest little price of ten cents per quart for it.

I picked up an egg in front of our door which some obliging hen had laid before the shell was formed, and with two others which our faithful Green obtained for us we succeeded in "getting up," with assistance of bread and milk, quite a palatable pudding, which we *spiced* with figs, and baked upon the coals on our hearth.

We've no table linen, but we have a very convenient substitute in the *Commercial*, of which we have a supply, two numbers of which furnish an ample cover for our plain pine table. Mrs. Sherwood has five small silver teaspoons, and two large table spoons which fortunately she brought with her, and these are all that we need in that line. They were made away back during revolutionary times, and are relics of days when men battled for Freedom, as we are battling now—and in which a

Nation was born, and our glorious heritage of constitutional Liberty bequeathed to us, and, we trust, to latest time.

I received a letter last evening from Mrs. Terry. Her heart was in it, as it is in all of her letters to me, and I was gladdened by its perusal. She sent me her picture—It's like herself. The noble, womanly face that I love. God bless her and hers.

The flies are buzzing thickly about me. They have swarmed here, whole armies of them since we came. They with the little mice keep us company.

I've a bouquet on my table—the gift of a soldier friend. It has in it, mingled with the flowers, a small, delicate quince, which looks pretty enough among the rich leaves of the flowers. I've received many such little favors since I've been here, and I'm grateful for them.

Drs. Graham and Buck called again this evening. Sat until ten o'clock. The evening is calm and lovely, The moon has stolen out from behind her cloudy pillars, and her silver beams flood hill and dale. The high mountains sleep away off against the sky, and there's perfect stillness all around.

Holy thoughts come stealing down like the starlight, and the soul is flooded with them as is the still world, with the silver moonbeams.

SATURDAY, JUNE 27. [1863]

This morning the sun arose in an almost unclouded sky, and we early made arrangements to visit Hines Point—We had received such glowing descriptions of the almost unprecedented grandeur and wildness of the view that we felt unwilling to leave Fayette without a glimpse, at least of the beautiful [word omitted] to be seen in that vicinity.

Harry went over to camp to attend to a few moments' business, and while he was gone we prepared our lunch of sandwiches and cake, which we proposed eating in the woods.

An hour or two passed away yet Harry had not returned. We wondered at his delay, and grew almost impatient because he did not come. I went out on the street and met Major Carey, of the Twelfth. He was hurrying along, but he stopped just long enough to bid me good morning, and added "Now the rebels have you surrounded." O, well I can stay here awhile then said I—"I'll have a few days more with my Husband." He passed on, and I noticed that there was hurry and bustle everywhere.

I went to my room and soon My Husband came in. "We'll not go to Hines Point this morning," he said. "It's reported that the rebs. have come in below us, and we must be in readiness for any attack they may make. I must be in camp."

I did not wish to detain him from duty, and in the midst of all the excitement and uncertainty I felt scarce a shadow of fear. I packed my trunk, and Harry's valise that they might be ready for any emergency, and feeling a little tired, I laid down and slept.

In the afternoon the excitement had subsided and in company with Lieutenant-Colonel Hines,[3] Dr. Graham, Lieutenant McMillen,[4] Mrs. Sherwood and Harry I set out for the Point.

We rode for nearly a mile in an ambulance—out through the

3. Lieutenant Colonel Jonathan D. Hines, Twelfth Regiment. *Roster*, vol. 2, 253.

4. Lieutenant Jonathan H. McMillen, Twelfth Regiment. *Roster*, vol. 2, 357.

fields—over rough places, where we were jolted and shaken almost from our seats.

When we came into the woods we were obliged to dispense with our *"carraige"* and make our way on foot.

The sun was obscured by clouds, and the cool air came stealing through the leafy boughs, breathing *rest* upon us even as we passed along.

For about a mile we took the same course through which Harry led us when we were out with him—then we turned to the left into an almost pathless thicket of laurel huckleberry bushes. The leaves were heavy with the rain drops which lay scattered like pearls everywhere, and we shook them off in showers as we passed, till our feet received a perfect baptism.

Lieutenant McMillen was my escort, and he loves Nature. The Beautiful has a voice for him—It has the utterance of eloquence—Its great truths go sounding down through the Ages, and lay the touch of their infinite fingers upon the Past, the Present and the Future. To the hearts of all good men Nature speaks as a Mother speaks to her child.

I'll not attempt to describe our walk through the forest. All such walks one can appreciate who loves them. In the silence of the dim old woods, I always *grow away* from the world. Not from the sympathy of its human hearts do I mean—but from its vanities, and the shallowness of its life.

The deep undercurrents of my being are stirred by the baptism of Nature's stillness, and Heaven seems hardly above the tree tops.

After forcing our way for a long distance through the underbrush, and stealing along the edge of dizzy heights over narrow paths, treacherous and slippery, with scarce a foothold among their rocks, our guide conducted us to the broad, smooth platform of rock that rested like a crown upon the head of Hines Point. I stood still, feeling as if I wanted to uncover my head and worship.

Down through the leafy, emerald roof above us came stealing the golden sunshine. The clouds' heads parted overhead, and dimpled and white they lay along the edge of the little field of blue, that we caught bending over the tree tops. The leaves rustled and whispered their secrets, and there was cheerfulness in their murmur, but as it deepened it seemed like a sort of breezy prayer floating out like incense, the words so spiritual that we could not catch them.

The beautiful laurel flowers, with delicate petals, some white and pale, others with a slight pink blush, were scattered everywhere in the sunlight and in the shadows. But my eye did not linger long on these, the simply beautiful, for the grandeur, the inutterable magnificence of heaven-reaching mountains—of great, swelling forest—waves of hues, of huge precipices, and yawning chasms, of valleys so deep it seemed as if they belonged to a world below us, were all there as [they] had been for limitless years, unchanged by Time, untouched by man, with the glory of their first creation unshadowed, all standing still, and vast and changeless. New River rolled along in its bed nearly half a mile below us, its roar sounding through the old aisles of the forest, and its waters dashing with musical rhythms and cadences over the rocks where the ripples chased each other in eternal laughter.

I crept to the edge of the huge cliff where I stood, and looked down—down three hundred feet into the *abyss* of greenness and verdure. I leaned there till I felt dizzy—dizzy with the deepness, and with wonder at the river before me. In the mingling of that grandeur and beauty—in the mild sublimity of mountain, the magnificence of vales and of waters, it seems as though an eternal Presence stood revealed and Infinite Power had unfolded itself in living, tangible forms.

We stood there an hour or more, till the sound of thunder startled us.

The clouds had gathered in the blackness, and shortly the rain came down dashing most unceremoniously in our faces. We didn't find fault with its lack of ceremony, but shook hands with it as it lay on the bushes, and laughed while it drenched us thoroughly. The day was warm, and a real dashing shower-burst, free of charges wasn't unacceptable.

SUNDAY, JUNE 28. [1863]

I have been on the invalid list all day, but feeling a little better this evening we all accepted an invitation to take tea at the Hospital. The good genius of the place, Dr. Graham, met us as we went in, and seated us in his office where we enjoyed a pleasant chat until tea was ready.

The table was spread with good things—fresh pork, nicely bucked [?]; warm, light biscuits, canned tomatoes, new cheese, lemon pie—charming [illegible] butter, Gingerbread, and real tempting little sweet cakes, fresh sweet milk, tea with a real fragrant smell, served in Uncle Sam's best tin cups, which by the way though had grown a little less shiny from half a year's use.

Our china ware consisted of genuine tin plates, big enough to reflect our faces with rather a distorted smile, but nevertheless answering every practical purpose.

Dr. Buck sat nearly opposite me, wearing his quiet, pleasant smile, talking now and then, while his face said I am happy to have you all here. He is a young man—not more than twenty four or five years of age—with rich, chestnut colored hair, eyes large, dark and brown, a small mouth folded like a rose leaf, yet with the lines of decision and manliness about it—complexion rather fair, forehead high, shielded a little by the brown locks, and not touched in the least by time's fingers. I'll remember the face, almost like a brother's—with the looks that show a soul beneath them.

Dr. Graham sat at the head of the table, and looked after all our wants. His lips always look as if there were sunshine struggling through them, the sunshine of a great, genial, human soul. He is tall and somewhat stately in appearance, hair dark as the night, with large eyes mirroring a world of goodness, dancing and sparkling with laughter sometimes, and then looking serious as if the wants of the world had trembled before their glance. The whole face is one that you look into again and again. You don't call it a handsome face really, and yet, it has a charm for you—there's the beauty of generous feeling in it—the impress of a noble manhood on every feature.

We enjoyed our tea drinking at the Hospital, though there were hordes of flies buzzing about us, which the poor black boy with the hurried sweep of his green bough could not chase away, and I chatted lightly with the pleasant young man who sat next me, and whom they all teased about the pretty Miss Tompkins, who lives with her aristocratic mother in her home on the Kanawha, and who sings her secesh[5] songs so sweetly, and plays rebel marches on her rosewood piano, and talks of the chivalrous South, and its brave "Stonewall Jackson," whom they he-

5. "Secesh" was Northern slang for any aspect of the culture of the Confederacy.

roize and make his memory green with their praises, forgetting that he was a traitor to his Country, and was striking his deadliest blows at Liberty and Freedom.

Returned home as the sun was setting, sending up its glory beams in the West, and flooding it with gold like a river.

In the evening several of the officers of the Twelfth and Ninety-first came in to say their farewells. They sat talking of home life, and home scenes, of the battlefield, its strife and rushing death—of war, and peace—and how their words rippled out in gladness, and their faces lightened up at this thought of home—and the loved ones there.[6]

They sat with us until ten o'clock. Captains Wilson and Caldwell, Lieutenants Ludlum, McMillen and Glotfelter—and then they bade us goodbye—with their best wishes for our happiness, and the utterance of the wish that somewhere in the great future we might meet again.

The night—our last one at Fayette—is as beautiful as cloudless June nights always are, when flooded with starlight and moonbeams. The air is soft—and balmy, but has none of the earthiness of July heats. I'll go to rest with the sentinel mountains guarding us. Their vast forms almost lose themselves in the blue, misty veil about them. The moonlight hangs like a glory over them—in still pulseless waves like the presence of a spirit.

I would like to linger here and dream until the morning, amid this impressive stillness, this hush of Nature—this starry

6. A wonderful picture of the life of the ordinary soldier in the Union army is presented in Reid Mitchell, *The Vacant Chair: The Northern Soldier Leaves Home* (New York: Oxford University Press, 1993). An earlier, classic description is provided in Bell Irvin Wiley, *The Life of Billy Yank* (Indianapolis: Bobbs-Merrill, 1952).

radiance. My heart lingers here, and its feelings ebb and flow with the waving trees. My pulses keep time with them—and I wish that the morrow would a long time delay its coming.

But I must go to rest. All is still in the camps. The city of tents is quiet. The steady tread of the sentinel, as he passes on his measured beat is almost the only sound that breaks the stillness. Hours like this are holy, and they bring their inspiration.

MONDAY, JUNE 29. [1863]

We leave this morning. Rose about half past six, and dressed for our journey.

Harry set the table for breakfast—and made up our bunk, while I finished packing my trunk.

Breakfasted on fried ham, fresh baker's bread, delicious June butter, honey, orange jelly, canned tomatoes, and sweet cake from the sutlers.

Tempting as our meal was, I had no appetite for it. I ate but little, drank a cup of coffee, with a little condensed milk in it, which by the way is a very good substitute for the real article.

Evening. I feel tonight as if I had gone out from home. Old Time has cast me, a strong waif on his billows, and I expect I'll be tossed here and there, without anchor or sail till I drop off into the great ocean from which I shall come back nevermore.

I sometimes half feel now as I used to when I was a very happy little child, when I would say to my mother—the dear mother whose head is under the sod now—"Ma, I wish that things could be just so always." But riper years teach me that change is necessary to progress. It's a law of restless human nature, of the world, and even of hoary old eternity.

We left Fayetteville about ten o'clock this morning. Harry put his heart into the good bye that he said to me, and I—well no matter!

Several of our friends called on us this morning, among them Dr. Graham, Lieutenant Busbee,[7] C. T. Crooks and others.

As we passed Mrs. Jones' we halted a few moments at the gate. Mrs. Jones came out with a perfectly despairing look on her face—She was alarmed at the idea of the order which prevented our longer stay in camp. We tried to assure her that there was no immediate danger of an attack, but we could not make her feel quite secure.

We rode on with now and then an unpleasant thought of rebel bushwhackers, starting out from the thick woods on our roadside, and making a sudden dash upon us. But we got no glimpse of any—We rode through green valleys—and made our way up the long, winding road over Cotton Mountain, seeing scarce a human face, save those of our scouts and pickets.

As we came over the mountain, and down into the valley we enjoyed with a quiet wonder and soul thrilling delight, the grand mountainous view before us. There's scarce a shadow that lay on the forest, changing ever though the shadows are, but what I remember—scarce a frowning cliff that I looked upon whose form and place is not daguerrotyped clearly in the great picture gallery of the soul—and they will glow there forever, finished, and complete there, their forest greenness—their rugged rocky sides untouched by frost or time.

We took dinner at Mrs. Huddleston's and were kindly entertained. The family are strongly secesh, but they did not intrude their sentiments upon.

7. Lieutenant John M. Busbee, Twelfth Regiment, acting company quartermaster. See *Roster*, vol. 2, 353, 371.

Just as we drove up to Mrs. Tompkins this evening, dark wrathful looking clouds hung over the brow of the mountains. The thunder rolled in heavy, sullen murmurs, and the lightning shot out its forked tongues of flame and at times lighted the sky with its livid angry glare. We were hardly in the house before the storm was upon us in all its fury. The winds sent out their echoing roar through all the caverns of the woods—the tall trees jostled against each other, and their long branches were clenched together as if in an agony of fear.

The rain came down in great sheets—till by and by the wrath of the elements subsided, and a calm, like the hush that falls on our hearts when we hear a good man's prayer, fell on the world. It was still, calm twilight when I went to my room—after passing a pleasant hour in the parlor with Mrs. Tompkins and the younger ladies.

Mrs. Tompkins is a lady of about fifty—dignified and ladylike, with charming powers of agreeableness, and a pleasant womanly face, which still has the traces of more than usual beauty. She is an aunt of Major General Grant[8]—to whom the hearts of the Nation are turning, trusting for him to win for Freedom our American Gibraltar—Vicksburg—the city which he has "girt with fire."

Mrs. T. is heart and soul a Southern woman—Her sympathies are with the rebellion—her hopes are for its success.

"Pennsylvania is passing through a fiery ordeal now" she remarked to us, "and she may as well suffer as Virginia, whose soil her sons have invaded, and desolated its homes."

We made but little reply to her remarks, for while compelled

8. Ulysses S. Grant, the new commander of the Northern army and later the eighteenth president of the United States.

to share her hospitality we did not care to invite a discussion where there was so much room for unpleasant differences.

Mrs. Sherwood and myself occupy a large pleasant chamber, with windows looking out upon the river, and towards the east. It is nicely furnished, and I think I'll dream home dreams to-night—on this soft, yielding spring mattress, and the high posts of the French bedstead watching me. I'll give myself and loved ones to the keeping of Our Father, and go to sleep. God bless all whom I know and love, and may his Angels guard them.

TUESDAY, JUNE 30. [1863]

I am back in Mrs. Newton's again, and a sort of home feeling crept over me as she extended me her warm welcome back again. I was glad to meet her, and others in her home—for I've garnered up pleasant friendships here—friendships that I shall take with me through all time—and *over the river too*, I hope, into the eternal years where friendships are perfected and purified, and grow into the deep love of immortality.

Left Mrs. Tompkins about eight o'clock this morning. The sky looked a little threatening, and the atmosphere was heavy and damp. As we came down the Valley I watched the white mists as they crept up the sides of the mountains raking with their fleecy whiteness those eternal hills as if there was to be a bridal between the earth and sky. The Kanawha sang for us all the way along, and its voice was musical and varied, full of murmurs and lullabies, and the willows on its bank looked as if they had listened themselves to sleep—and their long arms were reached down as if they would clasp the waves in their slumber.

We passed long trains of government wagons, and now and

then a cavalry soldier with his equipment on would ride dashing past us. Some nodded to us pleasantly, with a cheerful good morning, others passed by as if they saw nothing but the path before them, and their thoughts were busy with the world within them.

How my heart saddened and grew sick as I met ragged dirty little children, hovering around smoky, rude hovels which they called home. All along our route from Cannelton to Charleston, like ulcers on the fresh, green, beautiful earth, every now and then appeared these homes of the Virginia laborer. I've no horror of a log house be it fresh and clean. With white curtains, draping its little windows, and a few climbing roses and woodbines creeping over its walls, and the rough boards overhead mirroring the cheerful look which the touch of the white washers brush would give them—with the floor carpetless but nicely scoured, bearing no trace of muddy feet, or negligent indolence, one might even feel at home, and let the sunshine come in at the heart as well as at the open door. Giant minds might grow up here that should rule the world—and refinement and purity and womanly grace bred and expand till it permeated the atmosphere of home, as the sunlight pervades the air. But at Cannelton and all along our way down, the poor miserable dwellings, with their low roofs, and their one or two crowded dirty rooms, could have nothing of the sacredness of home about them. How could holy, hallowed associations spring up around such hearthstones? How could beautiful and sacred memories, such as bless some who go out from the dear old roof that sheltered them in childhood, moving them from temptation and from sin, follow those whose little feet trod only amid haunts like these? Poverty is crime when it dooms the young to life like this.

Evening. The hours are trembling between light and darkness, and day is fast losing itself in night. One by one the clouds are throwing by the bright mantle which the glowing sunset cast upon them, and are coming up like pensive mourners from the West, clad in sable, and gliding along with a lingering tread, as if they had just looked their last on some bright, loved face, and were loath to leave it alone in the gathering shadows.

FRIDAY, JULY 3. [1863]

I was reading today the notice of the "Autobiography of Anna Cora Mowatt," the celebrated stage actress.[9] I read the work some years ago. She endeavors to throw around her theatrical life a soft, sweet atmosphere of delight—to make it an inviting picture. But you can see plainly that the effort is a labored one, and that she cannot succeed in hiding the soulless reality of the thing. I like what she says of Mr. Mowatt. She seems to think his name only another one for perfection. I think that I should like his character, mostly though he had some very mistaken ideas of duty, if I judge rightly.

Theirs was love at first sight, but it was life long notwithstanding. He superintended her education and took her to his heart and home when she was but fifteen.

He was a gentlemen of great wealth, and his beautiful country seat was almost another Eden. But after a time he, by means of unfortunate speculations became involved, and in order to repair their broken fortunes, Mrs. M. was first induced to appear upon the stage.

9. See Eric Wollencott Barnes, *The Lady of Fashion: The Life and the Theatre of Anna Cora Mowatt* (New York: Charles Scribner's Sons, 1954).

She was eight years an actress, and during much of this time, Mr. Mowatt was a suffering invalid. But—where was the Wife—the dove that he had taken to his bosom and sheltered in her timid weakness from the cold, harsh world? Where was she who should now be his ministering angel, and with her soft hands soothe his aching head, and by her gentle presence beguile the long hours of weariness and pain? Away, far away from him, amid the glitter, the show, the dazzling fascinations, the mockery of the stage.

He died, but she was not with him. The hand that should have held his as he went down to the cold grave was busy elsewhere. The heart that should have throbbed close to his own as it beat slower and slower was throbbing at the adulations which it received from the heartless votaries of pleasure.

The eyes that should have looked lovingly into his and wept as they saw the light of life grow dim in his were looking on scenes of mirth and gaiety, and the lips that should have kissed their farewell to the dying were breathing words to cheat the soul with fancied good or ill. Poor man! as I read the account of his death I almost wished that I could kiss him for his Wife, his dying seemed so sad with one so loved away.

CHAPTER 8

The Glorious Kanawha Valley

[SEPTEMBER 1863.]

We left Charleston at ten on Tuesday morning, September 1st for our tour of the Kanawha Valley—and beyond to the outposts of our army—in one of Uncle Sam's easy ambulances. The morning was bright and sunny, not a cloud in the deep blue above us save over the top of a high mountain whose feet were kissed by the sparkling waters of the Kanawha, and there one little cloudlet, fleecy and white, rested like a crown. The hills, clothed in their rich greenness, covered with forests like a garment, the broad rich valley, with its wide sweeping meadows, its waving fields of corn, and the bare brown patches that had been robbed of their green mantle by the mower's scythe, and now lifted up their faces to the sun, yellow and faded, all mingled together made a beautiful and varied picture.

Our driver was a sturdy, quiet young man of perhaps twenty years. He wore a pair of trousers of coarse material, the color of which I could hardly determine. A stripped flannel shirt, a thick, heavy pair of boots, and a little round cloth cap of the same material as his pantaloons completed his attire.

My only companion was a boy friend of sixteen or seventeen years. A man though yet a boy he was.

The valley was new to him, and he set out on his day's journey as a child would sit down to a feast of good things. His fine, intelligent face was all aglow as he said, "I shall enjoy this wild, beautiful scenery."

"I know you will," said I. "Look at the mountains yonder. Even now they beckon us on. One could fancy himself amid Alpine scenery here. That old hill hasn't got off its night cap of mist yet. I wonder if its head isn't up among the stars, and if they are not telling it secrets that keep it a-dreaming there."

For a while then we leaned back thoughtfully. Only the eye and the soul were busy.

As you pass out from Charleston, fine broad fields of meadow and land reach from the river to the hills—those old hills so rich in mineral wealth, with coal enough to furnish fuel for the Ages. Every now and then we passed the mouth of a coal mine, and once I noticed a new railway track (there were many old ones) running over a steep hillside where the miners had been busy. The track glistened like silver as the sun shone on it.

When [we] arrived here our driver remembered that he had forgotten his pass, and without it he could not go on. "I will telegraph for it," said he, "it will not detain us long." He stopped his horses and jumping out made his way to the operator's tent. The tent was pitched in the shadow of a large tree. Soldiers were sitting or lounging everywhere in its shade. Some on the ground with pleasant looking faces, and the neat, clean uniforms which so visually distinguish our Yankee soldiers. There were several officers sitting on canvass stools, or leaning back in easy chairs comfortably smoking their nice Havanas, and looking for all the world as if man was not such a disagreeable thing after all;

and as they sent out the white clouds of smoke which curled slowly and lazily till they mingled, and were lost in the blue hazy atmosphere.

Our driver came back with the intelligence that we must wait one hour before his pass could be received. "Will you stay in the ambulance," said he, "or go into some of these houses? You might get out here at Headquarters."

"No, I'll sit here and look about me a little. I'll find plenty to amuse me. I will read the history that is written on some of these brave, brown faces." "How fast our soldiers grow old, Henry," said I to my friend. "Now there's a young face, but see the lines of care about the mouth. Those cheeks ought not to have a furrow in them yet, but the mailed hands of War and Time when they work together make sad havoc."

"Yes," says he, "I learned something of this when I was in the three months service. Those long marches if made every day would soon wear out sinews of iron. And then there's something in the experience which War brings that makes us men before our time; how I hardly know.

"I can tell you," said I. "Childhood, boyhood, doesn't have anything to do with *real* life. Its stern realities are in the future, when the man appears, but War brings you face to face with it at once. It ends your dreaming. It makes you feel that Life is real, life is earnest. That it isn't a long playtime, and so you put by your playthings and go to work. You say goodby to the cunning little romances which you were building, and stand face to face with peril. You grapple with Death, and if you come out unscathed you feel that if you have won life it isn't yours; that you have no time to rest for your Country needs you and with this sense of responsibility you are a man. Isn't it so?"

I looked into his face for a reply. "Yes, yes," he answered, half dreamingly, half absently, for his thoughts were away; gone out after his vanished boyhood. Its pleasant memories stirred his Soul. He could still see its sunlight in the past, and he felt its breath upon him yet. But in the Future lay only his Manhood, and its path looked to him rugged and thorny. He had glided out past the sweet isles of Fancy. Dreamland was behind him with its smooth waters—before him the sea was tempest tost and he must battle with its waves, guide his bark unerringly, or he was lost. Such revelations come to us all. To some they seem real from the first—to others like a dream from which they hope to awaken.

I left him to his thoughts. I knew that it was best that he should face them. He would be reconciled to all this by and by and feel that a life of earnest action was the only thing that would satisfy his chafed and troubled spirit.

Just by the roadside was a long white frame building which was occupied as a grocery and a Government bakery. Some four or five soldiers were sitting in front of it. One little contraband[1] was there too who reminded me of the immortal Topsy in Mrs. Stowe's Uncle Tom's Cabin. He looked the very personification of fun and mischief. He clawed the backs of the soldiers with the agility of a cat—pulled their ears, and tickled the noses of the *braves* who lay asleep, most unmercifully with a shawl, while any impatient movement on their part was received with a hearty yaw, yaw, yaw which denoted the most genuine and complete satisfaction on his part at the result of his pranks.

I sent to the grocery for some refreshments but could obtain nothing but crackers and cheese. But a hungry man would not

1. Eliza seems to mean mischief maker rather than an escaped slave.

starve with these before him, so we made a very comfortable dinner of them.

It's strange how small our needs really are. Sitting in our ambulance with no riches before us we felt satisfied, and why? Simply because we could get nothing better and with that fact in view we could reason logically that we had enough.

The hours glided away before we were aware, as one sat there with our busy eyes, and at one touch of the whip our horses dashed forward bearing us at a rapid pace up the valley.

The heat of that September noon made us cast eager, wistful glances at the cool, leafy woods, amidst the green depths of which the shadows lay so invitingly, and yet so mockingly because we could not reach them.

"This is the way to go through life, Henry," said I. "The unattained is always before us, and the unattainable we are always reaching after. With the almost torrid heat of this sun above us what would be more delightful than the cool shade of this long line of forest? Isn't it tantalizing to think of the breezes stirring there, of the little bird songs of which we get but just the echoes while we ride out here in the broad glare of this feverish sunshine."

"Yes," he replied, "but I don't quite believe you that life is all like this, for there are hopes that have their fulfilment—and don't we often reach what we are striving for?"

"I don't know if we ever do or not—indeed I don't believe that we do fully—or if we do we find that our expectations have cheated us. Are we ever satisfied? Can there ever come to us a feeling of full and deep content? Supposing that we reach out after any one thing—I am talking of the things that belong to the inner life now—and after a long struggle grasp it, don't we often find that we've clutched the shadow, and that the real substance is beyond our reaching—that it lies where our hands cannot touch it? I wouldn't darken your day-dreams; I wouldn't crush your hopes. Let them grow—let them reach out into eternity—they'll have their fulfilment there if you live rightly—but in Time there will always be unanswered yearnings—and you'll always feel that the greatest disappointments that you meet with in life is that which you are to yourself."

He turned towards me with a pained, troubled look that said as plainly as words—I do hope this is only a theory of yours, one that you haven't tested—and then his lips added—"Has this been your experience?"

"I believe it has. When I was a child I used to map out the future for myself. There were planted in my soul the germs of high hopes. I felt in my little child's heart a distaste for grovelling, unprogressive life. I would be great. Knowledge should open her whole vast store house to me. I wouldn't plod along as the great mass did. I didn't think such a life worth living. I studied and while I studied Fancy built her palaces. Weren't they gorgeous with their crystal bars and varnished pillars? And I reached out into the invisible. How the sky over my castle grew starred with fame. Life grew great, and vast, and full of meaning. My ideals traversed higher and higher, and all this while the years were stealing silently away, and at length I was a child no longer. But these hopes they are mocking me—my Soul reaches out its unseen arms, but they glide out from them and are beyond me still, and I stand today no better, no higher than thousands of others, feeling my life's incompleteness, its want and waste, still reaching upwards, still grasping for the unattained. But then, notwithstanding all this life is noble if we choose to make it so—and vast enough. Every day that comes into the

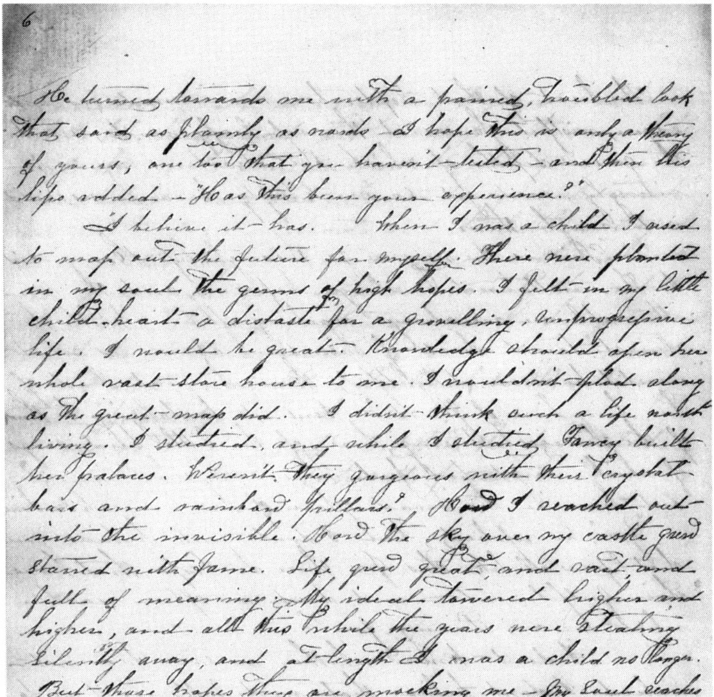
6

He turned towards me with a pained, troubled look that said as plainly as words "I hope this is only a theory of yours, one too that you haven't tested,"—and then his lips added—"Has this been your experience?"

I believe it has. When I was a child I used to map out the future for myself. There were planted in my soul the germs of high hopes. I felt in my little child-heart a distaste for a grovelling, unprogressive life. I would be great. Knowledge should open her whole vast store house to me. I wouldn't plod along as the great mass did. I didn't think such a life worth living. I studied, and while I studied, Fancy built her palaces. Weren't they gorgeous with their crystal bars and rainbow pillars? And I reached out into the invisible. And the sky over my castle grew starred with fame. Life grew great, and vast, and full of meaning. My ideal towered higher and higher, and all this while the years were stealing silently away, and at length I was a child no longer. But those hopes they are mocking me. My soul reaches out its unseen arms, but they glide out from them and are beyond me still, and I stand to day no better, no higher than thousands of others, feeling my life's incompleteness, its want and variety, still reaching upward, still grasping for the unattained. But then, notwithstanding all this life is noble if we choose to make it so—and vast enough. Every day that comes into the world opens a new path for progress. God meant man to be great—to be next to His own infinity.

But there—look at that mountain. One would think our way was wholly hedged up by it. Isn't it grand? The very mists sweep along below its summit, and its forest boughs heave like ocean billows when the wind rocks them—but it says to me "While I perish you endure."

It is great to live. Great to have souls that can take in this

Entry for September 1863, wherein Eliza relates her youthful ambitions and how she now feels mocked by her failure to fulfill them. (Huntington Library)

world opens a new path for progress. God meant man to be great, to be next to his own infinity."

"But there look at that mountain. One would think one's way was wholly hedged up by it. Isn't it grand? The very mists sweep along below its summit, and its forests boughs heave like ocean billows when the wind rocks them—but it says to me 'while I perish or endure' it is great to live. Great to have souls that can take in this wonderful beauty. A part of this vast creation we are thrilled by it, while we stand at the head of it, its noblest part, crown and glory."

We rode on while those giant hills seemed to have closed all about us. I never saw a view quite like it before. One wouldn't think there could be an opening found any where. Behind and before us, on our right hand and our left, they looked as if they had joined hands. Their high precipitate fronts, and long sloping sides waived their green banners at us, yet lifted up themselves like a huge wall against us everywhere. But our road threaded itself along at their feet—wound itself around like a serpent, stretching itself out on the banks of the rippling river, over which the mountains bent and mirrored themselves—their shadows lying slumberously in its cool depths, and tinging them with their beauty.

There are a few fine old residences scattered along the Valley on either bank of the river. Some times where there is a rich sweep of meadow land, and the mountains have fallen back from the stream these homesteads peep out from behind giant poplars, or the dark sighing cypress, or rich holly with a cheerful well-to-do air that is not the least in the world in sympathy with War or its desolation. The sun shines on them as brightly as ever, and the rich harvests come to them, and the pampered, selfish souls which they shelter are at ease, caring nothing for a Nation's peril—sympathizing only with its foes.

Meeting a little girl with a bright, sunny face, and a look of intelligence that interested me, we stopped for a few words with her.

Simple, artless and frank, as childhood always is in its perfect trust, the child amused us with her innocent prattle—her confidential story of baby brother, whose rosy, dimpled feet, so wonderful in her loving eyes, were just beginning to walk. "It was so funny"—it made her and darling mama—the prettiest and "goodest" mama the world ever saw laugh so to see baby brother toddle along. She wishes we could see him too. "And where do you live, little one?" "O, over there where those great trees are—don't you see?"

"Yes, and you have a pretty home, have not you? And you are a good little Union girl and your papa and mama, are they Union too?"

The great blue eyes looked up into our own—and over the pretty face that looked so innocent of all guile came a half smiling, half serious look as she answered. "O, we'se Union when the Union soldiers is here, and we'se Secesh when the Secesh soldiers came."[2]

"Isn't there an ample commentary in that simple reply on the loyalty of the people in this Valley?" said I to my friend as we rode onward.

"Yes, Loyalty here is generally a thing of policy rather than principle. It's an outgrowth from the pocket, an excrescence

2. James McPherson reports that "most of the Kanawha Valley" voted for secession in the referendum of May 23, 1862. See *Battle Cry of Freedom*, 303.

that is tolerated, that isn't lopped off, because it is balanced by dollars and cents."

"There's a deep undercurrent of hatred to our Cause flowing as steadily and surely through this Valley as the waters of the Kanawha flow—moving along often without a ripple on the surface, but daily upheaving."

Thus conversing of many things we rode up the Valley—the beautiful Valley of which one can give you but faint word pictures. There was an atmosphere of delight about it—a feeling of sympathy with that long line of majestic hills that seemed like the world's elder brothers in whose great breasts were hidden all the mysteries of the ages.

Old as Nature is She always seems fresh and young in all her summer times. We should be like her. A perpetual summer should be in our hearts. Even amid our mortality should mingle the freshness of immortal being. What though now and then comes to us the chilling wintertime of Sorrow, Hope and Faith should melt away the very bands which it clasps about—the tide of our joys and make the inner streams of gladness babble again with their old music.

A government train came in sight—winding its long length around the quick turns of the road in our advance, creeping slowly on in the hot Sunshine. The poor mules looked as if they had been driven hard and long, and the drivers appeared listless and wearied and only first lifted their eyes to us as we passed, and they had in their faces an expression that seemed like a revelation of what life was to them—a mere treadmill existence that wasn't expansive, that never went out beyond the toil or the pleasure of today.

There were some exceptions to this. There were a few faces on

Eliza (with her daughter Mabel) in 1878,
when she was living in Santa Barbara, California,
the mother of three daughters, and her husband's partner
in publishing the Daily Press. *The entire family moved to*
Los Angeles in 1882 to begin their historic connection with
the Los Angeles Times. (*California, "Where Sets the Sun"*)

which were the looks of intelligence, but it was an intelligence that had not been quickened by study or refined by thought.

The teamsters in the train were nearly all civilians, raised in this vicinity—their knowledge of the world limited mostly to the distance lying between Fayette and Charleston. The great world beyond, with its activity and progress must be like an old myth or fable to them—a dreamland of improbabilities—an Ideal into which the Actual never reaches.

Nineteen miles above Charleston is the residence of the widow T.[3] The afternoon shadows had lengthened somewhat when we reached it and I almost wished that we could make it a stopping place. I had passed a night there some months before and had been kindly received and entertained. The house is half way between Charleston and the Falls of the Kanawha, and is usually made a stopping place by our officers and soldiers in passing up and down the Valley. It is a pretty place. The house is embowered in trees, and the river flows along in front making with the high hills and rich valley a beautiful picture.[4]

Mrs. T. is a person of fifty or fifty-five years, dignified and lady like, with charming powers of agreeableness, and a pleasant, womanly face which still bears the trace of more than usual beauty. She is an aunt of Major General Grant to whom the hearts of the Nation are turning since he has won for Freedom our American Gibraltar—Vicksburg—being the city which he "girt with fire."

Mrs. T. is heart and soul a Southern woman. Her sympathies are with the rebellion, her hopes are for its success. She has two sons in the Confederate service. Yet with all her devotion to the

3. The Mrs. Tompkins described in chapter 7.

4. Much of this paragraph and the next two repeat material in chapter 7.

Southern cause, she is wont to expatiate freely upon the rising military fame of her kinsman "Ulysses," as she patronizingly terms the hero of Vicksburg. Evidently her family pride is as powerful as her treasonable instincts.

Speaking of Gen. Grant's growing popularity the remark was made to her by one of our officers that "he evidently possessed decided military skill and the hope was expressed that he might achieve still more important victories for the cause of the country. To this Mrs. T. replied that she thought "Ulysses" had many of the qualities of a military chieftain but her mighty prayer for him was that he might be led to see the error of his ways, abandon the cruel crusade which he is now waging against his unoffending and outraged brethren of the South and lend his influence to the cause of Southern independence.

Just beyond the house a little stream flows along between verdure-lined banks with a sweet rippling manner. Passing that our road wound gradually up one of the lesser hills that are scattered here and there at the foot of the more towering heights that seem almost as much the children of the sky as of the solid earth where they have their foundations.

As we rode up this elevation we noticed on the right of our road a small brick church which we were told had been built a few years since by one of the daughters of Mrs. T. whose generous heart had felt the needs of a churchless people. But the building stands now as a monument of War's desolating power. Vandal hands have dismantled it, and but little save roof and walls are remaining, and the owl and the raven hoot and cry amid its ruins.

From Malden, a small town a few miles above Charleston, to Lewisburg, a distance of one hundred miles—the land seems to have forgotten her sabbaths. The two or three churches which are left standing, where treason was taught instead of the pure Gospel of peace are now occupied as storehouses for our army, and day and night you hear before them the Sound of the sentinel's tread as he walks his measured beat. "How little friends at home, with the music of Sabbath bells unhushed, and with the quiet of the Sabbath day about them realize anything of War's desolation Henry," said I.

"I had hardly realized it before myself," he said, "but it saddens me now."

And well it may, for day by day the Present slips into the Past and never a voice nor a sound in all this valley to say "prepare."

Beyond this we passed sometimes fine old farm houses with broad fields of meadow land about them, flanked by extensive orchards, their trees laden with golden apples, as [and?] blushing red ones, their branches bending almost to the ground with the weight of their juicy treasures; and here and there limbs heavy with tempting peaches hung over the walls making our mouths water till we felt almost unable to resist the temptation to confiscate a little of the fruit which appealed so invitingly to our now sharpened appetites.

But these old farmhouses with their look of plenty were not the only homes passed. Here and there were the simple cottages of the Virginia laborer.[5] Some of these were log huts without windows, and the pleasant September sunlight could only steal gingerly in at them around often closed doors.

Such pitiful looking little children as we saw about them, with dirty faces and tangled hair, and clothes soiled and tat-

5. Technically now West Virginia, which had separated from the state of Virginia in 1863 in order to remain within the Union.

tered and such mothers! Loud voiced and rough, with faces brown and brawny, all the beauty of womanhood in eclipse.

But there were other of these houses with vine-covered windows, and white washed walls, with well kept gardens and beds of flowers that looked homelike though humble, and fair faced, rosy cheeked children played in the cool shadows of the trees overhanging the low roofs, and pleasant womanly faces would sometimes look out at us, nodding in a friendly way as their eyes met our own.

The shadows had crept up the beautiful Valley till the river and all the low lands were wrapped in them and half way up the high mountains they had stolen as we neared Cannelton.

"I never saw before so beautiful a landscape as this, Henry," I said, "Look at that gem of an island lying like an emerald in the water, and those old cliffs with their bare, bold brows standing out amidst that world of verdure—and see the different shades of green in the forests—the dark ferns and hemlock, the lighter shade of oak and maple and then the never resting water mirroring cloud, and sky and roads—just behind us on our right which we can see all of that rolling grand Valley, those smooth meadows stretching out to the river's brink. I'd love to paint here, full guarded by these sentinel mountains."

"It's painted on my soul," he answered, "and memory will never let its colors fade. But what is that amidst the rocks and trees away up near the top of that high mountain?"

"O that's the High House at Cannelton built by one of the superintendents of the works there. It looks as inaccessible as an eagle's eyrie. Look at its woods, all below it is in shadow, but the sunlight gilding it makes its windows look like shining topaz or amethyst. As you see it now you might fancy it a dryad's castle,

The three Otis daughters in 1876: Beulah Lilian (born 1864), Emma Marian (born 1866), and Mabel (born 1871).
(Los Angeles Times History Center)

built of rainbows and rubies and all wonderful things which they hide in their mountain caves."

"Yes it wouldn't be difficult to do so, and fill all these woods the while with forest genie. What a glorious world this would be if man was only right wouldn't it."

"Yes 'twould be as Moore has said, I fancy:

> O could we do with this world of ours,
> As thou dost with thy garden bowers
> Refect the needs & keep the flowers
> What a heaven on earthe we'd make it!
> So bright a dwelling should be our own
> So warranted free from sigh or frown
> That angels soon would be coming down
> By the week or month to take it.[6]

"Yes, he replied laughingly, "Moore has it all in a nutshell." "But turning from fancy to fact—what ever induced a man to build up there among the rocks at a point so difficult of access?"

" 'Twas a happy thought, for it placed him above the clouds of smoke, the nauseous gas, and the grime and dirt that is over everything at Cannelton. The town is made up mostly of the poor dwellings of the miners and workmen, at best but little more than miserable hovels, the abodes of filth, and dirt, and squalor. These steep mountains come down almost to the river's brink, there's but just room for the road at their base, and many of the buildings stand part way down the river's bank, and you go down to them from the road by means of rude plank steps."

It was nearly dark when we entered the place and the burning

6. Eliza and her companion were perhaps referring to Thomas Moore (1779–1852), the Irish romantic poet; this verse, however, does not appear in *The Poetical Works of Thomas Moore* (Edinburgh,1873).

gas escaping from the works, and the grim smoked faces of the workmen, together with the aspect of their miserable dwellings crowded out for the moment every cheerful, pleasant thought. We drove on quickly, and breathed a little more freely as we reached the upper part of the town which had decidedly a more Christian like looking air, with its two stores and neatly painted houses, and we noticed across the river, on its opposite banks some fine looking residences, built of brick, which spoke of both wealth and culture.

Beyond Cannelton the Valley widens a little again, and there are pleasant grounds for building, and it seems a little strange that they should not be occupied, it would be so delightful when one's day's work was done to go out from the smoke and dirt and breathe the pure, sweet untainted air.

The golden tints of the sunset had faded, and the shadows had deepened on mountain-top and valley as we reached the residence of the Widow H.[7] three miles above Cannelton where my friend Mrs. S. the wife of our brigade Quartermaster was waiting to greet me.

The house is a two story frame building, painted white and built in true Southern style, with broad verandahs above and below and three doors opening out to each from the chambers, and the lower floor. Here in the cool of evening the inmates love to gather and watch the shadows fall, while delightful breezes steal down from mountain top and forest, while the little stream flowing on just beyond the house keeps time with its sweet rhythmical murmur with the bass notes of the rolling river.

My friend Mrs. S. gave me a most cordial welcome and soon conducted us, not unwillingly, to a table laden with delicacies,

7. Presumably Mrs. Huddleston, with whom Eliza had stayed before.

and choice titbits—that would have led appetites sharpened less than our own into the temptation of overmuch eating. After doing ample justice to the good things before us we retired to the parlor where we found several military guests, but wearied with our long ride we soon excused ourselves.

Before retiring to my room I said good bye to my young friend who could accompany me no further on my journey. "This whole ride has been a feast to me," he said, "and I dont like to go back without going further and seeing more. Just come out on the verandah and let me take a good look at these old mountains with you. I'd like to look on them feeling that I am not alone in my appreciation of their grandeur. So we went out & gazed at them while like huge giants they lay asleep in the moonlight, and the quiet stars seemed trembling scarce an arm's length above them. Far as the eye could reach on all sides they stood, and the little valley where we were lay as if it were a world within a world, still & solemn & soundless save as only the waters sang their choral anthems, and the breeze stirred lightly the rustling leaves.

"I shall be off before daybreak, so I'll not see you again," he said at length.

So we said good bye & thus the day ended. Almost every day in life has its farewells.

SECTION THREE

The Civil War Diary of Harrison Gray Otis, 1862–1863

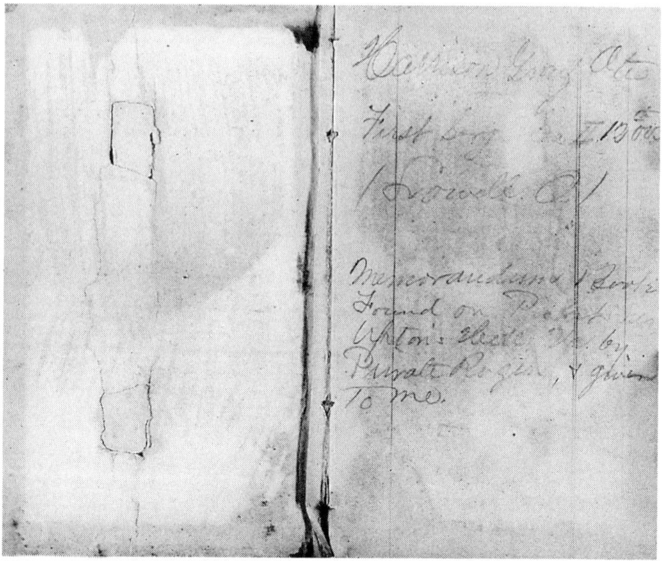

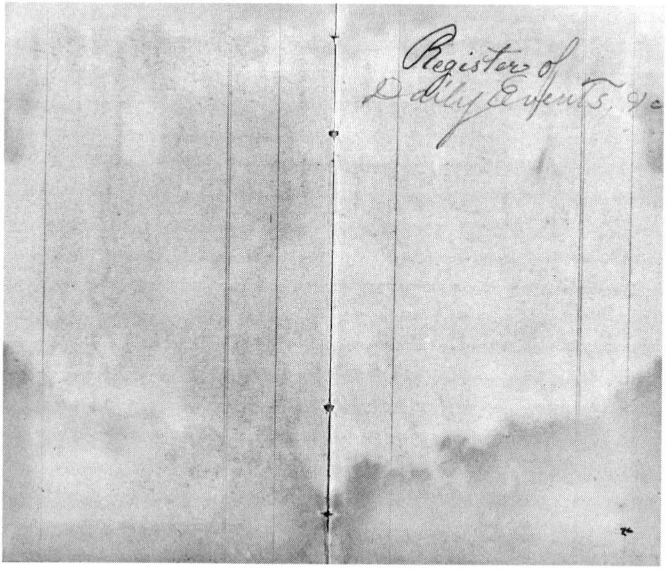

Title pages of Harrison Gray Otis's Civil War diary. (Family Collection)

SUNDAY, AUG 24, 1862

Arrived in Washington City by rail from Parkersburg, Va.—having left camp at Top Mountain, Aug 15, 1862; from thence marching to the Kanawha River; there took boats and reached Parkersburg on the 20th. At Parkersburg *Lizzie* came to meet me, with her brother Eddie,[1] whom I had never before seen. Saw Joe Dyar, wounded and a host of Rainbow folks.

MONDAY, AUG 25, 1862

Encamped on Common in Alexandria yesterday without tents and still here. House where Ellsworth died nearby.[2]—Eleventh Ohio and thirty-third Mass alongside.—Dust suffocating—Took a glorious wash in the Potomac.—Waiting for orders.—

1. Edwin Wetherby (born 1840), Eliza's brother.

2. Colonel Elmer Ellsworth, the first Union officer to die in the war. He was shot while trying to tear down a Confederate flag flying atop a hotel in Alexandria, Virginia, an escapade deemed "silly" by some military historians. See Herman Hattaway and Archer Jones, *How the North Won: A Military History of the Civil War* (Urbana: University of Illinois Press, 1983), 36. Eliza Ann Otis later wrote an elaborate poetic tribute to his heroism; see *California, "Where Sets the Sun,"* 813.

Wagon train and baggage not yet come up—Cox's[3] division—11th, 12th, 23rd, 28th, 30th, & 36th Reg'ts—arrived or arriving—30th and 36th ahead at Warrenton.

TUESDAY, AUG. 26, 1862

Still in position of yesterday—Dust unendurable, *almost.*—McClellan's[4] troops passing through town from the Peninsula to form junction with Pope[5]—Heintz—Elman's corps, Hooker's[6] Division & other veterans gone or going.—Three days ration—cooked and put in haversacks—Expecting to move every hour—anxious to get off.

WEDNESDAY, AUG. 27, 1862

Started very early this morning by Orange & Alexandria R.R. for Manassas.—At Bull's Run Bridge met Taylor's New Jersey Brigade falling back from the old Bull's Run battleground—repulsed by large force of Rebel artillery, cavalry, & infantry—

3. Jacob A. Cox, brigadier general in charge of the Ohio militia, was a highly regarded commander; his campaign history is collected in Robert U. Johnson and Clarence C. Buel, eds., *Battles and Leaders of the Civil War*, vol. 2 (1888; reprint, Secaucus, New Jersey, 1982).

4. George B. McClellan was then commander of the Army of the Potomac, the North's principal field army. He was later relieved of his command for failure to be sufficiently aggressive. See McPherson, *Battle Cry of Freedom*, 359–65.

5. General John Pope, notorious for his tough tactics, was commander of the Army of the Mississippi but later transferred to the Virginia campaign. He was held responsible for losing the Battle of Bull Run. Ibid., 415, 499–500, 525–33.

6. General Joseph Hooker, a bold, popular leader, fought unsuccessfully at Chancellorsville and Gettysburg. Ibid., 639–45, 651–2.

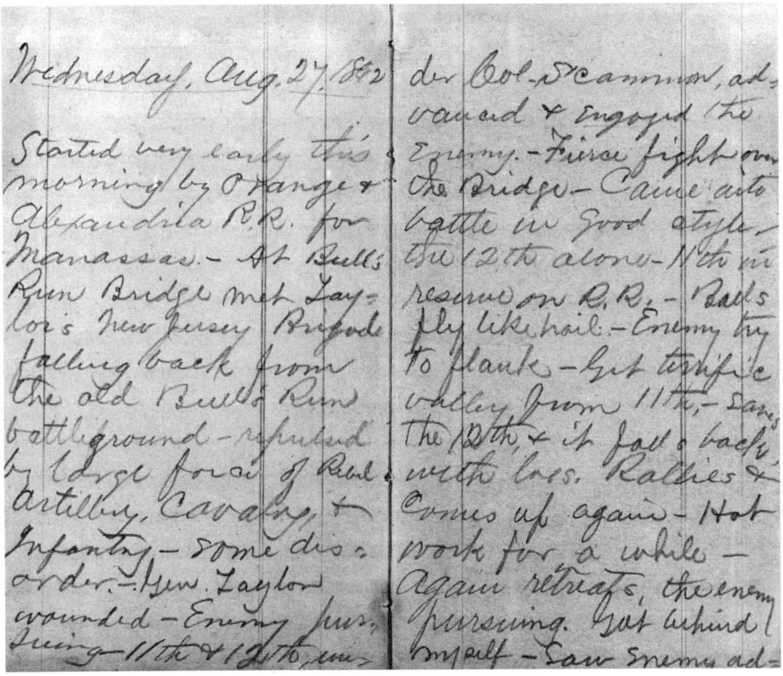
Wednesday, Aug. 27, 1862

Started very early this morning by Orange & Alexandria R.R. for Manassas. – At Bull's Run Bridge met Taylor's New Jersey Brigade falling back from the old Bull's Run battleground – repulsed by large force of Rebel artillery, Cavalry, & Infantry – some disorder. – Gen. Taylor wounded – Enemy pursuing – 11th & 12th under Col. Scammon, advanced & engaged the Enemy. – Fierce fight over the Bridge – Came into battle in good style – the 12th alone – 11th in reserve on R.R. – Balls fly like hail. – Enemy try to flank – Get terrific volley from 11th, – Saves the 12th, & it falls back with loss. Rallies & Comes up again – Hot work for a while – again retreats, the enemy pursuing. Got behind myself – Saw Enemy ad-

Entry for August 27, 1863: the beginning of Harry's account of the Battle of Bull Run. (Family Collection) some disorder. Gen. Taylor wounded.—Enemy pursuing 11th and 12th under Col. Scammon,[7] advanced and engaged the enemy. Fierce fight over the Bridge—Came into battle in good style—the 12th alone—11th in reserve on R.R.—Bullets fly like hail.—Enemy try to flank—Get terrific volley from 11th—saves the 12th and it falls back with loss. Rallies & comes up again—Hot work for a while—Again retreats, the enemy pursuing. Got behind myself—Saw enemy advance and form line of battle in open field on right of railroad—Two flags in full view—one red, the other white with black crop.—They send volley after our rear. I fire at flag & then "get up & dust"—Bullets fly like mad. Retreat through open fields and woods, with but two or three of 12th along. Reach the R.R. again—just as 11th is passing—overtake my Reg't, & again fall back to look after Sal. Smith, wounded—Rebel Cavalry came dashing up, crying "*Halt*!" "Nary Halt" for me—"Light out," with two guns & sword. Pursuers scattered by a few shots from rear of the 11th. Pop on to Fairfax Station—Column halts part of the night—12th in hollow square, ready for Cavalry (28th)—Up long before daylight, & on retreat by Fairfax C.H. road. Wounded left at station—Jersey Brigade in front—Troops nearly exhausted. No sleep, no food, no rest for 24 hours.—Killed, wounded, & missing in my company, 14. 44 only in action. Reached camp near Cloud's Mills, 2 miles from Alexandria, about noon—Got some rest & food. Thousands of new troops coming in—one vast camp all round.

7. Colonel Eliakim P. Scammon, Third Division, Eighth Corps, Ohio Volunteers (known as the "Kanawha Division"). *Roster*, vol. 3, 71.

FRIDAY, AUG. 29, 1862

Good sleep last night. Rations drawn & cooked. Marched to Munson's Hill, 4 or 5 miles.—Left wing on picket—news of heavy fighting in front—Muster Rolls to be made out.—Don't like the task.—Wagons come up, tents are pitched & make us comfortable. Boys forage a great deal & plenty to eat—Green corn, apples, peaches etc.

SATURDAY, AUG. 30/62

Still on Picket duty—Troops passing this evening—Sumner's[8] corps marching to the front. 4th Ohio with them. Young Davis, my nephew, stopped to see me—Glad to meet him. Looks like a good soldier & talks well. "Old Bull Sumner" himself passed and Thos. Francis Meagher[9] & other Generals—Saw the lamented Baker's[10] Old Reg't.

SUNDAY, AUG. 31, 1862

Troops passed all night & still passing—Heavy cannonading heard all day in direction of Centerville—A terrific battle going

8. General Edwin V. "Bull" Sumner was the sixty-five-year-old commander who led one of the four corps that composed the Army of the Potomac. His nickname was originally "Bull Head" because a musket ball was alleged to have bounced off his head. See Hattaway and Jones, *How the North Won*, 173–4.

9. General Thomas Francis Meagher was a "political general," appointed by Lincoln to gratify the Irish-American community. See McPherson, *Battle Cry of Freedom*, 328.

10. Colonel Nathan G. "Shanks" Baker, a senator from Oregon, is described by McPherson as "brave but tactically inept." He was ambushed and killed early in the war in the Battle of Ball's Bluff. Ibid., 81–2.

on—Wild reports brought in by stragglers.—Many scattered along the road—A few wounded in ambulances going by. Mostly taken to Washington by rail—letters for C.O. at Cairo in steamboat service & from Liz.

MONDAY, SEPT. 1, 1862

Still on Picket—Retrograde movement by the army in front commenced. Large herds of cattle & horses being brought back. Troops commence falling back—mostly stragglers.—Wrote to Brother Charles and Wife Lizzie—Great vigilance on outposts.

TUESDAY, SEPT. 2, 1862

Up in line of battle last night "in a jiffy." Guards foolish and frightened. Old English Ed Allston mighty near insane—False alarm—go to bed again—Troop falling back in large bodies. The dead body of Gen. Kearney[11] passed in an ambulance.

WEDNESDAY, SEPT. 3

Up again last night & formed line of battle in a mighty hurry. Cavalry spotted the enemy advancing. Tents struck & baggage loaded & wagons sent to the rear. Another false alarm—Laid down on the ground in line till morning.

11. General Philip Kearney of New Jersey, a professional soldier who had lost an arm in the Mexican War, urged a much more aggressive strategy upon McClellan. Ibid., p. 470.

THURSDAY, SEPT. 4

Left companies relieved on picket by 56th Pa. & marched back to Munson's Hill, joining the right again. Cannonading heard today in direction of Fall's Church—not more than two or three miles from our position. Large army massed at Munson's & Upton's Hills. Teams out foraging, came thundering back from direction of firing this evening—Saw a body of Lancers today. Report a victory by Wool[12] at Harper's Ferry—Churned up. Ready to fight to the death. The Country must be saved. God be with the Nation's defenders![13]

FRIDAY, SEPT. 5, 1862

Nothing exciting today. Dress Parade this evening—order to drill and establish garrison regulations—Later in evening got orders to march in two hours with five days rations—Talk of going across the Potomac. Two hours now up, all quiet, & I'm going to bed.

SATURDAY, SEPT. 6, 1862

Up about 2 o'clock this morning, took some coffee & started on the march about 7. Marched thru Georgetown & Washington—

12. General John Wool, an aging professional soldier, was given diverse commands to utilize his experience. The fight over control of Harper's Ferry led directly to the massive Battle of Antietam. See Hattaway and Jones, *How the North Won*, 503, and McPherson, *Battle Cry of Freedom*, 534–6.

13. Historian James McPherson believes that the intense ideological commitment expressed here by Harry was a widespread feeling among soldiers in the Civil War. See his *For Cause and Comrades*.

Twelfth Regiment Ohio Volunteer Infantry.

THREE YEARS' SERVICE.

This Regiment was organized at Camp Dennison, Ohio, from June 19 to June 29, 1861, to serve three years. It was mustered out July 11, 1864, by reason of expiration of term of service, and the veterans and recruits transferred to the Twenty-third Regiment Ohio Volunteer Infantry.

The official list of battles in which this Regiment bore an honorable part is not yet published in orders of the War Department; but the following list is submitted as the most accurate and complete that can be prepared from records at the disposal of this office:

SCARY CREEK, W. VA., ...	July 17, 1861.
GAULEY BRIDGE, W. VA., ...	August 25, 1861.
CARNIFAX FERRY, W. VA., . .	September 10, 1861.
BULL RUN BRIDGE, VA., ...	August 27, 1862.
FREDERICK, MD., ...	September 12, 1862.
SOUTH MOUNTAIN, MD., ...	September 14, 1862.
ANTIETAM, MD., ...	September 17, 1862.
FAYETTEVILLE, W. VA., ...	May 17–20, 1863.
MEADOW BLUFF, W. VA., . .	Dec. 12, 1863.
CLOYD'S MOUNTAIN, VA., ...	May 9–10, 1864.
LYNCHBURG, VA., ...	June 17–18, 1864.

Regimental roster of the Twelfth Ohio Volunteers, 1864, which lists the major battles in which the regiment fought. (Reid, *Ohio in the War*, vol. 2, 351) streets very dirty—Saw the White House. Encamped very tired, near the Soldier's Home. Some of Burnside's[14] troops nearby. Went to see Capt. [illegible] of the 30th. Found him sick.—Old Ruse [?][15] came back to pester us.

SUNDAY, SEPT. 7, 1862

Marched 6 or 8 miles today, over a dusty road, lined with troops, artillery, & baggage trains, end encamped for the night on the Edward's Ferry Road, near Leesboro. Enemy reported across the Potomac, with outpost not far from us. Got plenty of force to meet him. Took a wash just now & now I'm going to bed—This written by moonlight.

TUESDAY, SEPT. 9, 1862

Started just before night yesterday from camp near Leesboro, and marched to Brookville, Md.—8 or 9 miles. Arrived about 10 or 11 at night, very exhausted with fatigue and loss of sleep. Laid down in open air and slept soundly—no tents in use in the Reg't. Enemy reported, 8 miles ahead.—Baltimore 28 & Frederick 25 miles off. Letter to Lizzie.

WEDNESDAY, SEPTEMBER 10, 1862

Marched about 10 miles yesterday, first in a northerly direction, then west. Encamped at dark. Beautiful country. Fine old

14. General Ambrose E. Burnside, one of the most important generals in the Army of the Potomac, resigned after defeat at Fredericksburg. See McPherson, *Battle Cry of Freedom*, 584–5.

15. Possibly a misspelling of the name of Captain Andrew J. Rooso, Twelfth Regiment. See *Roster*, vol. 2, 353.

Twelfth Regiment Ohio Volunteer Infantry. 377

COMPANY I.

Names.	Rank.	Age.	Date of Entering the Service.	Period of Service.	Remarks.
Ferdinand Gunckle	Captain.	32	June 28, 1861	3 yrs.	Resigned Aug. 24, 1861; reappointed Oct. 23, 1861; resigned March 20, 1862.
Jonathan C. Wallace	...do...	31	June 22, 1861	3 yrs.	Promoted from 1st Lieutenant and Regt. Quartermaster March 20, 1862; mustered out with company July 11, 1864.
Ashley Brown	1st Lieut.	21	June 25, 1861	3 yrs.	Promoted to Captain Dec. 9, 1862; not mustered until Feb. 1, 1864; assigned to Co. D Feb. 1, 1864.
Thomas F. Hill	...do...	24	June 4, 1861	3 yrs.	Transferred from Co. H April 10, 1864; mustered out with company July 11, 1864.
Horatio G. Tibbals	2d Lieut.	29	June 25, 1861	3 yrs.	Promoted from 1st Sergeant June 28, 1861; 1st Lieutenant Co. D April 18, 1862.
William H. Glotfelter	...do...	23	June 5, 1861	3 yrs.	Transferred from Co. B June 13, 1862; promoted to 1st Lieutenant Co. E Sept. 30, 1862.
Harrison G. Otis	...do...	24	June 25, 1861	3 yrs.	Appointed 1st Sergeant from Sergeant March 1, 1862; promoted to 2d Lieutenant Sept. 30, 1862; 1st Lieutenant Co. B March 21, 1863.
John M. Busby	...do...	25	June 5, 1861	3 yrs.	Assigned from 2d Lientenant and Acting Regt. Quartermaster Aug. 1, 1863; resigned Oct. 12, 1863.
Henry W. Orvis	1st Sergt.	29	June 25, 1861	3 yrs.	Appointed from Sergeant June 29, 1861.
Joseph R. Wright	...do...	24	June 5, 1861	3 yrs.	Appointed Sergeant from Corporal April 14, 1862; 1st Sergeant Mar. 1, 1864; transferred to Co. K, 23d O. V. I., July 1, 1864; veteran.
Peter Smith	Sergeant	27	June 25, 1861	3 yrs.	Appointed from Corporal July 1, 1863; transferred to Co. K, 23d O. V. I., July 1, 1864; veteran.
James H. Kizer	...do...	19	Jan. 27, 1862	3 yrs.	Mustered as private; appointed Sergeant Feb. 1, 1864; transferred to Co. K, 23d O. V. I., July 1, 1864.
Jacob Weikel	...do...	18	June 25, 1861	3 yrs.	Appointed Corporal Nov. 24, 1862; Sergeant April 1, 1864; transferred to Co. K, 23d O. V. I., July 1, 1864; veteran.
William Kilyrzynski	...do...	27	June 25, 1861	3 yrs.	Mustered out with company July 11, 1864.
John Shoen	...do...	35	June 25, 1861	3 yrs.	Appointed from Corporal July 26, 1861; discharged Dec. 24, 1862, for wounds received in action.
Leonard Doersam	Corporal	21	June 25, 1861	3 yrs.	Captured near Raleigh, W. Va., Jan. 30, 1864. No record of muster-out found.
David Allbaugh	...do...	18	July 2, 1861	3 yrs.	Appointed Corporal Nov. 1, 1862; wounded at battle of Cloyd's Mountain, Va., May 9, 1864; left in hospital and captured ——; mustered out Nov. 1, 1864, at Columbus, O.
James Gorsuch	...do...	18	June 25, 1861	3 yrs.	Appointed Corporal Jan. 1, 1863; mustered out with company July 11, 1864.
Calvin Belt	...do...	18	July 2, 1861	3 yrs.	Appointed Corporal March 10, 1864; mustered out with company July 11, 1864.
Gottfried App	...do...	28	June 25, 1861	3 yrs.	Appointed Corporal June 29, 1861; discharged July 31, 1862, on Surgeon's certificate of disability.
William H. Phillips	...do...	30	June 25, 1861	3 yrs.	Appointed Corporal Aug. —, 1861; discharged Jan. —, 1862.
Solomon R. Smith	...do...	31	June 25, 1861	3 yrs.	Appointed Corporal June 20, 1861; discharged Oct. 29, 1862, for wounds received in action.
Simon P. Stubbs	...do...	20	June 25, 1861	3 yrs.	Appointed Corporal June 29, 1861; discharged Dec. 18, 1861, on Surgeon's certificate of disability.
Henry C. Light	...do...	23	June 25, 1861	3 yrs.	Appointed Corporal Aug. —, 1861; died ——, from wounds received at battle of South Mountain, Md., Sept. 14, 1862.
Joseph W. Meekins	...do...	27	Aug. 14, 1862	3 yrs.	Appointed Corporal July 25, 1863; transferred to Co. —, 23d O. V. I., July 1, 1864.
William Archer	...do...	18	June 25, 1861	3 yrs.	Appointed Corporal April 1, 1864; transferred to Co. —, 23d O. V. I., July 1, 1864; veteran.
George Collins	Musician	30	June 25, 1861	3 yrs.	Transferred to Captain West's 1st Virginia Cavalry Aug. 26, 1861.
Samuel Trimble	...do...	32	June 25, 1861	3 yrs.	
Adams, David F.	Private.	33	June 25, 1861	3 yrs.	Transferred to Co. B July —, 1861.
Atkinson, Thomas	...do...	18	June 13, 1861	3 yrs.	Transferred to Co. B July —, 1861.
Abbot, John B.	...do...	18	June 25, 1861	3 yrs.	Transferred to Co. B July —, 1861.
Allston, Edward	...do...	40	June 25, 1861	3 yrs.	Killed in battle of South Mountain, Md., Sept 14, 1862.
Briggs, Abner	...do...	23	June 25, 1861	3 yrs.	Transferred to Co. B July —, 1861.
Bailey, Michael	...do...	18	June 3, 1861	3 yrs.	Transferred from Co. F June 3, 1862.
Bryant, Jacob	...do...	43	June 25, 1861	3 yrs.	Transferred to Co. B July —, 1861.
Beemer, Jacob	...do...	....	July 2, 1861	3 yrs.	
Brooks, Jonas	...do...	18	June 25, 1861	3 yrs.	Transferred to Co. B July —, 1861.
Bauman, Jacob	...do...	43	June 25, 1861	3 yrs.	Transferred to Co. G July —, 1861.
Breelman, John	...do...	30	June 25, 1861	3 yrs.	Transferred to Co. B July —, 1861.
Bush, David	...do...	22	June 20, 1861	3 yrs.	Transferred from Co. B July —, 1861; transferred to Co. D July —, 1861.
Bener, Thomas	...do...	21	July 2, 1861	3 yrs.	Mustered out with company July 11, 1864.

Regimental roster of the Twelfth Ohio Volunteers, 1864. The list of officers shows Harrison G. Otis as a Second Lieutenant. (Reid, *Ohio in the War*, vol. 2, 351) mansions & good farms, though seemingly much worn. Ladies by the roadside wave pocket handkerchiefs. Expecting to march every moment today. Gathered lots of delicious grapes.

THURSDAY, SEPT. 11, 1862

Laid in camp yesterday and today. Marched about 10 miles to Ridgeville, Md. Encamped in a fine clover field near town. Day cool & cloudy. Slight rain & no dust. Not yet come up with the enemy. Reported by citizens to be just ahead. Saw Burnside on the road today. No letters from Liz since coming East.

SATURDAY, SEPT. 13, 1862

Frederick City occupied by our forces yesterday afternoon. Smart fight between part of our Division and rear guard of the Rebels. (Stuart's[16] Cavalry.) at Monocacy Bridge & in edge of town. Rebels driven & we passed through town amidst the wildest demonstrations of delight from citizens.

MONDAY, SEPTEMBER 15, 1862

Great battle fought yesterday at South Mountain Gap, 3 miles from Middletown, Md. Our division opened the infantry fighting. The 12th, 23rd and 36th charged the Rebel position in the forenoon, & drove them from behind a stone wall & into the

16. Lieutenant James Ewell Brown ("Jeb") Stuart, a dashing, daredevil Confederate commander, was called the "Cavalier of Dixie." The nemesis of the Army of the Potomac, he was killed in 1864 at Yellow Tavern. See McPherson, *Battle Cry of Freedom*, 462–4, 728, and Hattaway and Jones, *How the North Won*, 560.

woods in utter confusion. Many bayonetted & many more taken prisoners. The North Carolinians turned their backs upon the gleaming bayonets of the "Hirelings"[17] & threw away guns & equipment in profusion. Gen. Garland of N.C. killed.

Later in the day the battle raged even more furiously. Our Division again charged through a dense laurel thicket advancing with yells terrific upon a strong position of the enemy behind another stone wall. Here the fighting was indeed desperate. Our loss, severe, but the enemy's double. The ground lay strewn with dead & dying & hundreds were captured. We have gained a glorious but a dearly bought victory. Our loss is heavy. In Cox's Division the chief loss was sustained on the left. At night the enemy fell back. Citizens say in confused state towards Boonesboro, leaving dead & wounded upon the field. The sight was awful to look upon. We have captured guns, knapsacks, clothing & other trash which the chivalry[18] are wont to tote.

God has spared my life & I am once more ready to meet my Country's enemies.

How full of suspense are these days to Lizzie, my Best & Dearest Love. And yet they, who would ruin her pure name say she is not true! Palsied be the tongues of slander. Her unwavering constancy gives the lie to their every calumnious tale.[19]

17. This was obviously a Confederate taunt that Otis enjoyed throwing back in their faces. The reference is to the Southern claim that many Northern troops enlisted only for money not for love of country.

18. This is a rare sarcastic comment from Harrison on the pretensions of the Confederate officers. Most Northern soldiers shared his contempt for Southern pretensions of "chivalry."

19. This is a reference to Eliza's difficulties with her family. See Introduction.

SUNDAY, SEPT. 21, 1862

My record is often interrupted now. The rough fortunes of war make sad havoc in the pages of a diary, as well as in the ranks of an army. Since my last date, another great battle has been fought. On the 16th our army came up with the enemy at Antietam Creek near Sharpsburg. Some fighting occurred, but without definite result the first day. The night of the 16th was occupied by our troops in getting into position, and early on the following morning the great battle opened with tremendous cannonading from our side & tremendous replies from the enemy.

All day the battle raged. The left did not become engaged till afternoon, when one Division with others was thrown across the creek, and advanced through open fields into the face of the enemy, who occupied a corn field by scores. Here we encountered a destructive fire which threw us back for a time. The 12th rallied and advanced once more amidst a terrific fire of grape & shell to the edge of the cornfield. Got into confusion by supposing the enemy in the cornfields to be friends. Again fell back to banks of creek. Laid there during the night. The following day nothing but skirmishing took place between the contending armies. Towards night our Division was relieved by a portion of Fitz John Porter's[20] troops, and we gladly marched to the rear for a little rest & sleep. On the 19th the enemy having retreated & commenced the passage of the Potomac, we once more moved forward, and today rest upon the bank of the Antietam,

20. General Fitz-John Porter, one of General George McClellan's key commanders, was relieved of command with him in late 1862 and later court-martialed. See McPherson, *Battle Cry of Freedom*, 463–7, 529.

near the Shepardstown Ferry on the Potomac. The enemy's rear has been fiercely shelled by us, & he no doubt returns to Virginia with shattered columns.

The good God has once more taken me through a time of peril safely, though I was severely scratched by a stray ball on Wednesday, which glanced my left shoulder blade.

How thankful I am to God for his Mercy! & yet how undeserving I am.

It would relieve me could the sorely anxious heart of my faithful Lizzie be consoled by news of my safety. But "All's well that ends well."

FAYETTE C.H., VA. JAN'Y 9, 1863

A long interval since my last record! The old year has gone, a new one opens, finding me still alive and well, and able to defend my Country. *Thank God for that!* And in the early opening of the new year I resume my imperfect, uncertain record, interrupted more than a quarter of a year agone. Since my last notes, made in the Camp of our "Army of the Potomac," near the bloody field of Antietam, our Regiment has once more returned to the familiar field of Western Virginia. Landing at Clarksburg about Oct. 18, having left Antietam Creek, Oct. 8, we staid there several days to be clothed, then marched to Summersville, remaining in that place several days, thence to Gauley Bridge, and after camping there (in a state of suspense as to our destination, for the winter) several weeks, we finally came up to Fayette Dec. 4, and have built magnificent quarters for ourselves, which make us comfortable as soldiers usually get,—and more so. Plenty of drill, study, and guard duty—our time is pretty

Rock beside the Gauley Bridge. The mountains bordering the Kanawha River forced both Confederate and Union soldiers to engage in guerrilla warfare. (West Virginia Archives)

thoroughly occupied, & some of it pretty well, I venture to say. But this is hardly a record to be welcome & interesting to Lizzie, whose dear eyes shall fall upon it ere the "Ides of May."[21] The dear girl wants to know my daily thoughts, and if they be worthy of her, she shall know them. Many a loved missive comes to me now from her sweet hand and faithful heart. They are my joy in the long absence from her dear presence which my Country imposes upon me as a soldier of the Republic. In them my Darling sends me her heart and they are treasures indeed.

Since my last record, the Executive of my State has seen fit to promote me—his most humble servant.[22] I have tried to be worthy of trust, whether in the camp, the field, or before the enemy. I will try to redeem that trust.

Today I have slept some, having been Officer of the Guard last night, read a little, and recited a lesson in "Tactics" at the Colonel's quarters.

I write this by a splendid fire in our old-style fire-place. I'll soon be under the blankets. No mail last night, nor tonight. Darling's letters are delayed, and I must wait. I've thought of the dear, good girl often today, and I must get home to see and kiss her this winter.

"Up at reveille in the morning" is the order—Ugh! how cold it will be!

21. Presumably meant to read "the Ides of March" from Shakespeare's *Julius Caesar*. The text suggests that Otis certainly hoped to see his wife sooner than May.

22. Otis was officially promoted to first sergeant on March 1, 1862. He became a first lieutenant on May 20, 1863 and a captain on July 1,1864. See Otis-Chandler Family Papers, *Los Angeles Times* Archives.

SATURDAY, JANY. 10, 1863

Rained hard most of the day, the floor of our tent was twice nearly half-covered by water coming in at the door. Staid close in doors all day. Darling sends me a New Year's Day letter, and I commence a reply tonight. In a few days I'll have some books from her dear hand. Her letter says Cousin Joe will have my clothes made & sent to me as requested, and she'll send books, etc.

SUNDAY, JAN'Y 11, 1863

Spent the day quietly in my tent. Inspected the Company in the morning. Boys all looked neat & clean, & guns in good order. Had chicken for dinner, and some of Lizzie's sage tea. Col. Hines called me to his tent to advise close study of "Tactics and Regulations," to ease going before Examining Board at Charleston. Lt. Sherwood arrived with verbal message from Dave Newton about my wife coming to their house this winter. News of Rosecrans'[23] victory cheering, but with them, not so Sherman's repulse.[24]

23. The reference is to General William S. Rosecrans ("Old Rosy") and the Battle of Stones River, the prelude to Vicksburg. See McPherson, *Battle Cry of Freedom*, 579–82.

24. William Tecumseh Sherman, perhaps the most ferocious of all Northern generals. His "repulse" refers to his inability to surmount the defenses at Chicksaw Bayou, north of Vicksburg. McPherson, *Battle Cry of Freedom*, 579. Sherman's subsequent "march to the sea," through Georgia and the Carolinas, remains the stuff of legend.

MONDAY, JAN'Y 12, 1863

Spent the day mainly in our regular routine—drills & recitations. Col. gave us long lesson for tomorrow. "Grand Mounting, Guards, Grand Guards & outposts, and some 'Tactics.'"

Went over to Provost Marshall's office this evening, and saw three Rebel deserters from Edgar's Battalion, just in from a daring foray with Paxton's Cavalry, whom they guided. Big fellows & served with Rebels for months. Finished letter to Lizzie.

TUESDAY, JAN'Y 13, 1863

Nothing new today. In forenoon, made invoice of Arms & other property in the Co. to be transferred to Capt. Wallace.[25] In the afternoon took the Co. on Battalion Drill (left wing). Drilled in Manual of Arms by Col. Hines. All did well. Attended the regular recitation after drill. Capt. Wilson returned, looking well. No mail tonight, except papers. I find there is an artist in town, and Lizzie shall have my picture.

FRIDAY, JAN'Y 16, 1863

Stormed hard nearly all day. Snow and wind . . . .Pretty cold. The Colonel would have the Companies out on drill in it. Double-quicked to keep warm. Recitation in the afternoon, finishing "School of the Soldier." No letter from Liz today. Wrote her tonight. How her dear heart will love it if she can

25. Captain Jonathan A. Wallace, Twelfth Regiment. Reid, *Ohio in the War*, vol. 2, 88.

Drawing etched in stone of Hawk's Nest, West Virginia. Harry spent the last three years of the war fighting in this territory. (West Virginia State Archives, Nep Roesler Collection)

meet me at Charleston!—and mine! Cisco arrived with intelligence of Col. White's departure for Reg.

SATURDAY, JANUARY 17, 1863

Two letters from Darling to-day, and one from Cousin Joe about my clothes and valise, which are on the way here. Joe has had me a suit made, costing $36.00, and I can pay at will. He is an obliging boy, and has done me a substantial favor. Tomorrow Lizzie shall have my heart's reply. Wrote to Loup Creek to have my valise sent on. Had 1st [illegible] made.

SUNDAY, JANUARY 18, 1863

Nothing new to-day. In the evening wrote a letter to Lizzie, which I wouldn't have fall into other hands for anything.

MONDAY, JANY 19, 1863

Same old programme carried out to-day. Recitation in skirmish drill in the afternoon.

TUESDAY, JAN'Y 20, 1863

On Battalion Drill this afternoon in Command of "Squad II." Received a long letter from Dave Newton, marked "Official Business." He wants Mrs. Otis and I to come and see them and thinks 'twill do Rebecca good. Surely I must get down there sometime this winter, to meet Lizzie. Expecting Paymaster hourly.

WEDNESDAY, JANY 21, 1863

Not well to-night, and have felt badly all day with a dull, heavy headache. Damp snow falling.

THURSDAY, JANY 22, 1863

Wrote to Lizzie this evening, advising her to go out from the desert of Lowell, and come to meet me at Charleston. *God speed* her, and vindicate her good name. I wait impatiently for my money, so that I may be able to go down to Charleston.

Col. White returned to-day. Glad to meet the hero. *Poor soldier*! He suffers from distaste.

FRIDAY, JAN'Y 23, 1863

On Batallion drill with the *Squad* this afternoon. Still improving.

Wrote to Dave Newton this evening about visit at his house and a note to Mrs. Newton asking for a reply if she is ready for Lizzie to come up.

Dispatch yesterday from Gen. Cox to the "Heroic" says Paymasters are now receiving funds to pay Valley Troops.

SATURDAY, JANY 24 [1863]
SUNDAY, JAN'Y 25 [1863]
MONDAY, JANY 26 [1863]

Excitement in Camp about rebels in vicinity. Co. "H" sent out to reconnoitre. "Officer of the Day" Buck Smith flying around like mad this evening. Summoned to the Brigade Commander's (Toland's) quarters. Expects to be attacked every minute, being

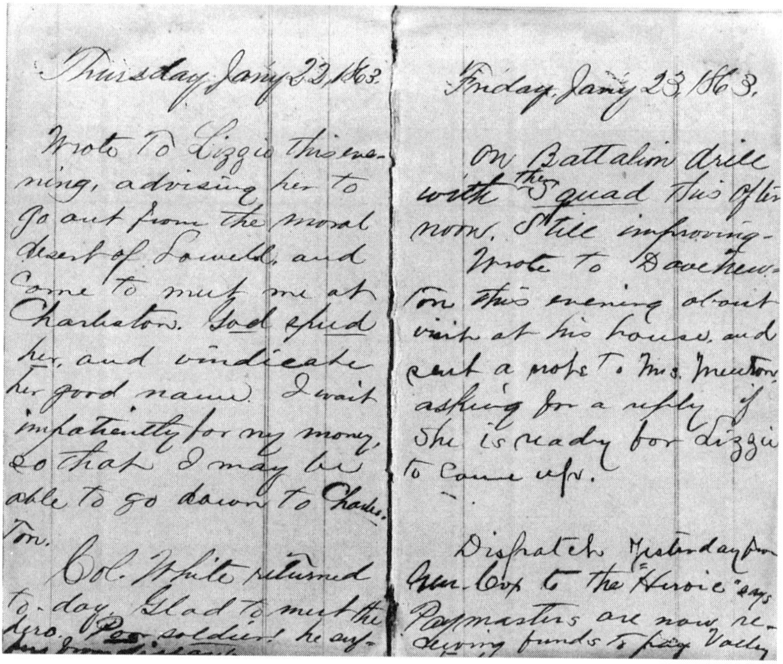
Thursday Jany 22, 1863.

Wrote to Lizzie this evening, advising her to go out from the moral desert of Lowell, and come to meet me at Charleston. God speed her, and vindicate her good name. I wait impatiently for my money, so that I may be able to go down to Charleston.

Col. White returned to-day. Glad to meet the hero. Poor soldier! he suf-

Friday Jany 23, 1863.

On Battalion drill with the squad this afternoon. Still improving.

Wrote to Doc Newton this evening about visit at his house, and sent a note to Mrs. Newton, asking for a reply if she is ready for Lizzie to come up.

Dispatch yesterday from Gen. Cox to the "Heroic" says Paymasters are now receiving funds to pay Valley

Entry for January 22, 1863, contains Harry's scornful comments on Eliza's treatment by her family. (Family Collection)

unduly excited. "Hd. Qrs. 2d. Kan. Div'n" moving to Charleston today. Wrote to Lizzie. Will finish letter in the morning & borrow money if I can.

TUESDAY, JANY 27 [1863]

Alarm in Camp subsided. Co. H. returned this forenoon having seen nobody. Finished letter to Lizzie, enclosing $5.00 borrowed from Barrett (Sutler). Uneasy about my valise and box sent to me by Dallas from Loup Creek Saturday. I fear they are stolen by teamsters. Spent most of the evening at Capt. Hawke's office, "Hd. Qrs." still moving today.

WEDNESDAY, JANY 28 [1863]
THURSDAY, JANY 29 [1863]

No chance for notes last night. My tent filled by a drunken crowd of officers—or rather a crowd of very drunk officers. Ex-Lieut. Campbell,[26] the whiskey-bloat, who was not fit for the service among the crowd, "hand in glove" with the other tubs. Perish the hour when I come to such a pass! My self-respect will not allow me to associate willingly with such a crew. Vacated the premises and slept with Ludlum.

FRIDAY, JANY 30 [1863]
SATURDAY, JANUARY 31 [1863]

Monthly Inspection today by the Colonel and his *puppy* Adjt. Artillery practice by McMillen[27] in the afternoon. He did some very indifferent Shooting, the shells flying far from the mark.

26. Second Lieutenant John C. Campbell, Twelfth Regiment, resigned in December 1862. *Roster*, vol. 2, 88.

27. Jonathan H. McMillen, Twelfth Regiment. See *Roster*, vol. 2, 357.

Captain Harrison Gray Otis, 1865. At the end of the war, Harry was promoted to Captain and brevet Major and Lieutenant Colonel. Despite his excellent record, his effort to join the regular army in 1867 was denied.
(Francis Trevelyan Miller, *The Photographic History of the Civil War.* New York: Review of Reviews Company, X, 1911)

Long letter from Liz yesterday, to which I commenced reply this evening. Hope I may send it to omit duty at Charleston. No reply yet from Mrs. "R. Rosa" yet.[28] No signs of my valise either. *Confound* the man that stole it! Lett drunk again. The little whore.

SUNDAY, FEB'Y 1 [1863]

MONDAY, FEB'Y 2. [1863]

TUESDAY, FEBY 3 [1863]

WEDNESDAY, FEB'Y 4. [1863]

Returned from Loup Creek, from search for my valise—found by Lt. Sherwood. Had very hard trip—roads bad, weather cold, and my feet sore. Staid with Capt. Gilman at Loup Creek, and at Mr. Wilson's on Laurel last night. Very clever people, and a sprightly girl in the family. On my return rec'd letters from Mrs. Newton & Liz.

FRIDAY, FEB'Y 6 [1863]

Valise came up on Sherwood's train today. Every thing safe. Clothes fit tolerably well. Nice lot of books sent by Lizzie. *Thank you Darling*!

Little Callie (Clarke) sent Life of Washington—Box not rec'd. Letter for Clevenger about books in it delivered.

SUNDAY, FEBY 7 [1863]

Batallion drill this afternoon. I commanded a 6th Co. Used *numerous* [illegible][29] Brown on *detail* building redan &

28. Presumably a pet name for Dave Newton's wife, Rebecca.

29. Could be "St." or "Lt." Harry seems to be referring to a military manual rather than a person.

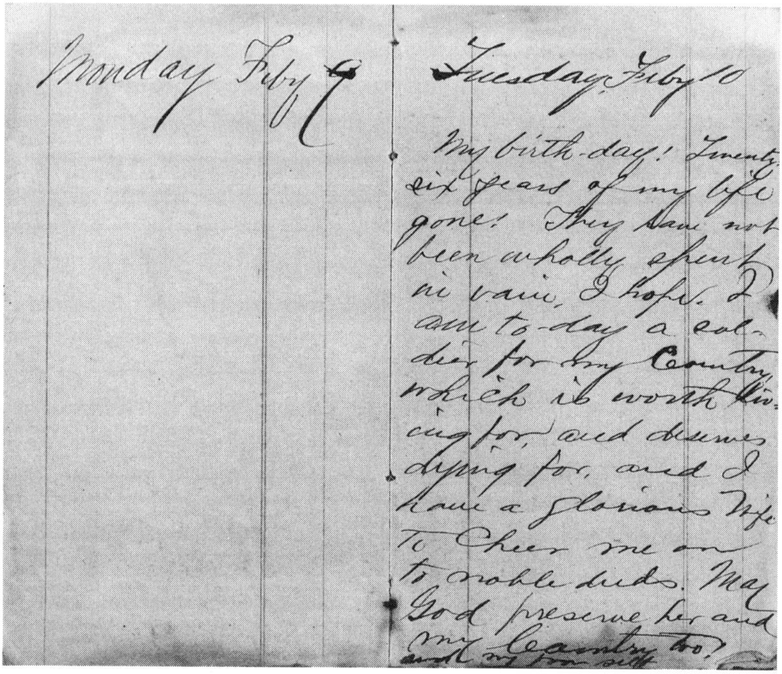

Monday Feby 9

Tuesday Feby 10

My birth-day! Twenty-six years of my life gone! They have not been wholly spent in vain, I hope. I am to-day a soldier for my Country which is worth living for, and deserves dying for, and I have a glorious Wife to cheer me on to noble deeds. May God preserve her and my Country too! and my poor self

His diary entry for February 10, 1863, reveals Harry's jubilant thoughts on his birthday. (Family Collection)

abbatis.[30] Qr. M. issued Clothing. Letter from Liz. Ready packed up to start for Charleston. *Dear*! I wish you could come right up. Mrs. Newton going to Chicago.

SUNDAY FEBY 8 [1863]

Inspected my Co. to-day in my new "rig." Read "Articles of War" to them.

Wrote to Mrs. Newton. Will write Liz in morning. Feel dull with a cold in the head tonight.

Going to bed.

MONDAY FEBY 9 [1863]

TUESDAY, FEBY 10 [1863]

My birthday! Twenty six years of my life gone! They have not been wholly spent in vain, I hope. I am today a soldier for my Country which is worth living for, and deserves dying for, and I have a glorious wife to Cheer me on to noble deeds. May God preserve her and my Country too and my poor self.

WEDNESDAY FEBY 11 [1863]

THURSDAY, FEBY 12. [1863]

The man with the "Greenbacks" has been entertaining the boys today. There's many a glad heart tonight among us. For there's many a soldier's family in need. My pay for 6 mos. & 11 days as 1st Sergt & 1 mo. and 19 days as 2nd Lt. with Clothing Bal. due was $301.75. I've some bills to pay.

30. Redan and abbatis are common terms for military fortifications. Eliza gives a fine description of an abbatis in her journal entry for June 9, 1863. A redan is a field work having two faces or parapets which form a salient angle.

BIBLIOGRAPHY

Primary Unpublished Sources

Correspondence and Papers of Harrison Gray Otis, 1859–1917. *Los Angeles Times* Archives.

Journal of Eliza Ann Wetherby Otis, 1860–1863. Private collection.

Letters of Harrison Gray Otis to Eliza Ann Wetherby Otis, 1860. *Los Angeles Times* Archives.

Otis-Chandler Family Papers. *Los Angeles Times* Archives.

Primary Published Sources

Chesnut, Mary Boykin. *Mary Chesnut's Civil War.* C. Vann Woodward, ed. New Haven, Connecticut, 1981.

Foraker, J. B., H. A. Axline, and J. S. Robinson, comps. *Official Roster of the Soldiers of the State of Ohio in the War of Rebellion, 1861–1866.* 3 vols. Cincinnati, 1886.

Irving, Washington. *The Sketch Book.* 1819–1820.

Longfellow, Henry Wadsworth. *A Psalm of Life.* 1839.

Louisville Directory and Business Advertiser, 1859–60.

Lummis, Charles F. "One of the Old Guard." *The Land of Sunshine* 12 (1900): 72–83.

Lytton, Edward George Earle Bulwer [Owen Meredith]. *Falkland.* London: H. Colburn, 1827.

Macaulay, Thomas Babington. *History of England.* 6 vols. (London, 1848–1860).

Moore, Thomas. *The Poetical Works of Thomas Moore.* Edinburgh, 1873.

Otis, Eliza Ann. *California, "Where Sets the Sun": The Writings of Eliza A. Otis in Poetry and Prose, 1876–1904.* Harrison Gray Otis, comp. Los Angeles, 1905.

———. *Christopher Columbus: A Poem in Blank Verse*. Los Angeles, 1909.

———. *Echoes from Elfland: Jack and the Beanstalk, Cinderella, Little Jack Horner, Little Boy Blue, and Other Juvenile Poems*. Los Angeles, 1896.

Secondary Published Sources

Aaron, Daniel. *Cincinnati: Queen City of the West*. Columbus, Ohio, 1942. Reprint, 1992.

———. *The Unwritten War: American Writers and the Civil War*. New York, 1973.

Andrews, Martin R., ed. and comp. *History of Marietta and Washington County, Ohio and Representative Citizens*. Chicago, 1902.

Athearn, Robert. *The Mythic West in Twentieth-Century America*. Lawrence, Kansas, 1986.

Babcock, Gwendolyn Garland. *The Ancestry of Marian Otis Chandler*. San Marino, California, 1991.

Barnes, Eric Wollencott. *The Lady of Fashion: The Life and the Theatre of Anna Cora Mowatt*. New York, 1954.

Bennion, Sheryl Cox. *Equal to the Occasion: Women Editors in the Nineteenth-Century West*. Reno, Nevada, 1990.

Billington, Ray Allen, with Martin Ridge. *Westward Expansion: A History of the American Frontier*. 5th ed. New York, 1982.

Boller, Paul. *American Transcendentalism, 1830–1860: An Intellectual Inquiry*. New York, 1974.

Brown, Dee. *The Gentle Tamers: Women of the Old Wild West*. Lincoln, Nebraska, 1968.

Cayton, Andrew R. L., and Peter S. Onuf. *The Midwest and the Nation: Rethinking the History of an American Region*. Bloomington, Indiana, 1990.

Cleland, Robert Glass. *The Cattle on a Thousand Hills: Southern California, 1850–1880*. San Marino, California, 1969.

Conrad, Margaret. "Recording Angels: The Private Chronicles of Women from the Maritime Provinces of Canada." In *The Neglected Majority: Essays in Canadian Women's History*, vol. 2. Alison Prentice and Susan Mann Trofimenkoff, eds. Toronto, 1985.

Cronon, William J. *Nature's Metropolis: Chicago and the Great West.* New York, 1991.

Dearing, Mary R. *Veterans in Politics: The Story of the G.A.R.* Baton Rouge, 1952.

Degler, Carl N. *At Odds: Women and the Family from the Revolution to the Present.* New York, 1980.

de Tocqueville, Alexis. *Democracy in America.* 2 vols. J. P. Mayer and Max Lerner, eds. New York, 1952.

Dickens-Garcia, Hazel. *Journalistic Standards in the Nineteenth Century.* Madison, Wisconsin, 1989.

Douglas, Anne. *The Feminization of American Culture.* New York, 1977.

Dumke, Glenn S. *The Boom of the Eighties in Southern California.* San Marino, California, 1944. Reprint, 1991.

Etcheson, Nicole. "Manliness and the Political Culture of the Old Northwest." *Journal of Early American History* 15, no. 1 (1995): 59–77.

Faragher, John Mack. "Americans, Mexicans, Métis: A Community Approach to the Comparative Study of North American Frontiers." In *Under an Open Sky: Rethinking America's Western Past.* William J. Cronon, George Miles, and Jay Gitlin, eds. New York, 1992, 28–51.

———. *Women and Men on the Overland Trail.* New Haven, Connecticut, 1979.

Faust, Drew Gilpin. "Altars of Sacrifice: Confederate Women and the Narrative of War." *Journal of American History* 76 (1990): 1200–28.

Foner, Eric. *Free Soil, Free Labor, Free Men: The Ideology of the American Revolution before the Civil War.* New York, 1970.

———. *Reconstruction: America's Unfinished Revolution, 1863–1877.* New York, 1988.

Gottlieb, Robert, and Irene Wolt. *Thinking Big: The Story of the Los Angeles Times, Its Publishers, and Their Influence on Southern California*. New York, 1977.

Halberstam, David. *The Powers That Be*. New York, 1979.

Hampsten, Elizabeth. *Read This Only to Yourself: The Private Writings of Midwestern Women, 1880–1910*. Bloomington, Indiana, 1982.

Hattaway, Herman, and Archer Jones. *How the North Won: A Military History of the Civil War*. Urbana, Illinois, 1983.

Hine, Robert H. *The American West: An Interpretive History*. 2nd ed. Boston, 1984.

Hofstadter, Richard. *The Age of Reform: Bryan to F.D.R.* New York, 1955.

———. *The Progressive Historians: Turner, Beard, Parrington*. New York, 1968.

———. *Social Darwinism in American Thought*. Rev. ed. New York, 1955.

Howe, Daniel Walker. *The Political Culture of the American Whigs*. Chicago, 1979.

Howe, John R. *From the Revolution through the Age of Jackson: Innocence and Empire in the Young Republic*. Englewood Cliffs, New Jersey, 1973.

Hunt, Rockwell Dennis, ed. *California and the Californians*. 5 vols. New York, 1926.

Jakle, John A. *Image of the Ohio Valley: A Historical Geography of Travel*. New York, 1977.

Jensen, Joan M., and Doris A. Miller. "The Genteel Tamers Revisited: New Approaches to the History of Women in the American West." *Pacific Historical Review* 49 (May 1980): 173–213.

Johnson, Allen, and Dumas Malone, eds. *Dictionary of American Biography*. 22 vols. New York, 1928–44.

Kelly, Mary. "The Making of Learned Women in Nineteenth Century Culture." *Journal of American History* 83, no. 2 (1996): 401–24.

———. *Private Women, Public Stage: Literary Domesticity in Nineteenth-Century America*. New York, 1984.

Kerber, Linda. "Separate Spheres, Female Worlds and Women's Place." *Journal of American History* 75 (June 1988): 9–39.

Lears, Jackson. *No Place of Grace: Antimodernism and the Transformation of American Culture, 1880–1920.* New York, 1981.

Limerick, Patricia. *The Legacy of Conquest: The Unbroken Past of the American West.* New York, 1987.

Lystra, Karen. *Searching the Heart: Women, Men, and Romantic Love in Nineteenth-Century America.* New York, 1989.

Marzolf, Marion. *Up from the Footnote.* New York, 1977.

McConnell, Stuart. *Glorious Contentment: The Grand Army of the Republic, 1865–1900.* Chapel Hill, North Carolina, 1992.

McKinney, Tim. *The Civil War in Fayette County, West Virginia.* Charleston, West Virginia, 1988.

McPherson, James M. *Battle Cry of Freedom: The Civil War Era.* New York, 1988.

———. *For Cause and Comrades: Why Men Fought in the Civil War.* New York, 1997.

McWilliams, Carey. *California: The Great Exception.* Santa Barbara, California, 1976.

———. *Southern California Country: An Island on the Land.* New York, 1946.

Merk, Frederick. *Manifest Destiny and Mission in American History: A Reinterpretation.* New York, 1963.

Mott, Frank Luther. *American Journalism: A History of Newspapers in the United States through 250 Years, 1690–1940.* 3rd. ed. New York, 1962.

Nash, Gerald D. *Creating the West: Historical Interpretations, 1890–1990.* Albuquerque, New Mexico, 1991.

Petrik, Paula. "The Gentle Tamers in Transition: Women in the Trans-Mississippi West." *Feminist Studies* 11, no. 3 (Fall 1985): 677–94.

Pomeroy, Earl. *The Pacific Slope: A History of California, Oregon, Washington, Idaho, Utah, and Nevada.* Lincoln, Nebraska, 1965.

Reid, Whitelaw. *Ohio in the War: Her Statesmen, Her Generals, and Soldiers.* 2 vols. New York, 1868.

Rose, Anne C. *Victorian America and the Civil War.* New York, 1992.

Schneider, Norris F. *History of Lowell and Adams Townships.* Lowell, Ohio, 1946.

Schroeder, Ralph. *History of Washington County, Ohio, 1798–1881.* Marietta, Ohio, 1881.

Sherwin, Louis. "The Walrus of Moron-Land." *American Mercury* 13 (February 1928): 190–7.

Sherwood, Midge. "Eliza Ann Otis, Co-Founder of the *Los Angeles Times.*" *The Pacific Historian* 28, no. 3 (1984): 45–52.

Slotkin, Richard. *Regeneration through Violence: The Mythology of the American Frontier.* Middletown, Connecticut, 1973.

Smith, Henry Nash. *Virgin Land: The American West as Symbol and Myth.* New York, 1950.

Somkin, Fred. *Unquiet Eagle: History and Desire in the Idea of American Freedom.* Ithaca, New York, 1965.

Starr, Kevin. *Inventing the Dream: California through the Progressive Era.* New York, 1985.

———. *Material Dreams: Southern California through the 1920's.* New York, 1990.

Stillwell, Lewis D. *Migration from Vermont (1776–1860).* Montpelier, Vermont, 1948.

Trachtenberg, Alan. *The Incorporation of American Society: Culture and Society in the Gilded Age.* New York, 1982.

Van Alstyne, Richard W. *The Rising American Empire.* Oxford, 1960.

Volpe, Vernon. *Forlorn Hope of Freedom: The Liberty Party in the Old Northwest, 1838–1948.* Kent, Ohio, 1990.

Walker, Cheryl. *American Women Poets of the Nineteenth Century: An Anthology.* New Brunswick, New Jersey, 1992.

———. *The Nightingale's Burden: Women Poets and American Culture before 1900.* Bloomington, Indiana, 1982.

Wecter, Dixon. "Instruments of Culture on the Frontier." *Yale Review* 36 (1947): 242–56.

Weinberg, Albert K. *Manifest Destiny: A Study of Nationalist Expansion in American History.* Baltimore, 1935.

White, G. Edward. *The Eastern Establishment and the Western*

Experience: The West of Frederic Remington, Theodore Roosevelt, and Owen Wister. New Haven, Connecticut, 1968.

White, Richard. *"It's Your Misfortune and None of My Own": A New History of the American West.* Norman, Oklahoma, 1991.

Wiebe, Robert H. *The Search for Order, 1877–1920.* New York, 1967.

Wiley, Bell Irwin. *The Life of Billy Yank.* Indianapolis, 1952.

Wilson, Edmund. *Patriotic Gore: Studies in the Literature of the American Civil War.* New York, 1963.

Wish, Harvey. *Society and Thought in Early America: A Social and Intellectual History of the American People.* New York, 1950.

Wright, Louis B. *Culture on the Moving Frontier.* Bloomington, Indiana, 1955.

Wyatt, David. *The Fall into Eden: Landscape and Imagination in California.* New York, 1986.

Secondary Unpublished Sources

Henry, Susan. "'Journalistic Comrade': Eliza Otis and the Beginnings of a Newspaper Dynasty." Unpublished monograph, 1986. *Los Angeles Times* Archives.

Miller, Richard Connolly. "Otis and His *Times*: The Career of Harrison Gray Otis of Los Angeles." Ph.D. diss., University of California, Berkeley, 1961.

This book was designed

and composed in Bauer Bodoni by

Wilsted & Taylor Publishing Services

of Oakland, California.

It was printed by Thomson-Shore, Inc.

on Glatfelter Supple Opaque Recycled Natural paper.